FROM
Growing up
pains
TO THE Sacred
Diary

Also by Adrian Plass

FROM

Growing up pains

TO THE Sacred Diary

NOTHING IS WASTED

Adrian Plass

ZONDERVAN™

GRAND RAPIDS, MICHIGAN 49530 USA

ZONDERVAN™

From Growing Up Pains to the Sacred Diary
First published by Zondervan in 2002

The Growing Up Pains of Adrian Plass first published in Great Britain in 1986 by Marshall Pickering. Copyright © 1986 by Adrian Plass.

The Sacred Diary of Adrian Plass (aged 37³/4) first published in Great Britain in 1987 by Marshall Pickering. Text copyright © 1987 by Adrian Plass. Illustrations copyright © 1987 by Dan Donovan.

Requests for information should be addressed to:

Zondervan, *Grand Rapids, Michigan 49530*

Adrian Plass and Dan Donovan assert the moral right to be identified as the author and illustrator of this work.

ISBN 0-310-27857-0

Interior design by Nancy Wilson

Printed and bound in the United States of America

02 03 04 05 06 07 08 /❖ DC/ 10 9 8 7 6 5 4 3 2 1

Contents

Preface

They almost always get it wrong. When people talk to me about my 'first' book, they are invariably referring to *The Sacred Diary of Adrian Plass, Aged 37 3/4.* This is very understandable. It was in the pages of *The Sacred Diary* that most of my readers met me for the first time, but in fact the whole thing started with a book called *Join the Company,* later renamed *The Growing Up Pains of Adrian Plass.*

I take a particular pleasure in the fact that these two books are now to be published in one volume, because they are, in a sense, two sides of the same coin. I was asked to write *Growing Up Pains* whilst in the process of recovering from a stress illness that laid me very low in the mid-eighties. It is a strange mixture of a book, a combination of fairly intimate autobiography, several sketches of fellow-contributors to the television programme 'Company' that my wife and I were involved with for some years, and an account of the illness that ultimately brought about such changes in my life. It is a somewhat 'lumpy' piece of work, but as I re-read it today I thank God that it was written before I was fully recovered. There are no loose ends tied in this book. There couldn't be, because I had not the first idea how to tie them. My experience of God and the church and being a Christian had simply fallen apart and there seemed little point in telling anything other than the truth about how rotten I was feeling. It has given me great pleasure to learn how, over the years, many suffering and lost people have taken heart from the vulnerability expressed in *The Growing Up Pains of Adrian Plass.* At the time when I wrote it, it would never have occurred to me that the book could have much of a ministering role for others. Putting pen to paper was a useful therapy for me, and a way to fill the many hours that had become available in my life, but it seemed likely that after selling a couple of thousand copies it, and my hypothetical writing career, would disappear without trace.

That is probably exactly what would have happened if it had not been for *The Sacred Diary of Adrian Plass*. This little book began its life as a column in a Christian publication called *Family* magazine, and was actually entitled *The 'Secret' Diary* at that stage. Writing this monthly column provided me with an opportunity to get a veritable tidal wave of dirty water off my chest. It was the perfect way to express many of the church-linked frustrations and confusions and fears that had helped to bring about my illness. There was a part of me that had wanted to write bitter, angry words about all those dark things, but, as my wife so rightly pointed out, making people laugh was far more likely to succeed than telling them off or doing a sort of public sulk.

Those early writings seemed to pour out of me. Ideas tumbled over one another in the race to reach the page. It was an experience that has rarely been repeated in my writing career since that time. Later, when the columns were expanded, added to and published in one volume, nobody could have been more surprised than I was at the immediate success of the book. Could there really be that many people out there who so readily identified with the foolishness and foibles of a central character who appeared to spend much of his life battling with inadequacies in himself and his church? Apparently there were.

I don't think I shall ever be unhappy enough to write such a funny book again.

There it is then. It might be a good idea to read these two books in the order that they were written, but in a way it doesn't matter. They sprang from the same negative source, and both, despite an emphasis on the problematic side of faith, offer the same flickering candle-flame of hope. That hope is Jesus, my friend and saviour. Have a good read.

The Growing Up
Pains of
Adrian Plass

Preface

God really brought me down to earth once. He's rather good at that sort of thing.

We'd gone to Cornwall for a winter holiday, something that we'd always yearned to do as a family. It was early December, bitingly cold, but brilliantly lit by one of those water-colour winter suns that seem to drip liquid light through the atmosphere. Our little white rented cottage overlooked an indescribably beautiful part of the northern coast. That coast must have been planned, built and illuminated by a creator with time on his hands, and a fine, excited eye for detail.

One morning, after a long, lingering, excessive breakfast, we all dressed in layer upon layer of the warmest clothes we could find, and set off, a procession of human barrels, to go for a walk in the ice-cream air. We went a new way. Through a white farm gate, and across an expanse of wind-flattened, metallic green grass, towards what looked like a cliff edge a few hundred yards away. Beyond that the sea stretched away for ever, merging with the sky in the strange pale distance.

I walked with Matthew, aged eight, whose every utterance at that time began with an interrogative. My wife, Bridget, strolled beside four-year-old Joseph, deep and thoughtful beyond his years. The smallest barrel, David, aged two, ran ahead of us chuckling delightedly, applauding the seagulls who keeled around us for a few minutes, performing impossible aerobatics with casual vanity.

As we neared the edge of the cliff, I reflected on the fact that we were happy – all of us. We are a close family, but it didn't often happen that we all achieved contentment, all at the same time, when we were all together. You have to work hard to keep a family of five reasonably happy. It's like the circus act where all those plates are kept spinning on the top of tall, thin sticks by someone rushing from one to the other at great speed. The difference with a family is that you never get a chance to stop and take a bow. You just carry on, and get tired. Holidays had always been an opportunity for Bridget and myself to enjoy an awareness of our whole selves, and to give some thought to what we needed to keep our plates spinning.

We had reached the edge. Far beneath us, enclosed by a horse-shoe of unscaleable cliffs, lay one of the most magically secluded bays I had ever seen. Perfect shape, perfect sea, perfect sand, perfect rock pools. There was no way down. We could never use it. We could only look at it. It was as though one of God's success-ful creation prototypes had been overlooked when the workbench was cleared.

I forgot everything else as I gazed out over this hidden corner of the world. I felt a sudden surge of pride about belonging to the same world as the vast shining sea, the blue-white wash of the sky, and the massive, granulated bulk of the cliffs. These, surely, were symbols of God. Huge, beautiful, sublime, desirable, yet impossible to contain or define narrowly. I was lost in wonder ...

'Daddy, want to go loo, daddy!'

My youngest son's voice arrived in my consciousness with urgent haste. David's little face was strained with the knowledge that disaster was imminent. As I struggled to reduce his Michelin-like proportions to an appropriate state of undress, I spoke to God in my mind with some truculence.

'Goodness knows,' I complained, 'I get little enough time as it is to actually relax and enjoy beautiful things. Why should I have to come down from where I was to cope with little problems like this?'

'I did,' said God.

Chapter One

Early photographs show that I was little more than a huge pair of ears mounted on two long skinny legs. In most of those early pictures I look slightly troubled and very earnest.

Each week I attended the local church at the other end of the village, an activity that seemed to me to have very little to do with God. The Roman Catholic chapel in Rusthall was a converted private house, and therefore lacked the atmosphere of sublime mystery and divine confidence that I rather enjoyed on our occasional visits to St Augustine's, the huge and ornate mother church in Tunbridge Wells. There were few points of interest for a small child in an hour spent in one of three physical postures, listening to someone speaking a language that he didn't understand, to a God who seemed as distant and irrelevant as the dark side of the moon. Some of those services seemed to be several days long. Afterwards, my father, my two brothers and I would proceed sedately back along the path into the village, all my little springs of boredom and tension popping and pinging into relaxation as I looked forward to Sunday lunch and the traditional midday comedy half-hour on the radio.

Nowadays I have a great respect and fondness for the Roman Catholic Church and many friends who are members of it, but if you had asked me at the age of eight or nine to tell you what I enjoyed most about the mass, I could have named only one thing. I did rather look forward to that point in the proceedings when the priest placed a wafer in the open mouths of the communicants, as they knelt in a semicircle around him. There was a satisfyingly repellent fleshiness about all those extended tongues, and a fascinating vulnerability about the grown-ups, waiting like baby birds to be fed with something that, once inside them, (I was told) would turn into the body of Jesus Christ and nourish them in a way that I couldn't begin to understand.

That the church seemed to me to have very little to do with God may have had something to do with the fact that, while my father was a convert to the Catholic Church, my mother, whose religious background was the Congregational Church, remained a Protestant and didn't come to church with us on Sundays.

We frequently experienced our own domestic version of 'The Troubles' and I can recall how, as a small child, I felt painfully bewildered about the religious separation between my parents.

Why didn't mummy come to church with us? Did she know a different God? No? Well, in that case why didn't she come to church with us? I would understand when I was older, I was told.

The shadow of conflict darkened those Sunday morning services throughout my early childhood and had a strongly negative effect on my feelings about God, who clearly wouldn't or couldn't sort out our family.

If my poor father had been a more secure man the boredom of the services and even the parental conflict over religion might not have mattered too much. As it was, his inability to trust the love of his family resulted in twenty-five very difficult years for my mother, and, in my case, a very confused and troubled perception of what love, adulthood and Christianity meant. Two incidents spring to mind as being typical of the kind of emotional half-nelson that he was expert in applying and which must have contributed heavily to the emotional constipation which led to a breakdown in my own life years later in 1984, and from which I am only just emerging as I write.

The first concerned my father's black prayer book. It was a small, plump, much thumbed little volume, whose wafer-thin pages were edged with gold. As a child it seemed to me a miniature treasure chest, filled with immense wealth that had somehow been compressed into a tiny space for easy portage.

Dad's prayer book was part of him, like the little round boxes of Beecham's pills, the tin full of old and foreign coins, the trilby hat, and the tortoise-shell reading spectacles that made my sight worse when I was allowed to try them on, before they were put away again in the case that snapped shut with a pleasing hollow 'plock' sound.

One day we had all been naughty – all three of us. One of my brothers was two years older than me, the other was two years younger. I must have been about eight years old at the time. We seemed to spend our lives pursuing one of three activities. The first involved the consumption of vast slices of white crusty bread, spread thickly with butter and marmalade. We often accounted for three long loaves in a single day.

The second activity was simply playing together, and the third, which usually grew naturally out of the second, was simply fighting each other. Today, the eating and playing stages had passed all too quickly. We three boys had argued and squabbled and cried and fought for most of a long rainy Saturday. My parents' patience had been tried and tested in a way that, with three boys of my own, I now fully understand. They had tried everything: the gentle rebuke, the not-so-gentle rebuke, the appeal to reason, the bribe, the threat, the repeated threat, the repeated-yet-again threat, the last chance option and finally the shriek of fury. Nothing had worked. My father had long since abandoned any attempt to play an adult role in the proceedings. He was an angry child, hurt by our refusal to make it easy for him to be grown-up. His idea of an appropriate solution to this problem was bizarre, to say the least. He picked up his prayer book from its place next to the biscuit barrel on the sideboard, and holding it dramatically over his head, announced that if we didn't behave ourselves, we would drive him to the point where he would be forced to throw it at us, and if he had to do *that*, it really would be 'the end'.

Children believe things.

The end of what? Pictures flashed through my mind of the little book, stuffed with condensed divinity, crashing to the floor, bursting like some ripe, heavy fruit, and losing all its goodness for ever. Was that what he meant? Would I be to blame for that? Had I said or done something in the course of that long day of bickering, that was more serious – more wicked than I had realised? When he did finally, with a sort of orgasmic zeal, fling the book in the general direction of my younger brother and me, I was surprised to find that the world seemed unaffected by the gesture. No thunderbolts – no voice from heaven. The book lay, almost unharmed, on the floor, one or two pages detached by the impact and protruding slightly from the others, but otherwise, just the same.

I wasn't just the same though. I had made my father throw his prayer book at me, and he had said that it would be 'the end'. That book contained God. I had made him throw God away.

The devils grinned as they snapped home the padlock on another chain of guilt.

The other incident was so painful, that, even now, I find it difficult to record.

My father was a very jealous man. He found it almost impossible to believe that he was loved and wanted by those closest to him. Happiness and peace were just clever devices designed to lull him into a state where he could more easily be cheated and victimised, especially by his wife – my mother – who was, and still is, one of the most loving and innocent people I have ever met. People outside the family were 'all right'. They could never give him things that he feared losing in the same way. It was us, the family, and my mother particularly, who were obliged to trip and stumble through the dark forest of his fear and insecurity. In the middle of a pleasant family walk, when it seemed impossible that anything could go wrong, he would quite suddenly stop, and with that expression of tight-lipped anger on his face, that we all dreaded, announce that we were going back.

'Why, Dad?'

'Ask your mother.'

My mother, it usually transpired, had 'looked' at a man passing along on the other side of the road, or working in a field, or sitting on a gate, or driving a car. This kind of innocent glance was enough to shatter my father's self-esteem, and send him into a brooding sulky state for hours, or days, or even weeks. Eventually my mother would find a way to bring him round, but only by accepting and playing out the role of penitent, which was a very risky business, as he would only accept her penitence if she was innocent as well. He saw rivals everywhere. The man who came to build the extension onto our kitchen was, he told me, a 'naughty' man.

'What do you mean?'

'I'll tell you when you're older.'

'Why can't you tell me now?'

'It's not very nice.'

The man who took us for catechism lessons in a tall dark room in St Augustine's presbytery was also on the list of suspects. He was a big man with a large impressive moustache, a profound understanding of the catechism, and an almost total inability to communicate it to children. He was also, so my father said, not a good man.

'Bad, you mean?'

'Yes, very bad.'

'What's he done?'

'You wouldn't understand.'

'I would!'

'I'll tell you when you're older . . .'

There were so many things that I was going to be told when I was older! So many little clouds of half-knowledge were massing around my understanding, shutting out the light until much later in my life.

The most painful instance of my father's insane jealousy (most painful from my point of view, that is), happened just before my tenth birthday. I arrived home one afternoon after playing some sort of tracking game through the bracken up on the common. Tired, hot and hungry, I came through the back door into the kitchen, and was about to get a drink of water and a wedge of the all-sustaining bread and marmalade, when I heard my father's raised voice coming from the other side of the dining room door. My very heartbeat seemed to fade, as it always did when I realised that 'it' was happening again. What now? I opened the door and slipped quietly into the room, thinking vaguely that I might be able to protect someone from something. My mother was shaking her head tearfully, sobbing out the words, 'It's just not true, it's just not true!'

My father, with an odd mixture of pain, anger and relish filling his face and voice, was jabbing his finger towards her and shouting, 'I saw you! I saw you with him! I looked through the window and saw you on the bed with him!'

My sympathy fluttered around the room like a nervous butterfly, uncertain where to alight, unsure where to lend the tiny weight of its concern.

'You can't have done – you really can't have done! It's not true ...!'

Despite ample evidence from the past that plain denial was an absolute waste of time, my mother continued her tearful protest, until my father, suddenly inspired, took a step forward and pointed at me.

'Adrian was with me. He saw it too! Didn't you?'

There was a wild plea in his eyes.

My mother was crying.

They were my parents. You should support your parents. My father was appealing to me to lie for him. My mother needed me to tell the truth. Someone was going to be let down, and we were all going to suffer anyway. My voice was very small as I answered.

'I wasn't with you. I didn't see anything.'

I don't think I looked at my father's face. I had failed him by telling the truth. I was a cold mess inside. Angry, unhappy, and of course – guilty.

As an adult, I have come to understand how profoundly my father suffered through his inability to believe in happiness, and I am now able to offer him posthumous forgiveness and feel more peaceful about the past. There is no doubt, though, that the development of my perception of God as a father was sadly distorted by the way in which he presented himself to me both as a Christian and a parent. It is fortunate that my mother was able to provide warmth and consistent care throughout my childhood, and for that I shall always be grateful.

The other great pleasure in my life, apart from eating bread and marmalade, was reading. I was an avid but non-discriminating reader. Various aged relatives died during my childhood, leaving large and generally rather sombre collections of books to my father, who placed many of them in a big dark-brown bookcase in my bedroom, presumably to aid the process of 'doing better than he did'. I read everything. I would sit, cross-legged, on the bedroom floor, in my baggy grey flannel shirt, and my even baggier grey flannel shorts, surrounded by little stacks of novels, poetry collections and biographies. Each book was like a stone in a rock pool. Lift it up, investigate closely, and you might discover something exciting – something alive! Nor was I handicapped by snobbery. There was no such thing as a classic. I was quite happy to give someone called Joseph Conrad a fair trial, but he had to succeed on his own merits, or be replaced by a really great writer, such as W E Johns, or Richmal Crompton. I was in love with words and ideas, but it never occurred to me, until one momentous day, that something I read in a book could actually change my attitude to real people in the real world.

It was my earliest encounter with the truth, although I certainly wouldn't have called it a religious experience at the time, and it happened on the top deck of the number 81 bus which used to run between Rusthall and Tunbridge Wells. The journey only took twelve minutes, but on this occasion that was long enough for a startling new truth to penetrate my ten-year-old consciousness so profoundly that it has affected almost everything I have done since that day. It was connected with something I had read that morning.

As I sat on the front seat of the big green Maidstone and District bus, a sixpenny bit and a penny clutched in my hand ready for the conductor, a phrase I had read earlier repeated itself over and over in my mind.

'Everybody is *I*.'

For some reason, I sensed an important inner core of meaning in the words, but I was unable to dig it out. I was frustrated and fascinated by the problem. If only the answer – the secret, had been a solid thing. I wanted to stretch out my hand and grasp it firmly – make it mine.

'Yes, son?'

So absorbed was I by the intensity of my quest for understanding, that the bus conductor's perfectly reasonable attempt to collect a fare from me seemed an unforgivable intrusion into my privacy. The friendly smile under the shiny-peaked cap wilted in the heat of a ferocious glare from this odd, skinny little boy. The poor man hastily took the two coins from my extended palm, turned the handle on his machine, and handed me a green seven-penny ticket, before returning to more congenial company on the lower deck.

I stared out through the big front windows at the road ahead. We were nearly at Toad Rock. Didn't like Toad Rock very much. Why not? Didn't know really ... Everybody is *I* ... Everybody is *I* ...

Everybody is *I* ... Everybody is *I* ...

We were passing the white frontage of the Swan Hotel now, turning slowly into the lower end of Tunbridge Wells High Street. Good old Tunbridge Wells, like a collection of huge dolls' houses. Lovely day, lots of people about – hundreds of people in fact. Probably going to the fair on the common. Everybody is ...

Suddenly I stiffened. Body erect, hands flat on the ledge below the window, I pressed my forehead against the glass and stared in amazement at the crowds on the pavement below. The true meaning of those three simple, but puzzling words had exploded into my mind, destroying the illusion that I was the centre of the universe, and leaving me to cope, for the rest of my life, with the burden of knowledge. Every one of those people down there in the street, walking the pavements, driving cars, waiting for buses – every single one, whatever they were, whatever they looked like, whatever I thought of them, were as important to themselves as I was to myself! I shook my head, trying to clear it of this incredible notion. Everybody is I . . . That funny, bent old lady with the mouth drooping on one side – she mattered, she was vital – central. The bus conductor who had interrupted my mental churning earlier; he wasn't just a bit player in my world. He was the star in his own. He had a head full of thoughts and feelings; a life inside him; he was the reason that the earth went on turning. My own father and mother, my brothers, aunts, uncles, all my friends – all were 'I'. Everybody was I, and at that moment I was somehow aware that I would probably never learn a more important lesson.

This new understanding did not transform me into a nice person. It enabled me to understand a great deal more about others, but that understanding could be used to help or to harm. In the years that followed, the latter seemed more useful than the former.

Between the ages of ten and sixteen I was desperately engaged in the task of trying to cobble together something in the way of a usable personality. Other people seemed to have one. Why shouldn't I? Somehow I had to batten down the chaos, and construct a facade that would be both acceptable and impenetrable. I certainly didn't want anyone catching a glimpse of the earnest but confused little wretch that I felt myself to be. I discovered that sarcasm, skilfully used, was a means, not only of holding people at a distance, but also of acquiring a certain power. Lowest form of wit it might be, but it was also the most effective. I became an expert in the art of diminishing, belittling, and hurting with words. I blush when I recall the relish with which I applied this weapon at times, to people who can have had no idea of the yearning unhappiness that lay beneath such an alienating strategy. I had postponed happiness in order to concentrate on safety. I learned how to bob and duck and weave in my dealings with school friends and adults, though with more and more difficulty as I moved into the highly competitive world of the boys' grammar school.

Things like homework, and PE kit, and pens that worked, and tidy school uniform, were constant nightmares. I felt grubbier, less equipped in all ways, and more disorganised than any other boy in the school. I had seen other people's houses and families. They seemed almost impossibly ordered and relaxed in comparison with mine. How did they manage it? I had no idea. Our house was a place of loud, moving bodies, swirling emotions and constant television. My mother always did her best, but it was not a place where you did homework. In any case, how could I spare any attention for things like homework or schoolwork, when every ounce of my inventive and mental energy was required for basic social survival?

I was still a voracious reader, and I had considerable natural ability in the subject of English language, but by my second year at secondary school I had already slipped gloomily down into the 'D' stream, the Hades of an establishment like ours, where academic achievement was the road to heaven. My reading nowadays was a way of escape, often into the world of those very dated public-school stories that used to be published in solid thick-paged volumes with a dramatic illustration etched on the front. In these books, clean-living, square-jawed chaps who inhabited something called the Shell, or the Remove, did and said manly things in a highly organised atmosphere of Victorian morality. They had names like 'Goodman' or 'Mainworthy'. Such cads as did exist were called 'Badstone' or 'Munger', and were either reformed or expelled in the final chapter. The teachers always included a young and enthusiastic ex-blue who unobtrusively guided the hero along his path to ultimate manliness, and a God-like headmaster who combined the wisdom of Socrates with the judgement of Solomon. The trinity was completed by a mysterious moving force known generally as 'good form'. Ridiculous though it was, I yearned for such a world. It offered so many things that I had never had.

My other avenue of escape was the fantasy of stardom as a film actor. I nursed a secret conviction that I was the greatest undiscovered thespian in the country, and that it was only a matter of time before, in one of the scenarios that I spent much of my time imagining, I would be discovered by an astonished director and immediately begin a glittering career on the silver screen.

I secretly bought a book entitled *Teach Yourself Amateur Acting,* and studied it in private, so that when the great day came I should be absolutely prepared. My first part would be a leading role in a film that also starred Hayley Mills, with whom I had been deeply in love ever since the day when I sat in the indescribably delicious darkness of the Essoldo cinema, watching *Whistle down the Wind* three times in a row. It was in connection with my passionate feelings about Miss Mills that I learned the second great lesson of my life.

One day, when I was thirteen or so, I made the fatal mistake of trying to turn fantasy into reality. At that time the Mills family lived a few miles away from my home, in a little country village called Cowden. I had often pictured myself accidentally bumping into my beloved in Cowden High Street. It is a fair indication of my naivety that I usually saw this romantic encounter developing from the fact that her bicycle tyre had gone flat. Her knight in shining armour would then pedal suavely on to the scene, flourishing not a sword, but a pump. She would be overwhelmed by my resourcefulness and charity, and subsequently bowled over by my natural charm, which, in my fantasy at least, was irresistible. Marriage would follow at an appropriate age. Large close-ups, glistening tears, stirring music – the lot!

One day I got tired of pretending. I wanted something real to happen for once. I had never actually been to Cowden, but on this warm, sunny, Saturday morning, I decided that the time had come. I set off on my shiny blue bicycle, tense with excitement, to make my dream come true. My belief in a satisfactory outcome to this expedition lasted for several miles, until the moment when I found myself confronted by a nameplate at the side of the road, which said simply, Cowden. I stopped my bike and, balancing on my left foot, reached over to touch the cold metal of the sign with my hand. It was real. Cowden really did exist. I straightened up again and looked around. Beyond the sign the road continued, bordered by trees, flowers and bushes. I could see the tops of one or two houses in the distance – Cowden houses. They were all real. Everything was real. By implication, then, Cowden High

23

Street must be real, Hayley Mills must be real. She was a real person, who didn't spend her life hanging around the village street with an incapacitated bicycle, waiting for some scruffy little twit to rescue her with his pump. It was a sad moment. The world was real. As the full absurdity of my daydream dawned on me, I quietly turned my bike around and pedalled grimly back to Rusthall. Another lesson learned – hard but necessary. I would never find what I wanted in fantasy. That frightened me. Where *would* I find what I wanted?

By the time I began my fifth year at the grammar school, the whole area of education stank of dismal failure. I had never managed to acquire the work habit, and I was so far behind in all subjects except English language, that any hope of passing 'O' level exams had long since evaporated. I felt ugly, and awkward, and useless. The teachers were puzzled. I wasn't typical of the types who failed, but I was impossible to reach by then. It is also impossible to describe to someone who had not experienced it, the leaden misery of daily attendance at an establishment in which you are a legal obligation and nothing more. In all but fantasy (and that was discredited) I was worth nothing. The very school buildings themselves with their grand, mellowed, red-brick frontage seemed to mock my outer and inner disarray as I toiled through the big wrought-iron gates each morning.

I began to truant, setting off for school each morning, dressed in the distinctive grammar school uniform, and ending up walking round and round the recreation ground opposite the school, watching the old men playing bowls, or sitting with a book on the slowly revolving roundabout in the children's corner. Sometimes, at lunchtime, boys from the school would gather in a noisy group behind the bowls pavilion to smoke illicit cigarettes, often cadged from 'Jack', a highly questionable old character whose suspicious enthusiasm for the company of schoolboys was redeemed by his generosity with Kensitas cigarettes, of which he seemed to have an endless supply. Every school seemed to have its 'Jack'. Occasionally I would join this group, pretending to myself that I was normal and involved like them; that, after a morning's work in school, I was relaxing in an enjoyable, forbidden way before returning for the afternoon lessons.

When they left, the game ended, of course, and I would return to the intense solitariness of my truancy. I longed to be part of something, to be genuinely wanted by ordinary people, to be caught up in the warm casualness of relaxed friendship. Those endless months of morbidly aimless wandering while others were busy 'belonging', scarred my self-image more deeply than ever.

Eventually, and inevitably, I was 'asked to leave' by the headmaster. I felt no relief when this happened – only resentment, confusion and shame. I threw my school uniform away for ever, and stepped warily into the adult world.

Chapter Two

Tunbridge Wells in the mid-sixties was an experiential chocolate box. Every flavour of sensation was available in one form or another, and the notorious 'Disgusted of Tunbridge Wells' would need to take only a short walk through his own town to find ample cause for complaint. If you sat in a coffee bar at the lower end of the town, you were as likely to be offered marijuana as a religious tract. If you stayed long enough you would probably get both, and if you lingered even longer you might be approached by a glassy-eyed scientologist offering the chance to learn how to walk through walls in ten easy but very expensive lessons. If group violence was more to your taste, you would become either a mod, in which case you would wear a parka and ride a motor scooter, or a rocker, in which case you would need a leather jacket, long hair, and, at the very least, a regular place on the pillion of somebody's motorcycle. Membership of either of these groups effectively removed the problem of boredom at weekends and on bank holidays, which were spent planning, running from, or seeking mass conflict.

There were other possibilities. Eastern religions and philosophies were available in paperback, and once the jargon was learned, could be adopted as a way of life for a day or two. I remember experiencing some confusion over this when I walked into 'La Rue', one day. La Rue was a small cafe at the busy end of the town, where the pseudointelligentsia (of which I was one) met to discuss something called 'life' at interminable length, with no great profit to the proprietor who viewed with some coldness our tendency to sit in a group around one shallow glass cup of frothy coffee for hours on end. One morning I sauntered intelligently into the cafe, to find a friend called John sitting in the corner, with *I have undergone a change* written all over him. The ensuing conversation went something like this.

ME: You're early, John.

JOHN: *(Unwilling to be drawn into small talk that might dissipate the impact of his new image)* Yes.

ME: Any fags?

JOHN: *(Irritated by my failure to say he seemed different somehow)* No!

ME: Why are you out so early?

JOHN: *(Dreamily)* Because the sky is blue.

ME: Pardon?

JOHN: Because the grass is green, because birds fly, and hair grows.

ME: Right ... hair grows ... right. I'm with you now, John. (What the hell was he on about?)

SILENCE

JOHN: *(Further irritated by my refusal to admit ignorance)* I don't see things in the same way any more.

ME: *(A generous concession)* Why not?

JOHN: *(Triumphantly)* Because the world is round!

It turned out that John had sat up for most of the night reading a Penguin publication about Zen Buddhism, and his peculiar responses to my questions were evidences of his exciting discovery that, not only was he a Zen Buddhist now, but he always *had* been one without realising it. This made life a little difficult for him, as the book made it clear that the true adherent would never dream of actually stating crudely that he was a Zen Buddhist. Hence, the rather strange dialogue when I came into the cafe. I believe John went on to become a totally committed Marxist – for a week.

If the 'isms' failed to attract, one could always become a novelist who also wrote poetry. The attraction of this occupation in the sixties, was that it was unnecessary to actually write anything beyond the first line or two of what would undoubtedly have been a great psychological work of fiction if it had ever been finished. In addition, one might compose a few lines of totally obscure poetry, unadulterated by such dated devices as metre, rhyme, or even meaning, and designed to break the stranglehold of the old classical poets like Milton, Dryden, and other people whose works one had never read. Today, twenty years later, there are still, to my certain knowledge, two people continuing to circulate the cafes and pubs of Tunbridge Wells with exercise books and biros, who were doing exactly the same thing in 1965. Tunbridge Wells can do that to people. It can allow them to decay with such a sense of style, that they hardly notice the process until it is too late.

This was particularly so in the sixties because educationalists thought they had discovered that each human being was, potentially, a creative genius. It would have been sacrilege for any one person to criticise another's artistic efforts. The real casualties were those who never recovered from flattery.

So, the choice was mine. Which flavour would I choose? I needed something badly, but it would have to go very deep to make a real difference. My facade of ironic indifference was brittle, but effective, and it was all I had. I sensed the shallowness of all that was on offer, but it didn't surprise me. Everybody is I. Did all these others carry around inside them the same tight ball of tearful chaos that I did? At one point my disguise included a violently checked jacket, a pair of dark glasses that I wore at all times and in all weathers, and a black billiard ball which I repeatedly threw up and caught with my right hand. Nobody was going to get inside me! I must have looked, to borrow a powerful expression of my son's, a real 'super-nurd'.

There were three good and important things in my life at this point. The first, my mother, had always been there, although on reflection I can see that my appreciation and treatment of her had been variable. Often, during this difficult period, I would arrive home very late at night to find that my father had switched off the electricity at the mains. This meant that the one light-bulb which travelled from room to room as it was needed, was useless to me. The dark house was doom-laden at one o'clock in the morning, but as I groped my way upstairs – still wearing the dark glasses – I knew that, nine times out of ten, my mother would have left beside my bed a little pile of sandwiches – usually Marmite – and a large glass of milk. People say they are curious about heaven. I have tasted heaven. It consists of reading escapist literature by candlelight while eating Marmite sandwiches and drinking cold milk, in a dark house in a dark world.

The second good thing was a real live girlfriend called Anthea. She was a talented, kind girl, whose parents were predictably aghast to find that the apple of their eye had trawled in an apparent lunatic, whose taste in clothes and obsession with dark glasses and billiard balls must have suggested that placement in a locked institution was imminent.

Anthea and I were together for four years, and I owe her a great deal. She was the first person outside my family to dispel my personal myth that I was unlovable, and she put up with a lot of testing in the process. I remember her with great affection.

The third important thing was my acquisition of three friends. The first, John Hall, had attended one of those traditional public schools I was so fond of reading about, though his description of life in his particular establishment bore little relation to fictional accounts. John's natural courtesy and generosity thawed me, often allowing the vulnerable little boy of six years ago to risk a brief excursion into the outside world. John is now an Anglican priest in the north of England, and still my closest friend. The other two friends were a married couple who lived in a rented cottage in the depths of the Sussex countryside, near Wadhurst. Murray and Vivien Staplehurst accepted me so unreservedly that I really began to feel – while I was with them at any rate – that life might be worth living after all. They switched me on with their approval, affection and appreciation of my sense of humour and fascinated me with their eccentricity and larger-than-life-ness. I value their friendship now, as then.

Every Sunday, the Anglican Church of St John's in Tunbridge Wells organised a coffee-bar evening in the upper room of a building called Byng Hall, next door to The Red Lion on one side, and my ex-grammar school on the other. In charge was a young and enthusiastic curate named Clive Sampson. He arrived after evensong each Sunday, accompanied by a small group of clean-looking teenagers to unlock the front door of the hall and admit the little knot of non-church attenders who usually gathered outside. I had got into the habit of coming along each week largely because there was very little else to do in Tunbridge Wells on a Sunday evening. The coffee was very cheap, and there were other, less material attractions. I sensed that, in a way I didn't quite understand, I was nibbling at someone's bait. Something in the studied casualness of the non-miniskirted Christian girls, and the short haired, jerseyed Christian boys suggested that they were all expecting something to happen in, for, or to me, one of these days. It soon became clear that they were waiting – and perhaps praying – for my conversion to Christianity, whatever that might mean.

I took an odd pleasure in paddling on the edge of this sea of expectation, never going in too far, but never withdrawing completely. The only formal religious content of these evenings was a three minute talk or 'epilogue' near the end, but I rather enjoyed the sport of 'cornering the curate'. Every week I would have a different question to ask, a fresh objection to make, or a new argument to introduce. Clive battled manfully with the problems, clearly feeling a little inadequate as he sorted out the whole question of universal suffering for me, and explained, on behalf of God, how predestination and free will are, actually, not incompatible at all. He half dreaded, half enjoyed these mind-stretching encounters. For me the whole thing had very little to do with God, any more than the Roman Catholic chapel had when I was a child. I enjoyed the discussions – I enjoyed seeing Clive out of his depth sometimes – but mainly I was just a sucker for being wanted. They let me talk and they seemed to want me in a slightly predatory sort of way. It was possible to relax and enjoy being large and different among these people who, though the same age as me, had skinnier arms and more innocent and organised lives.

Poor old Clive became aware after a number of weeks that talking me into any kind of Christian belief had about as much chance of success as striking a match on jelly. He had used all the illustrations, explanations, revelations and exhortations that he could think of. He was right out of '-ations'. The day came when his patience faded. His intellect stomped off in disgust, leaving his heart free to say something at last.

'I just love him!' he blurted out, smacking the palm of his hand down on the formica-topped coffee bar. 'I love him! That's all – I just love Jesus!'

This crashing service ace, coming at the end of a long succession of easily returned schoolgirl lobs, caught me totally wrong-footed. He'd broken the rules, hadn't he? Who said we were going to talk about things that really mattered to us? Because there was no doubt at all that Clive reacted to this Jesus from the gut. He'd taken a long time to say so, but it was a fact, and I was impressed. Not convinced, but definitely impressed, even a little shaken perhaps. Underneath Clive's words – and I knew all about words – lay a passionate feeling, or emotion, about someone who didn't exist, except as an historical figure.

Here we are, then, at a danger point. I can feel the temptation to embroider this incident and my reaction to it. I know how to do it. I would like to say that my spirit sensed the presence of the Lord. It didn't. I would like to say that from that moment I felt God calling me to him. I didn't. I would like to say all sorts of things that are not quite true. They might encourage people, but God wants the truth, and the truth is a funny, ragged old thing.

One instinct that Clive's outburst did arouse in me was curiosity. I was puzzled by the strength of his feelings and the process by which he had acquired them. Not that I equated strength of feeling with truth or goodness, necessarily. The Inquisition and the Nazi party were poor adverts for enthusiasm, to name but two. Clive had never burned anyone at the stake, or invaded Poland, as far as I knew, but, perhaps because of my father, I was very wary of emotion. I decided to maintain my air of indifference, and investigate as casually as I could.

I went to church. St John's was a very satisfactorily churchy-looking sort of church. Grey stone, and towers, and pointed arches, and dark wood and things. It was a heavy, comfortable, motherly sort of building, presided over by the Reverend Donald Edison, one of the sweetest-natured men I have known. Clive was his curate. I began to go to the service known as Evensong. This began at 6.30, and ended at 7.30, a long time for a devoted cigarette smoker like me, but I usually stuck it out for the hour. Soon I was settled into the new pattern. Tea at Anthea's house about five o'clock, down to the church for Evensong at half past six, and along the road to Byng Hall for the coffee bar at half past seven. The whole thing had a very pleasantly civilised feel about it. It was an oasis of order and freshness in the desert of unemployed gloom that filled the rest of the week. I remember my particular pleasure in the knowledge that Anthea's mother always ensured that Sunday tea included one of those beautifully labelled china pots of Patum Peperium – Gentleman's Relish. It was there for me.

The preacher at the evening service would usually be either Donald Edison or Clive Sampson, with the occasional visiting speaker.

One day a man called Denis Shepherd, from one of the London churches, came to speak to the evening congregation. He was a tall, broad man, with a quiet manner and an air of inner strength. As far as I can recall he had been in the Merchant Navy for some years before being ordained into the Anglican Church. I was still very much a spectator, and I would have rejected with scorn the suggestion that what this man said was going to bring real tears to my eyes, and, for better or worse, change the whole course of my life.

The talk he gave was about the brief conversation between Jesus, as he hung dying on the cross, and the two lawbreakers who were crucified on either side of him, an event which is recorded only in the Gospel of Luke. The preacher read the relevant passage before beginning his talk.

> One of the criminals hanging there abused him. 'Are you not the Christ?' he said. 'Save yourself and us as well.' But the other spoke up and rebuked him. 'Have you no fear of God at all?' he said. 'You got the same sentence as he did, but in our case we deserved it: we are paying for what we did. But this man has done nothing wrong. Jesus,' he said, 'remember me when you come into your kingdom.' 'Indeed, I promise you,' he replied, 'today you will be with me in paradise.'

The Reverend Shepherd went on to speak in more detail about the kind of interaction that must have occurred between these dirty, blood-streaked individuals as they hung side by side waiting for the relief of death. He spoke particularly about the man who had recognised something special in Jesus. He was a man who, to all intents and purposes, was finished. His life was over, and a wretched, useless life it had been. Any dreams of last minute reprieve had been shattered by the first of the executioner's nails, as it crunched through bone, sinew and flesh, impaling him to the rough wooden surface of his cross. It was the end of all reasonable hope. The dialogue between this fellow and Jesus was very uncomplicated. Presumably, it arose from what each saw in the other as they shared the same kind of physical agony. What did the criminal see in Jesus? Nobody knows for sure, but it was probably some kind of natural authority blended with deep compassion.

He obviously looked like someone who, despite his present circumstances, was going somewhere – an 'in-charge' sort of person, a grown-up. He must have known a bit about Jesus already, the conversation shows that: but perhaps he had never looked closely at him before, or believed it was possible to reach the heights of virtue that must surely be required from followers of such an uncompromisingly moral character. Whatever else he did or did not see, though, one thing is clear. He recognised a sudden, breath-taking opportunity to make everything all right. Morally naked as he was, there was no hope of convincing the Galilean that he deserved anything, nor was there time to live-a-better-life for a while in the hope of investing a little in his divine bank account. Perhaps what was happening was that the child in this hardened law-breaker, the part of him that still wanted to believe in something or someone, was yearning for the warmth and comfort that all children must have. In the eyes of the man beside him, he saw an invitation to be loved and wanted, not because of, nor despite, anything, but simply because that is what children need. Jesus' eyes, as they looked into the lost and dejected face of his neighbour, were full of the love of his father. They were saying, 'I don't care what you've done. I don't care what you are. I don't care what others say about you. I don't even care what you think of yourself. You're coming with me. Don't worry, everything's going to be all right.'

As I sat next to Anthea at the back of the crowded church, the preacher's words seemed to be meant specially for me. I felt like a child too. The puzzled little boy who had wanted so much to stop his mummy and daddy arguing so that they would be happy together, but had failed, not only at that, but at almost everything else since, wanted to shout out his hurt across the heads of the congregation, through the preacher who seemed a sort of conduit to God, and thence up to heaven itself.

'What about me? I'm lost too! I'm lonely and ragged inside. I've tried and tried, but I just don't know how to be like ordinary people. What about me? Do you love me like you loved that man on the cross? Will you be a father to me, whatever I am and whatever I say or do? Can I safely show you how hurt and wretched I am?'

Would Jesus look at me from the cross with those same loving eyes and say 'Don't worry, everything's okay. I know all about you, Adrian. It doesn't matter what's happened up to now. I'll look after you. I know you never wanted to be hurtful or sarcastic. I know how much you wanted to do well. I know you're not the person you wanted to be. It doesn't matter – I do understand.'

Suddenly my eyes were full of tears. How I wanted that kind of acceptance, the chance to start again and be real, to relax the constant strain that the maintenance of my artificial personality imposed on me. This man was saying that Jesus offered all these things in the twentieth century – right now. As I stood for the final hymn, my hands supporting my weight on the pew in front of me, I managed to control the tears, and after the blessing we joined the stream of people flowing down the centre aisle towards the big front doors where the preacher waited to shake hands with people as they left. Just before we reached him, Anthea and I looked at each other. Without speaking we knew that both of us had been affected by what we had just heard. As I shook hands with Denis Shepherd a few seconds later, I found myself saying quietly, 'Could we see you afterwards? We want to become Christians.'

Later, when the congregation had dispersed and all was quiet, we met him in a room at the back of the church and told him that we wanted to do 'whatever you did' in order to get 'whatever you got'. He seemed to understand this strange request, and suggested that we should say a prayer in which we asked Jesus into our hearts as Lord and Saviour. I didn't know what that meant, but I wasn't going to let mere technicalities put me off when real happiness was available. We found it hard to frame a prayer properly, so, in the end he prayed for us, while we joined in silently in our minds, and said 'amen' with him at the end. The prayer was short, but it included terms and concepts that, while appearing quite straightforward at the time, awe me nowadays with their depth and mystery.

'Heavenly Father, we know that we have sinned against you, like all mankind, by turning away from you. We thank you that Jesus died on the cross to pay for our sins and to offer a way back to you. We ask that Jesus will come and live in our hearts by the power of your Holy Spirit, and that we may be able to love and serve you for the rest of our lives, and be with you in heaven forever when we die. We ask this in the name of the Lord Jesus Christ, Amen.'

I didn't feel anything as I prayed this prayer – neither then nor immediately afterwards, but I had prayed it. My mind had said 'Yes' and I was a Christian.

There were many exciting Christian paperbacks on sale in the sixties. There are still, of course, but at that time it was something new. These books were so full of miraculous signs and wonders, that they made everyday life seem very drab and dull in comparison. After my conversion I, in common with many others, devoured this kind of literature in much the same way that large mammals are obliged to eat constantly in order to stay alive. They usually chronicled the background, conversion and subsequent spiritual adventures of a particular individual – often American. They made you gasp and weep and hope that, in time, God could use you in a similar way. Each new book that was published seemed to emphasise a different aspect of the Christian life, or a more reliable way to ensure that you had easy access to the divine machinery, and a working knowledge of its controls.

'Praise God in all adversity' said one. 'Don't be afraid to be angry and honest with God' said another.

'People who don't speak in tongues are not really Christians' claimed one writer. 'You don't need to speak in tongues to be a Christian' answered somebody else.

'God is working in the established church.' 'God had rejected the established church.'

All claimed to be right, all offered evidence to support their particular claim, and most included, somewhere on the front or back cover, the seductive phrase 'This is a true story'. I now know that there is a significant difference between a list of consecutive factual events, and an account in which things like atmosphere, interpretation and illustration have been woven – often very attractively – around those events. I try to do it myself. 'Truth' can be a very difficult thing to pin down. At the time, though, I was happy to collude with the writers of these books, which meant that I discovered the 'real answer', on average, about twice a week.

Many people were genuinely and lastingly helped, especially by such classics as *The Cross and the Switchblade*, but I fear that for me and many others, each new spiritual volume was like one more shot in the arm for an addict. It reassured for a time, and gave the world a rather tinny dazzle, but it didn't last for long.

One thing that nearly all these books had in common was the suggestion that conversion meant the end of the bad times, and the beginning of the good times. Much recent Christian literature, thankfully, avoids this grotesque and dangerous over-simplification, and is as honest as Jesus was, but at that time I got it firmly into my head that conversion equalled happy-ever-after, and there was little in the presentation of evangelical Christianity at the time to dispel this illusion. I had been converted. Go on then, God. Do something. Change me. Organise me. I've said the prayer. Away you go!

It wasn't working.

Soon after the day of our conversion, Anthea and I had been sent, through the post, a list of prayer meetings, Bible studies, and youth activities that were scheduled for the coming month. This list utterly dismayed me, and for some weeks I didn't go near the church. I felt confused and hurt. On the Sunday evening when Denis Shepherd had spoken, I had been deeply moved and attracted by the possibility of acceptance and love from this man – God, Jesus. It had been an encounter between two personalities, and it had seemed to promise change. What had a typed list of activities to do with that? My resentment was on a hair trigger, and the flimsy piece of formality that I held in my hand was enough to fire it full-blast at a church which seemed to think that 'putting me on the register' would help in some way. God had offered me bread to eat because he saw that I was hungry. Now I was being told that what this amounted to was a course of cookery lessons. What had I expected? I don't know. I was full of bitterness and anger, quite unable to think rationally. I felt like the army recruit who, having responded to the charm of the recruiting officer, finds that things change drastically after signing on the dotted line.

In hindsight I can see the extent to which vanity played a part in my response. Like most people who despise themselves in private, I found it very difficult to be an also-ran in public. Perhaps I thought that the whole of Christendom should have rejoiced mightily to find such a valuable asset added to its numbers. Perhaps, in a local sense, it should have done. We who call ourselves Christians should be constantly aware that when someone responds to a call from God, we may have access to the particular kind of bread that was promised in that encounter. Let's give it. Let's ignore our prissy concern that we may be feeding someone's vanity. Let's be extravagant and let God sort the rest out.

Whatever the rights and wrongs of the situation, by the time I did go back to the church, a month or so later, I had reassembled my defences, and was ready to take on my old role of guilty performer in the new context of the Young People's Fellowship, and the Christian community of St John's Church. I learned the ropes and the language (what someone recently called 'Christianese') quite quickly. On one level I enjoyed being a part of the group, and yet being different – more 'of the world', but on another I still felt alienated and unreal. In the middle of meetings and services it was possible to feel good, to shout 'Praise the Lord!' with the others, and even feel that I meant it, but the nights were black. God never came home with me. I would return from a lively bout of rejoicing to find that, on my own, there was only fear, fear that there was no God; fear even that in some peculiar way I only existed when other people were present. My own consciousness was embarrassingly there with me, watching as some other 'I' wrestled with panic and doubt. I had never heard of holograms then, but that was what I felt like – substantial only as a projection of the beliefs, attitudes and responses of others. But how could I tell anyone this? I was a Christian. I was converted. If things weren't going right; if I wasn't experiencing the love, joy and peace that God *always* brought into the hearts of believers, there were only three possible reasons that I could think of.

(1) There was no God. I had made a mistake.
(2) I had done, or failed to do, something that was crucially important.
(3) After taking a closer look, God had said, 'No thanks very much', and decided I wasn't up to scratch.

I didn't want to believe the first, hoped vaguely that it might be the second, and secretly believed and dreaded that it was actually the third. Sometimes, I read the parable of the sower, in which some of the seed falls on stony ground, and after springing up quickly, withers away in the sun because it has no real roots. Was that me? And were all these mild, tidily dressed young people, who didn't smoke and were working for exams or preparing to go to university or college, the seed that fell on rich soil and produced a crop, some a hundredfold, some sixty, some thirty? I felt they must be. No doubt they all woke each morning and had the much discussed and strongly advocated 'quiet time' with God. I didn't. I said I did, but I didn't, any more than I had done my homework while at school.

In fact, the whole experience became a kind of parallel of schooldays. My uniform was evangelical language and behaviour – as scruffy and ill-fitting as ever – and the headmaster was God, a distant being who was kind to those who succeeded, and eventually expelled the ones who didn't, or couldn't. What had happened to the Jesus who said he would look after me, and accept me whatever I was? I sang about him, discussed him, tried to talk to him. Where the heck was he? If there seems to be a lot of anger in these words, that's because there is. Even as I write, the memory of that feeling of angry disappointment floods into my mind and momentarily obscures the peace that I have now.

Now, of course, gentle reader, (I used to read a lot of Victorian literature as a child) I can see, as you can, that this scruffy, mixed up and over defended teenager was confusing God with middle class evangelical Christianity and that as long as I was trying to be like other people who were very different to me, I stood little chance of feeling that I was getting somewhere. Also, I recognise that my trusting mechanism had rusted with disuse, and was bound to require consistent applications of the oil of love, over a long period, before it ground into action again. Add to this my distorted perception of fatherhood and adult relationships, and it really is not difficult to account for the mess I found myself in. But I was by no means the only casualty. My heart goes out to all those others, who, in the sixties were attracted by Jesus, and tried unsuccessfully thereafter, to find him in the security of groups and jargon. In the group that I joined there was at least a handful of people who, because of difficult, painful backgrounds needed a special kind of love and discipline, but gave up in the end because the strain of copying was too great. They are at a particular disadvantage because, whereas most of the other attractions of the period – drugs or eastern philosophies or whatever – could be dropped without guilt, the abandonment of Christianity, as it was presented then and still is in many places, often left a shadow of guilt and failure darkening a corner of the spirit, that was not easily removed. This was intensified by the fact – puzzling and hurtful at the time – that whereas people in the church accepted you totally before conversion, they tended to find any deviation from the norm very annoying or unacceptable after you had 'crossed the line'.

So, the escape into reality that I had so longed for was simply not happening. Why *did* God disappear when I was on my own? Why was I still having to wear the masks that prevented people from coming close to me? Why, oh why was it all such a strain? I just didn't know.

Chapter Three

I arrived in Bristol after dark, clutching two badly fastened, string-reinforced suitcases, with not the slightest idea of where I would stay, or how I would look after myself. The city seemed terrifyingly large as I trudged out of the coach station, to find myself on one of those featureless roads that run dumbly behind large buildings. It was a viciously unwelcoming spot, and I was near to tears for a moment, as I put my bags down and tried to decide what to do next.

I suppose it was something of a miracle that I was there at all. Nearly three years had passed since I officially left school. After two or three disastrous attempts to enter the world of employment I had managed, on the strength of my ability with language, to enrol at the West Kent College of Further Education for a combined GCE and foundation drama course. Such a course could not have been better suited to one who, like me, was able to produce occasional flashes of brilliance in English Literature classes and drama exercises, this temporarily blinding tutors to the fact that I was doing next to no work at all.

A close friend, Hugh Card, wrote to me recently about those days.

We met in 1967, at a college Christian Union meeting. I was an engineering student. You were on a drama course. I noticed your size and untidiness. You sat at a table, dropping cigarette ash on the yellow formica, taking up more space than seemed reasonable. You talked rather than listened. As you explained your ideas, bits of paper spread across the table and on to the floor. An Agatha Christie fell out of your pocket. You were the untidiest Christian I'd met.

For two years I enjoyed a feeling of relative significance in this setting, especially as the second year was spent in the comfortable knowledge that I had secured a place on the Bristol Old Vic Theatre School acting course, to commence in the autumn of 1967.

I left the college, finally, with a B pass at 'A' level in English Literature, which delighted and (secretly) amazed me, and a scraped pass in French 'O' level, which left me with the ability to converse in the present tense with close members of the family on such useful and diverse topics as writing implements and dining rooms, but very little else. Now, I was about to pursue that old fantasy of stardom in the acting world, and I had a real place on a real course at a real and reputable theatre school, over a hundred miles away in the city of Bristol. If only I had been better prepared. For some reason I never got round to arranging a place to stay when I arrived. It was so easy to rationalise my disorganisation. I called it 'walking in faith'. Christians didn't need to trouble themselves with such trivial matters as booking accommodation in advance. God would provide.

Now, as I stood dismally next to my luggage in the darkness of a strange city, I wasn't so sure. There was one chance, though. A friend in Tunbridge Wells had told me about a church in the Redlands area of the city. She knew the vicar well. He was, she said, a wonderful Christian. If ever I needed anything I should go to him. He would help.

'Right!' I said to myself, picking up my cases, 'Redlands it is.'

After many enquiries, and a fairly lengthy walk, I found myself, at last, outside the front door of a house situated to one side of the church my friend had named. On a polished wooden nameplate beside the door, I could just make out the reassuring words 'The Vicarage'. I was very tired by now, and aching with hunger, but these basic needs were as nothing compared to my desperate desire to make real contact with someone in this alien world. Ever one for the dramatic moment, I planned my lines carefully before

44

raising my hand to the brass knocker in front of me. After all, this might be the beginning of chapter one in my own best-selling Christian saga one day.

The door was opened by a nicely dressed lady, probably in her fifties, who peered doubtfully out at the tall dark figure standing between what must have looked in silhouette, like two over-stuffed cardboard boxes.

'Yes?' she said, rather nervously.

'I'm starting at the theatre school this term,' said I, 'and I've just arrived from Tunbridge Wells tonight.'

'Yes?' she sounded even more nervous than before.

Time for my punchline.

'I've got nowhere to stay and the only person I know in Bristol is Jesus.'

Now she looked positively terrified.

'My husband's out at the moment, I'm afraid . . . I don't know . . .'

Something crumpled in me. Never mind my Christian saga, I just wanted a little mothering. My voice broke a little as I spoke.

'A friend suggested I should come if I needed help . . .' I named the friend.

'Oh, yes, I know.' It obviously didn't make any difference. 'I'm afraid that my husband won't be back for some time.' The door was closing, she was drawing back. 'Try again later, perhaps . . .' The latch clicked into place. She was gone.

What had gone wrong? Wrong script? Wrong house? Wrong city? Wrong world? I was desolated. My last emotional and physical reserves had been spent in reaching that front door. All the old horror of not belonging flooded into my heart as I picked up my luggage and trailed off into the darkness. The magic words hadn't done the trick. Much later that night I did finally find somewhere to stay, but the moment immediately after the door shut on that autumn night in 1967 remained as a nightmare memory for years. Christians, God, Jesus – no one kept their promises.

I was, of course, totally self-absorbed at the time, otherwise I might have understood that middle-aged ladies on their own late at night are, quite reasonably, unwilling to admit very large religious maniacs with great armfuls of murder weapons in cardboard boxes. I'm sure that the lady concerned was as charitable as the next person, and, in one sense, she has affected me positively. Since that night I have never turned anyone away from my door.

I had not realised that it was possible to be as lonely as I was during my first term at Bristol. I used to lie on my bed in the lodgings I had found, alternately pleading and raving in the direction of this God who seemed to exist only within the confines of St John's Church, Tunbridge Wells.

Not surprisingly, perhaps, the year that followed was not a successful one in terms of the acting course. There was no doubt that I had talent, but my application and self-discipline were very poor. I soon realised that I lacked the kind of consistency required from students of what is a very tough and demanding profession. Once again, the reality trampled all over the dream. I stumbled through the days and weeks in my usual ragged fashion, still clutching my large Bible like a talisman in the most inappropriate situations, hoping I suppose that God would eventually flesh out the bones of the identity that I still thought the Christian faith might offer me.

Now some of those who have been following the story closely so far, will be aware, and are probably dying to point out to me, that 'Old God', as Bishop Peter Ball sometimes affectionately refers to him, had been putting in some pretty useful work on my behalf for some time, and getting no credit whatsoever for it. From the year before my conversion there were no less than five people who were offering me the kind of love and acceptance that God had seemed to promise on the night when Denis Shepherd spoke in the church. Whether they knew this or not, whether they liked it or not, it was so. My mother, Murray and Vivien, John and Anthea, all were keeping God's promise, and in their own way contributing to the process of breaking up the stony ground in my heart to create the kind of rich soil that would make real growth possible in the future. I didn't know this at the time, of course, but how well I understand it now. Later, in my work with children I met so many disturbed youngsters for whom security was just a rumour put about by social workers. They could be surrounded by love, and not see it. Their conviction that the world did not want them was not a belief. It was knowledge. They could not simply be talked into happiness, nor could they be bribed or lured into feeling 'all right'. Often, all that one could do was to go on loving them, practically as well as emotionally, sometimes for years without much, if any, response. They could be aggressive, rejecting, sentimental and apathetic by turns. I once sat with a fifteen-year-old boy sobbing on my lap after he had broken all my windows.

During that excruciatingly lonely period in Bristol, my head was so full of myself, scripture, spiritual gifts, charismatic speakers and Christianese gobbledegook, that I probably wouldn't have recognised Jesus if he'd jumped out in front of me on the pavement and performed amazing miracles before my eyes. Much less was I able to see the quietly persistent love of God in the eyes and arms and voices of those who cared about me.

Blinking God! I'd have broken all his windows if I'd known where they were. Then, perhaps, he would have let *me* sob on *his* lap!

It was in Bristol, in that year of failure at the theatre school, that God gave me the most valuable gift of all. Bridget Ormerod was a fellow student. Like me, she was capable of great mood-swings, but she had a kindness and sense of humour that I found irresistible. Her surname, she told me, meant 'snake in the clearing', which suggested a sort of unconcealed evil. How inappropriate for someone who has brought nothing but care and kindness into people's lives for as long as I have known her.

We spent all our time together after the first term, sometimes spending the period from midnight to dawn in the all night cafe down in the Cumberland Basin, a place where the river and the main road met and crossed by means of a pivoting concrete bridge. The whole scene was lit up at night like a stage set, this appealing greatly to the sense of drama we had in common. It was a blissful time. After a long period of non-belief, Bridget had recently had a conversion experience of her own, and, for a while

I enjoyed the novel experience of feeling that God and the world and I belonged to each other, and to Bridget of course. I was in love. We were in love. We felt like two children whom God was leading by the hand into a future that seemed much more promising than I had dared to hope. Perhaps God was all right after all? Fingers crossed.

The immediate question was what to do next. We would get married. We were quite sure about that. We were also quite sure that our future did not lie in the theatre. Eventually, we decided that, although we knew very little about it, we wanted to work in child-care of some kind. Indeed we believed that this was what God was leading us to do. After one or two false starts, and a brief but very enjoyable period as domestic workers at Burrswood, the Christian Healing Home near Tunbridge Wells, we started work as housefather and housemother in a County Council boarding school for maladjusted boys, in the little town of Dursley in Gloucestershire. The school provided places for fifty teenage boys with educational and emotional problems. We occupied single staff flats at opposite ends of the building, which was set in the beautiful green-sculpted Gloucestershire countryside. We were to be married in the following year. On the day we started work it was difficult to see how anything could go very wrong.

At last I seemed to be secure enough to let my childhood insight that 'Everybody is I' work for the benefit of other people. I suppose I envisaged the children I would work with as little, neglected, empty pots, into which I, a combination of Danny Kaye and Doctor Barnardo would pour care, affection and sympathy until they were full and overflowing. They would be pathetically grateful.

I cannot recall any single child being willing to take part in this touching scenario, and after only one day's work with the boys, I drastically adapted my fantasy to one in which a child, any child, was willing to talk pleasantly for five whole minutes to a painfully inept and lonely house-parent.

Within a few weeks my dignity was in shreds. All the techniques and ploys that had just about kept me afloat in the sea of adult interaction were virtually useless against the tidal wave of raw feeling that emanated from these hurt and needy children. With the uncannily accurate insight that is born out of disappointment and failure, they saw through my assumed air of calm confidence and provoked me into responses that frightened me in their violence and intensity. One boy in particular, was a past master in the art of finding my psychological raw spot, and twisting his metaphorical finger into it with relish. He had been alternately beaten and rejected by his policeman father, and he set out to prove that I, tall and dark like his dad, would do the same. His lengthy campaign of aggression and cringing apology worked in the end. In the centre of the football field one day, I knew that my frustration and humiliation were about to find expression. I would either burst into tears or hit him. As we faced each other at that moment the only real difference between us was one of size. I hit him very hard, twice. He had revealed me for what I was; a very immature adult with far too much chaos of my own to be able to cope with his. I couldn't face that at the time, though. I needed so much to be a person who loved children. The guilt and confusion I felt over this and other occasions when I lost control, remained unexamined and unresolved, and were to result in profound problems later in my life.

That first year of work was a nightmare of demolished dignity, lost battles and periodic retreats into the bottom of my wardrobe, where the enclosed darkness offered temporary respite from this world that seemed determined to prove to me yet again, that it was horribly real. Thank goodness I had Bridget. God seemed to have gone on holiday.

The second year was a little easier, but it was marked by an event of considerable significance: the death of my father. The news came by telephone one evening, as Bridget and I, married by now, were preparing to take ten of the most difficult boys away for a hostelling holiday. My mother said that the cancer which had been diagnosed two years earlier had finally killed my father. I didn't really know how to react, and the holiday, which we decided should go ahead as planned, was actually a rather welcome distraction. The constant activity required in the job I was doing enabled me to postpone the uncomfortable task of looking at my feelings for some time. When I did finally risk a peep round the wall of my busy-ness, I discovered that I was deeply unhappy. I was unhappy for a specific reason. My father's death had not been unexpected. We had known for some time that his illness was terminal, so whenever I journeyed from Gloucestershire to Tunbridge Wells to visit my parents' home, I made sure that we 'got on' well. I felt sorry for him in his diminished, crumpled state, all the old jealousies and insecurities seeming so trivial now that he depended on my mother like a helpless child. Also, if I am honest, I was deliberately trying to put together a reasonable collection of positive memories, ready to pile up like sandbags against the inevitable attack of guilt after his death.

But my immediate unhappiness was not about anything that had happened during his life, but about what was happening *now*. Had the plump prayer book worked? Had the Roman Catholic Church worked? Had God worked? Where was my father now? I wanted to know the answer to that question more than I wanted anything else. I remembered moments from the distant past when, frustrated beyond measure by the unbridgeable gap between what he was and what his religion said he should be, he had knelt on the floor pounding a chair with his fist, and shouting through clenched teeth, 'Oh, Christ, help me! Oh, Christ, help me!' Had Christ heard him, or was it all just a cruel, meaningless game?

By now, my father would know – if there was anything to know – all about heaven and hell. I had only the vaguest notion of what terms like that might mean, but I asked God about it again and again.

'Tell me . . . please tell me. Where is he?'

I began to think that I would never find peace, until, one night, I had a dream.

There were two parts to the dream. In the first part, I didn't feel as if I was dreaming at all. Perhaps I wasn't. The period just before sleep can be an odd mixture of conscious thought, and unbidden, dream-like images. Awake or asleep – it doesn't really matter. I saw the face of Jesus, just above mine, as I lay in my bed in the darkness. It was a face that smiled, and the smile was one that comforted and reassured. It was there for a few seconds, and then it was gone, like a light being turned out. Don't ask me how I knew that it was Jesus' face. I just knew.

The second part of the dream was quite definitely just that – a dream. It began with a muffled knocking sound, someone was knocking on wood with their knuckles, trying to attract attention. Gradually, I became aware that the noise was coming from my left, and, turning slowly in that direction, I saw a coffin. As I stared at the brown wooden container, I knew with the absolute certainty that is peculiar to dreams, that my father was inside, alive, and anxïous to be released from the darkness. With that knowledge came the realisation that someone was standing quietly on my other side, waiting to speak to me. He was a traveller, a man from Tibet, the country I have always associated with hidden knowledge and mysticism. He had travelled a long way, he said, to bring me an important message.

I can hear his words as clearly today as I heard them that night, fourteen years ago.

'There is a rumour that your father has been resurrected.'

That was all; the dream ended with those words. In the morning I remembered the details, but it wasn't until later in the day that I connected the dream message with my constant requests to God for information. As soon as that connection was made, I felt peaceful about my father's whereabouts, although I reckoned that at most, I had been given a divine 'hint'.

This experience is of course a very good example of the kind of incident that can be wrapped in the cotton-wool of spiritual jargon and exhibited from time to time in one's personal museum of 'things that show there is a God'. Thus, in the past, I might, and probably have, described the events of that night in the following way.

'I was lying awake – absolutely wide awake – when the Lord manifested himself to me, and ministered to me through his spirit in great power, with a mightly blessing. I was then shown a vision as of a coffin, and a great knocking came from within. A messenger of the Lord then appeared, and brought wonderful news that my father was gloriously resurrected. From that moment my soul was at peace, and I knew that my prayers were indeed marvellously answered.'

Notice that Tibet has disappeared altogether, and the whole thing is much tidier and more presentable. No, I seemed to see Jesus smiling at me; a man in a dream hinted that my father might be okay; the next day I was no longer troubled; I had been asking God for reassurance. These were the things that happened and they were enough.

Bridget and I worked at the boarding school for three years, and although there was some success and satisfaction, some good relationships made, and some painful partings at the end, it was an overpowering relief to walk down the drive and out through the gates for the last time. As we sat surrounded by cases in the little Dursley bus station I reflected on my amazing capacity for nostalgia.

'If,' I said to Bridget, 'you ever hear me say that I wish we could go back to the good old days in Gloucestershire, just remind me that at this moment I KNOW that's not the way it was!'

She promised she would, and has, of course, had to do so on a number of occasions since.

From Gloucestershire we moved to Bromley, in Kent, where I had been offered a place at a teaching college. In those days, the main qualification for promotion in the child-care world was a teaching certificate, and despite having been reduced to my lowest common denominators by the children at Cam House School, I wanted to continue in that kind of work. I also wanted to have a higher education qualification just for the sake of having it. Bridget had obtained a degree at Bristol University before starting at the theatre school, and, although very humble, was annoyingly bright. So – little Adrian had to have a badge to wear, just like her! I got my badge in the end, a not very impressive B.Ed degree, but by then it didn't seem to matter so much. During the three year course, our first son, Matthew, was born. I was totally enchanted with this little scrap of humanity. He was an enduring novelty, a source of endless fascination and pleasure. I loved his uncompromising, openly expressed need for us, his parents. Every sound he made, every new expression or movement was vitally interesting. Dear Matthew was, and still very much is, another link in the chain of God's loving concern for me. So too are a number of folk who were members of the local church youth club which we helped to run. They are all grown up now (they claim), but are still our very close friends, including Madeleine Dawson, who later became as regular a contributor to Company as her teaching commitments allowed.

St Augustine's, the church we attended in Bromley was one of the best kinds of Anglican assembly. By this I mean that the general ethos was more reminiscent of a family than either a morgue or an obstacle race. At the centre of the congregation was a minority of people who had a genuine faith, and a profound regard for God, while the majority came in a wide variety of temperamental and spiritual shapes and sizes. It was a very warm and caring community, and the first church in which Bridget and I felt genuinely close to, and part of, a worshipping body. The various dramatic productions and youth services that we helped with are among our warmest memories.

Despite all these positive aspects of life in Bromley, however, I still agonised over my relationship with God. I found myself doubting to the point of total disbelief. Okay, things were good at home, and very good socially at church; college was a strain from beginning to end, but I didn't have to be there much. Generally speaking, things were good. We were sharing the house of the curate, who was none other than my best friend from Tunbridge Wells, John Hall. Together we played bad but enjoyable golf once a week on the municipal course, and renewed our old practice of sitting up until the early hours from time to time, talking about everything under the sun.

I was happily married. Matthew was a constant joy. What more could I ask?

I wanted God. I still wanted that God who had made all those promises back in St John's Church when I was sixteen. In what form did I want him? I wasn't sure. I just knew that there was a knot of pain and anger in me that would never be untied (no matter how many good things happened) until I *knew* that God loved me in the way I had always wanted to be loved by a father since I was just a small child. And, as I still didn't know that, maybe there was no God after all.

It is supremely ironic that when, towards the end of our stay in Bromley, I did at last experience reality in my contact with God, I was so frightened by what he wanted me to do that I turned my back on him and 'did a Jonah'.

I had been reading an extract from the writings of Meister Eckhart, a German mystic of the Middle Ages. Particularly interesting to me was his view that repentance was a happy thing. God, he said, was overjoyed when people wanted to change their lives for the better, and more than ready to forget and forgive if it meant that a real friendship could be established. The parable of the prodigal son says exactly the same thing, of course, but perhaps now, I was more ready to accept this truth. Eckhart's words inspired me. I developed a sort of meditation technique, which had an amazingly releasing effect. I would imagine that I was standing in a mist or cloud, surrounded by all the bad or negative things in my life. I would then make a pile of these things – they were easy to stack – and stand on the top of the pile, as tall as I could. The stack was always high enough to allow my head to rise above the level of the mist into the clean, clear, light of the sun. God, in some indefinable way, was in that light. Neither he nor I could see the disreputable heap of baggage under my feet, in the mist, and neither of us cared. It was just good to be in the light, and it made all the difference. Prayer started to feel like conversation, like friendship. It was so new and unusual that I felt slightly hysterical about the whole thing, but it was real, and that was what mattered. Then, one evening as I sat alone in the sitting room at home, a thought 'punched' me in the brain. I can think of no other way to describe it, nor do I care to classify it too precisely. The words were few, but the meaning was clear.

'You must love Jason.'

Clear though the injunction was, I was still rather puzzled. The person in question (his name was not Jason) certainly didn't give the impression of needing my particular care or affection. He was strong, competent, one of those large, hand-carved, independent Christian types. Why should I need to specially love him, and what would it involve? The next day, Jason drove in from Central London where he ran a drug rehabilitation centre. He wanted to confide in me, he said. After my experience of the night before I was all ears, as you can imagine. A real job to do for God at last? He wanted to talk about a dark and difficult area in his private life, something that contrasted starkly with his public image as a professional worker and a Christian. For some weeks we met at frequent intervals. Our meetings did not feel very productive. He talked and I listened, or made feeble attempts to offer advice. His situation grew more complicated, the burden on me seemed increasingly onerous. I was out of my depth and floundering helplessly. I hated the thought that, now, when things in general seemed so much better, I might be about to fail yet again. I wanted to retreat into safety, and just at that time I was presented with a way that seemed to offer just the opportunity I needed. Since the completion of my college course I had applied for a post in a regional assessment centre in the midlands. Now, after a rather alarming interview in the big grey city of Birmingham, I was offered a job as housemaster in a unit of twenty-four delinquent boys. At the same time Jason suggested that I should join him in the work he was doing in London.

'You must love Jason.'

We went to Birmingham.

My new-found relationship with God was too fragile to withstand this deliberate evasion. I know now that, in fact, God being the way he is, he would have been quite ready to heave a sigh, forgive me unreservedly for letting him down, and start again in Birmingham, but I was not prepared to forgive myself, and that was that.

The following five years were dominated by the work I was doing in Birmingham, Norwich and finally Hailsham in East Sussex. Shift work with disturbed children split my existence into two parts – periods when I was working, and periods when I was waiting to go to work. Free time was not free of the shadow of the shift to come, unless it was lengthy enough for stretched nerves to relax, and clouds of worry to disperse. There never seemed to be time to stop and reflect on the strange tension-ridden life that I was leading. I learned to cope in the world of residential child-care. I was even able to appear fairly consistently calm and strong, compassionate and caring. I probably helped many children in the process, but every encounter was a role play involving the selection of a suitable personality from the stock that I had accumulated. The growing inner chaos was pushed deep and well controlled.

Meanwhile I was assembling my own little residential unit at home. Joseph was born in 1978, and David in 1980. It was not until 1982 that we moved off campus to share a house with a young teacher friend. For six years the sounds, sights and tensions of the work situation had infected our attempts to relax.

Holidays away were refreshing, but there is something soul-destroying about returning, and being accosted outside your front door by an excited child who passes on, with relish, the news that Fred has run away, Gloria has slashed her wrists, and there is an epidemic of pubic lice. Instant involvement – instant tension. The family frequently had to make do with the fag-end of my good will at the end of a shift, or after the second or third 'sleep-in' in one week. As a family, we were all paying a very high price for the maintenance of my public role. The nervous and emotional expenditure required for a lengthy working period was often so great that there was little time left for my wife and children, who needed their own share of my time and affection.

All my old doubts about God had reappeared during these years. I tried to rationalise the business of Jason and my abandonment of him. Sometimes I prayed. Occasionally I seemed to sense God trying to get close to me, but generally speaking I was in a spiritual desert, and, although I didn't fully realise it at the time, the growing tension of my work environment was running parallel with a steadily intensifying anger towards this being who either didn't exist, or didn't like me. Back to square one! When people asked me what I believed, I dragged out the old unwieldy package of evangelical clichés, but my heart was not in it.

Then, at the beginning of 1981, Bridget and I were involved in a new group that called itself The Hailsham Christian Fellowship. It was relaxed, informal and refreshing. Both of us experienced a lightening of our spirits as we became part of this little community of Christians from a variety of church backgrounds. Perhaps, through this group, I would find God again and all would be well.

Later in the year, Bridget and I wrote and produced a Christian revue for the fellowship, which was performed on the local secondary school stage to an audience consisting mainly of Christians from the local churches. It was called 'A Place For You', and was specially intended to reassure those Christians for whom Christian living had seemed like a long slog through ankle-deep mud. At that time the fellowship was a welcome refuge for such people. The production had a valuable unifying function for the fellowship, most of whom were involved in the project in one way or another. For us it was like rebirth.

We felt that God really was with us in the writing and rehearsal of the revue, and that, at last, we were coming out of the desert, and taking a few tentative steps into the promised land. It was a truly satisfying experience, and it left Bridget and me with a warm sense of belonging to this group of people whose lives were becoming so intertwined as the weeks went by. I had recently helped to establish a new unit for older children in the children's centre where I worked, and found myself enjoying work much more. Overall, things were looking good, and although God and I still had a lot to settle, at least I was keen to hear what he had to say again.

It was at this point, when both Bridget and I felt more confident and stable than we had done for years, that a friend phoned me to ask if I had noticed a small article in the local paper about the new television company that was due to take over from

Southern Television in the new year. The company was to be called TVS, and the article described how Angus Wright, producer of religious programmes, was looking for six ordinary people to take part in a new kind of late-night religious programme.

'Why not write to him?' said my friend.

'All right,' I said. 'I will.'

Chapter Four

At various times, and in various parts of the country, I had found myself watching the late-night epilogue programme broadcast by the BBC, or the local independent television company. Occasionally they were interesting, but generally speaking I was not very impressed. They seemed to take one of two forms.

In the first, a single individual addressed the viewer with unstumbling ease, on subjects that were more or less religious in content. This kind of neatly packaged homily had a rather adverse effect on me. The speaker was heavily protected by the preparedness of his talk, and the fact that nobody was able to interrupt, or argue with what he was saying. At its best this kind of approach seemed harmless, but at its worst it could be positively intimidating. The impression often given was that the worthy person whose eyes followed you round the room as you collected the cocoa cups, had succeeded in tying up all the loose ends in his own understanding of the Christian faith, and was a living example of the way in which spiritual and psychological tidiness could be achieved. For people watching at home, whose lives were difficult and ragged at the edges, this was not always an inspiring example. If they had felt inadequate and confused before, they were likely to feel even more so now. The same thing happens, of course, in many churches, where there is a clear, if unspoken injunction to leave your 'shadow' by the door on your way in, before getting down to singing about how happy you are. There seems to be little room for people who desperately want to say, like Job, that life is wild and tragic and they don't like it, so isn't it a good thing that God can be trusted.

The second kind of programme took the form of a one-to-one interview between a questioner, who was either religiously connected in some way or just suitably genial, and a guest, who would probably appear each night for a week, to answer questions about his or her life and work. The background set was always very simple, the participants usually emerging from near darkness at the beginning of the programme, and disappearing into it again at the end. Occasionally, these encounters had life in them, but most of the programmes that I saw looked like two people trying to reproduce a real conversation that they had enjoyed the night before. Worthy, but dull, they reflected the generally poor presentation of the Christian faith that we have all become used to.

Angus Wright was interested in trying a new approach, which, as far as possible, would allow the viewer to feel involved with what was happening on the screen. Instead of one or two people delivering over-prepared lines to the camera or each other, there would be three or four folk seated around a kitchen table, in a proper kitchen set, having a genuinely unscripted conversation about real happenings and events in their lives. Hopefully, the viewer would, as it were, take a seat around the table and become involved with the lives and views of the participants in as real a way as possible, bearing in mind the obvious limitations of television. The programme would provide a familiar and consistent way to end the viewing day for those in the TVS region who for one reason or another were awake and still watching at that time of night. It would offer company, and it was this basic aim which suggested that the new programme should be called, simply, 'Company'.

Although it was years since Bridget and I had left theatre school, and abandoned the idea of acting as a profession, we had never lost our passion for everything to do with performance. At work, at church, and with the youth club in Bromley, we had never really been happier than when we were caught up in the rich complexity of 'putting on a show'. We both find the stage – any stage – tremendously exciting, whether we are working behind the scenes, or actually taking part in a performance. When I wrote to Angus after my friend's phone call, the performer in me certainly hoped that we might actually be able to take part in this new project, but it seemed more likely that he would simply thank me for contributing my ideas, and that would be that. When he wrote back, suggesting that an associate producer, Frances Tulloch, should visit us for a discussion, Bridget and I were quite ridiculously excited. I can understand that it might be difficult to see why the prospect of appearing on a tiny programme that wouldn't start until most people had gone to bed should give us such pleasure. I suppose that, at the time, it seemed like a sort of confirmation that things were looking up. Life was changing for the better. The fellowship that we had joined, the revue, a general easing of tension at work, and now this. It was as if God was saying 'Right! You've done your time, now you can relax for a while.' Yes, you're right. I still didn't understand God at all!

After our meeting with Frances, who subsequently took over production responsibility for Company, we were invited to take part in an audition, to be held in Frances' club in London. We were still very excited, but also very, very nervous.

Travelling in the same carriage as us on the train to London that day was Lionel Blair, who was appearing in Eastbourne for the season. We reflected ruefully on the ease with which he would have handled the ordeal that lay before us, and which was causing us such nervous apprehension as we clutched our cardboard cups of British Rail coffee, and passed through all stations to Victoria. I'm not quite sure what we expected of our first step into the world of television, something a lot less gentle and civilised, I suspect. For the audition, Frances had obtained the services of a charming old gentleman and his equally charming wife, who usually hired out themselves and their simple video equipment for the purpose of recording Christian meetings and events. Angus Wright turned out to be a tall, thoughtful man, with a slightly distracted air, but a very pleasant manner. He was rather like a serious Derek Nimmo. Finally, we were introduced to Maurice

Harper who was to direct Company. Maurice is a complex, attractive Irishman, who is still waiting for the world to deal him a really good hand. We were to become very fond of him.

The atmosphere was relaxed and warm as we took turns sitting in front of the single TV camera, but the five minute talks that we had been asked to prepare must have come over to our small audience as very tense and perspiring affairs. We were just learning how to breathe again when Maurice told us he was keen to see how we came over in conversation.

'Can you just talk?' he asked.

'Yes,' answered Adrian.

'No,' answered Bridget simultaneously.

Maurice ran a hand through his hair, a gesture that was to become familiar. He has always been able to subdue an oath when necessary. He subdued one now.

'Can't you discuss something that you both feel strongly about?'

We looked at each other.

'Well,' I replied tentatively, 'there is a problem we had a while ago when we did a church service. This lad. He was a bit of a nuisance – not turning up for rehearsals, that sort of thing. We weren't sure whether to get someone else or not. So we ...'

'Fine, fine!' said Maurice. 'Sit at that table. Away you go!'

So away we went, having a discussion that was two months out of date, in a big, strange room, watched by a group of people we had only just met, terribly aware that every word we said, every over-sincere expression on our faces, was being recorded by the expressionless eye of the camera and the microphone on its stand between us.

The general reaction to our efforts seemed quite positive, but as we sat, exhausted, on the southbound train an hour later, we still didn't know the outcome of the audition. The days passed, and we heard nothing. Then, one day when I was out at work, Frances rang and talked to Bridget.

I came home from work that day in my usual, slightly manic state, and flopped wearily onto the settee hoping that a cup of tea and the newspaper might somehow waft themselves in my direction. Bridget, the most likely wafting agent, was sitting very still on the edge of her seat, and something about the quality of her stillness made me forget work and tiredness and cups of tea. Something was wrong. The children? I felt a cold shiver pass through me that I always experienced when I thought something bad might have happened to the boys. Bridget spoke.

'Frances rang.'

Not the children then. Why did Bridget sound so troubled? At the worst Frances could only have rung to say that we had failed the audition. Upsetting, but hardly tragic.

'Yes . . . and?'

'Well . . .'

This was getting silly. I got up, grabbed an upright chair from its place by the wall, carried it over to where Bridget was perched on the edge of her armchair, and sat as close to her as I could. She didn't seem able to let her eyes meet mine.

'Bridget, what's the matter? What did Frances say?'

She raised her head and looked at me at last, eyes wide with apprehension.

'She said they want to use me for Company, but not you.' Her face was creased with pain. 'Oh, Adrian, I don't want to do it if you don't do it. You wrote the letter and I thought . . .'

Poor Bridget. She really and truly was more concerned with how I felt, than anything else. So, how *did* I feel? I felt as though I'd been banged on the head with a very heavy object. Drat God! It was happening all over again. Not wanted. Not accepted. Not good enough. Why not? Deep inside me the little boy collapsed in tears as his daddy let him down yet again.

Meanwhile, I was aware of Bridget's eyes searching my face for the slightest sign of hurt or upset. She has since told me that if she had detected the merest indication of what I was really feeling, she would have decided, on the spot, to ring Frances and say that she did not want to be included in the Company team.

Usually, I could not have concealed my feelings anyway. Like many husbands I am nothing more than a big baby at times, and if I get upset I make sure those around me know about it, or at the very least I carefully let them notice that I am concealing my feelings. But this was different. In the split second following Bridget's last speech I knew that the manner and content of my reply would either free her to pursue this interesting and novel activity, or prevent it altogether. It was not right or fair that it should be so, but it was a fact.

'Thank goodness for that. I thought it was something really awful for a moment.' I knew it sounded convincing.

'You mean you don't mind?' Bridget was puzzled, still wary.

I had myself completely under control now.

'In an odd sort of way, it's a relief,' I lied. 'Let's have a cup of tea. What about taking the children up along the old railway track for a picnic ... ?'

It was the only truly heroic thing I'd ever done, but it didn't give me very much satisfaction at the time. I was used to engineering rewards for my virtue, but in this case I knew that I just had to keep my mouth shut, and suffer. Ironically, if I had not responded as I did, it is possible that neither of us would have been involved with the programme. As it was, only a few weeks passed before I was also asked to join the Company team, and I could relax from the strain of pretending to be genial but unconcerned about being excluded from Bridget's new activity.

The first Company participants were not actually as 'ordinary' as the original concept had envisaged. There was, for instance, Peter Ball, the Anglican Bishop of Lewes, already quite a celebrity in the south-east and elsewhere. Bob Gordon was a distinguished lecturer in Old Testament studies, and about to join Colin Urquhart as a co-elder at the Hyde Christian community near Haywards Heath. Ken Gardner was an Anglican priest from the parish of St Philip and St Jacob, Waldeslade, near Gillingham, and Ann-Marie Stewart was a Franciscan nun who had left her convent after twenty years to start a new form of Franciscan life in Canterbury. Ann-Marie supported herself by taking on cleaning jobs in the mornings, while devoting the rest of the day to prayer and the occasional preaching or teaching engagement. Next to this line-up of religious experts, Bridget and I were very conscious of being 'token ordinary ones'. I was an expert in spiritual confusion, and Bridget was an expert in living with someone who was spiritually confused, but that was about all.

For a time, it was a little intimidating. The TVS world seemed to be full of incredibly expensive machinery and highly trained technicians. The atmosphere in the new studio at Gillingham was one of great enthusiasm. We were in at the beginning of, not only a new programme, but a new television company. Everyone seemed to be on their toes. We were amazed at the number of people that seemed to be necessary for the making of such a humble programme. Whenever a technical problem occurred, they seemed to come out of the woodwork in their droves, each one an expert in something or other. Cameras, lights, sound, make-up, props, wardrobe; there seemed no end to the specialised knowledge required to make this five minute programme in a small corner of the vast ex-cinema studio. So what were *we* doing there? What qualified us to sit with experts, surrounded by experts, saying things that thousands of southerners from Maldon in Essex to Dorchester in the West would hear every night? Not, I hasten to add, that our fellow participants in any way deliberately made us feel inadequate. Bob was aggressively confident on behalf of all of us, Ken was always warm and self-effacing, Ann-Marie was, by her own admission and despite wide experience of public speaking, quite paralysed by nerves for the first few weeks, and Peter – well, more about Peter later. Helpful and friendly though everyone was, the question remained for Bridget and me: what right did two ordinary people have, to talk about Christianity in front of thousands of viewers, when so many others were better informed, and certainly more consistent in the way they lived out their faith? The answer was, of course, none at all, and in realising this we realised what our contribution should be. If we could manage to be honest and open about the things, good and bad, that happened to us, and resist the temptation to make excuses for God by papering over the cracks in our lives, then we might offer hope and reassurance to people whose lives were just as frayed at the edges.

In theory, ours sounds a humble role, but in fact, we weren't really feeling very humble at all. We just *loved* the palaver of production meetings and make-up and work in the studio. It all smacked of the 'telly'. We were on the 'telly'! We developed a sort of compensatory nonchalance about the whole thing, which probably deceived nobody, least of all ourselves. That feeling of novelty and rich excitement did not last very long, and perhaps it was rather silly, but I think it was a good and necessary thing. It made us feel like children again, and that is always a healthy experience for Christians.

Some of those early programmes must have been awful. I wouldn't be able to count the number of times that Maurice, sometimes running *both* hands through his hair, would threaten to strangle the next person who started a sentence with the words 'As a Christian . . .'. Then there was our tendency to be terribly, terribly polite to each other while the cameras were on us. There is nothing wrong with politeness, of course, but quite often the relaxed and strongly animated discussion which followed the programme, would have been far more interesting to the viewer than the cosy, religious head-nodding exercise that had just appeared on the screen. We were in danger (and it has remained a danger) of doing exactly what the old-style epilogue programmes had done, only more expensively. Added to this were our two great fears. We were afraid of silence, and we were afraid that a programme might finish without the opportunity for us to contribute our particular little nugget of insight or wisdom to the conversation. I filled many a silence with absolute blithering nonsense in those days, and probably still do at times. I also remember sitting at that kitchen table, waiting for a gap – any kind of gap – in the conversation, so that I could thrust my little set-speech into the proceedings, regardless of context. With a little ingenuity it was possible to force a connection of some kind. Thus, the following conversation might have taken place:

ANN-MARIE: One of the most interesting things I ever saw, happened on a Monday, which is always a rather bad day for me.

ADRIAN: (Spotting a minute opening) Oddly enough, I was going to talk about something that happened on a Wednesday, which, as you know, is only two days after Monday. You see, my mother . . .

BRIDGET: (Determined not to be left out) Don't you think God is as much a mother as he is a father?

ADRIAN AND ANN-MARIE: (Both seething inwardly, but unwilling to display impatience in front of 50,000 people) Yes, yes, he probably is. How interesting . . . !

A slight exaggeration of course, but all these problems had to be faced. We discovered over the months that it *was* possible to be in conflict without throttling each other, and that a silence, if it was a natural one, was not only *not* to be feared, but could be more meaningful than a great deal of conversation.

The secret seemed to lie in two areas: honesty and listening. If the words we said came from the heart, and we really listened and responded to what others were saying, then it didn't matter whether we talked about potty-training or predestination. It would be real. As Angus has repeatedly said from the outset, people will only want to watch if something is *happening* on the screen. We are all still guilty of the same mistakes from time to time, but, one hopes, less often.

When Company first started, Bridget and I were naive enough to believe that the kitchen set, although obviously an aid to creating an appropriate atmosphere, was not something that would be much noticed by viewers. It was a rather basic kitchen as kitchens go, rather reminiscent of the fifties and not at all likely to attract attention. On the table at which we sat there might be a vase of flowers or a bowl of fruit, but generally speaking there was little that seemed interesting enough to distract viewers from our 'scintillating' conversation. We were wrong. One day, as we completed the purchase of a can of paint in a local shop, the lady who had served us cleared her throat in an 'I'm going to say something' sort of way, as we turned to go. She laid a hand on my wife's arm, and spoke earnestly.

'I do hope you don't mind me asking . . .' Her expression was very serious. Bridget smiled encouragingly. 'Only – you see, my husband and I have been watching your programme all this week and – well, we've got a question that we both want to ask. Would you mind?'

We were flattered. It was in the early days, and it felt good to be recognised in public. Now, here was this nice lady who'd listened, with her husband, to everything we'd said for a whole week, and wanted help with a problem. Some difficulty in their Christian lives no doubt. She and her husband saw us as people who might have some answers.

'If we can help, then of course . . .' Bridget's sincere tones matched the earnestness of the questioner.

'Only – it's been troubling us all week . . .'

'Yes?' Bridget was patience itself.

The lady leaned forward. She spoke even more confidentially than before.

'The fruit in that bowl . . . is it real?'

Later on, contact with viewers, through correspondence and in person was very important to us, especially in the very black days that were to come two and a half years after Company began, but at first, being recognised in the street was a strange and sometimes disconcerting experience.

One Saturday, Bridget lost her purse, containing most of our holiday savings, just drawn from the bank. Panic-stricken, she rushed around the town dragging our two preschool children behind her. Her face smudged with tears as she searched in vain for the missing money, she was reaching a fine pitch of hysteria, when a voice at her shoulder said, 'Excuse me, but haven't I seen you on telly?' Bridget is a very modest lady, but not even the most inflated super-Christian TV image would have survived that moment. I ought to add that the purse was found and later returned to us by a very honest gentleman who stumbled over it on his way home from work.

Then there was the lady who flung her arms round my neck and kissed me on the cheek as I queued outside a cinema with eight-year-old Matthew. She fixed me with the intense gaze of the semi-inebriate, and spoke with deep, throbbing sincerity.

'Are you and Bridget as happy in real life as you are on television?'

As she departed unsteadily along the pavement without waiting for an answer, Matthew looked from me to her and back to me in wonderment.

'Gosh, Daddy,' he said. 'You don't 'alf make friends quickly, don't you?'

Sometimes, when we made programmes separately, one of us would mention that we had been going through an irritable, argumentative patch. I was standing in a supermarket queue, one day, when a voice came from somewhere behind my left shoulder.

'Sorry to hear you and your wife had a row.'

It was a lady I had never seen before. Quickly, my mind made the necessary connection. Presumably Bridget had described our recent 'bad patch' to the south of England, late last night. What had she said? What did this lady in the queue know, that I didn't? I resisted the temptation to ask, and reflected on the fact that, while honesty on television might be the best policy, it could produce some very uncomfortable moments. Nevertheless, it became clearer than ever that it was just this willingness to be open about the darker side of our lives that would enable not just Bridget and me, but the Company team generally, as it changed and grew, to relate closely to viewers who needed to know that they were not alone in their experience of failure and difficulty.

Chapter Five

So what did we talk about evening after evening? Well, for a while we tried to solve most of the world's problems in double quick time. Death on Monday, forgiveness on Tuesday, suffering on Wednesday – we sorted them all out in five minutes or so each. Sometimes it was possible to have something approaching a reasonable discussion on these vast subjects in such a risibly short time, but I think we realised fairly early on that unless the things we said were grounded in experience we wouldn't sound very convincing.

Sometimes, for instance, we would pick up on the headline news of the day, and unless we had some specialist knowledge in a specific area, it was better to produce a kind of personal, uninformed response that the majority of viewers could identify with. Essentially, we were having a 'chat' rather than a discussion, and when friends chat they will probably talk about what they've been doing, making a passing comment on the day's news, and perhaps exchange gossip or 'have a laugh'. It is not easy to reproduce this kind of informality under laboratory conditions, as it were.

Apart from the specific area of child-care, the only thing I really knew about was 'being me', so for some time my contribution tended to be rather anecdotal. I suppose this was very fitting really, as my relationship with God had been rather anecdotal over the years. I enjoyed telling stories, and they did at least have the virtue of being true. There was the story, for instance, of the lorry driver and the rose.

It happened when I was hitch-hiking some years ago. I was in the cab of a huge lorry, somewhere on the M4 heading west.

I've always loved hitch-hiking. It's a wonderful blend of adventure and legitimate inactivity. G K Chesterton said that he knew few things more satisfying than the experience of being stranded at a railway station. I know what he meant. The flavour of accidental solitude is tastier than Marmite, and I've experienced it most while standing on the side of the road waiting for a lift. I relish the fact that only God and I know where I am. Add to this the knowledge that every lift means contact with an unknown and quite unique human being, and you have the perfect occupation for someone with my twin vices of laziness and curiosity.

On this particular day I'd been dropped off on one of the motorway exits, and I had to wait some time on the corresponding slip road for another lift. It was late afternoon when a very large lorry squealed to a halt beside me. The driver leaned across and pushed the passenger door open.

'You'd better get in, mate. You'll never get a lift standin' there.'

I smiled as I hauled myself up to the cab. People said this to me so often, that I quite frequently waited at 'impossible' spots, knowing that some kind person would pick me up in the end.

As the huge vehicle rumbled on to the motorway, my new companion and I began the pigeon-holing process that always preceded real conversation. Once he'd established that I was well-spoken, slightly naive, and not at all threatening, the man behind the wheel leaned towards me and spoke in the tone of one who has made an important decision.

'I'm goin' to tell you somethin' I've never told anyone before!'

He paused, flicking a glance around the cab as though checking for eavesdroppers.

'I wrote this effin' poem.'

He shot a look at me then went on, apparently reassured by my quiet interest.

'I saw this rose, see? In an effin' park. I was just sittin' there, and I looked at this effin' rose, and I thought, "Blow me! Look at that!" So I wrote this poem, didn't I?'

His vulnerability attracted and frightened me. His was a fragile trust.

'Have you said it to anybody?' I asked.

'You must be jokin'! If I told my mates I'd written a blinkin' poem I'd never 'ear the last of it. Just see me goin' down the local and sayin', "Oy, I've written a poem about an effin' rose." I don't think so!'

'Could I hear it?'

After some inward struggle he bawled the poem out over the noise of the engine. When he'd finished I said something appreciative, and the journey continued for some time without further conversation.

As I gazed sightlessly through the wide windscreen in front of me, I wondered what God would think about all this. After a few minutes I had to turn my face to the glass beside me. I didn't want the driver to see the tears in my eyes. I felt that I knew what God must think. All the way down the motorway and into the setting sun he probably wept with me for all the people who have poems in them, and can't believe that anyone else wants to hear them.

That story was especially poignant for me, perhaps, as I have always enjoyed expressing my feelings through poetry, some of which I have shared with Company viewers. One poem, in particular, seemed to sum up the tension that was my legacy from an uneasy childhood. Sending these words out through the camera lens had an oddly cleansing effect.

> When I was a small boy in a small school,
> With endless legs,
> And ears that widely proclaimed a head full of
> emergencies,
> When I clung by bleeding fingertips to thirty-three
> plus nine,
> And cognitive dissonance was a hard sum,
> There were only two crimes.
> The first was shouting in the corridors,
> The second was to be a fool.
> And when the bell, the blessed bell,
> Let me fling my body home,

I thought I might, at least, one day,
Aspire to rule in hell,
But now I never hear the bell,
And part of me will always be
A fool,
Screaming in some sacred corridor.

A less poetic but no less meaningful account, concerned the way in which I coped – or rather, didn't cope – with the first day of my new job in Sussex, after moving down from Norfolk.

It doesn't matter how experienced you are in residential child-care, it's always nerve-racking to confront a new and horribly unfamiliar group of children and staff, especially in the intense atmosphere of a large children's centre. I was due to start at 2.30. By half-past one I'd run out of distractions, courage, faith and saliva. I wanted Armageddon to happen within the hour. Then, a decision, a solution of sorts, crawled into my mind. If I really shifted – if I took the short cut along the old railway line and across the school playing-field, I could get to the Britannia Arms in time to pour at least three pints of bitter into my stomach. That should drown the butterflies; poor little beggars – they wouldn't stand a chance. I hurried out of the house wearing the inevitable load of guilt like a haversack on my back. I had not had much to say to God for some time, but I knew what he'd think of my dash to the pub. Eyebrows raised, fingers drumming on a cloud. I challenged him 'bravely'.

'There's nothing you can do about it, God. I'm going for a drink and that's that. I want a drink, I need a drink, I'm going to have a drink. And if you don't like it, you'll have to stop me!'

As I sped along the footpath between bushes and trees, I offered a couple of suggestions to the deity.

'What about muggers, God? Why don't you get someone to leap from behind a tree and knock me out? Or maybe a dramatic soil subsidence. I could just disappear into a crack in the ground. Is that what you're going to do?'

I laughed rather wildly as I crossed the sports ground and jogged up the hill towards the town. I really wasn't very proud of what I was doing. Here was the main road at last. On the other side the pub; the beer.

'Last chance, God. Road accident? Needn't be anything serious. Broken limb perhaps?'

I negotiated the busy road without incident, and walked into the saloon bar of the Britannia. I ordered a pint. I watched it being pulled; I licked my lips. I put my hand out and took the brimming glass. As I drew it carefully towards me I felt in my jacket pocket with my other hand for some money.

'Hard luck, God! Cheers!'

Suddenly, I froze. Panic – horror – no money! I'd changed my jacket. I hadn't a penny. The barman didn't know me from Adam.

'I'm sorry – I haven't got any money,' I said pathetically.

'In that case, we haven't got any beer,' replied the man – clearly an Old Testament type, and he reached over and took my pint back from me.

I didn't start laughing until I was halfway back to the Centre. I was still laughing inwardly as I went into work at half-past two.

It was rather like – being drunk.

After telling this story one night, I discovered that we had a hitherto unsuspected audience of publicans. As I visited pubs in and around the area over the next couple of weeks, I found that landlords and their wives were intrigued by the details of the account. Which pub was it? What kind of beer was it? They usually watched Company, they said, because once all the clearing up was done, it was nearly midnight anyway, and by the time they were able to put their feet up, our few minutes of chat was about all that was left of the evening's viewing.

It was also a good example of how openness can be a releasing agent. Having revealed that I was a Christian with a healthy liking for beer, and an unhealthy tendency to use it as a prop sometimes, it seemed easier for others to be frank about their own vices or failings. Although, at the time, I didn't know the answers to such problems, it did seem to me that it was better for people to feel free to talk about these things, rather than be paralysed by

75

feelings of guilt. A similar effect was produced by Bridget's lively descriptions of times when everything went disastrously wrong, just as she particularly wanted to look like a calm, confident wife and mother. Those who knew what it meant to wilt under the disapproving stare of 'mothers-whose-children-behave-well' whilst wrestling unsuccessfully with their own rebellious crew, found it refreshingly easy to identify with these graphic tales.

Of course, me being me, it wasn't long before I began to see myself as God's gift to the late night box-watchers, put at that table to offer hope to an army of insomniacs. What I didn't realise was that God intended to sort *me* out over the next three years, and the first step in his campaign, using my participation in Company as a lever, was to do something that I had been trying to do for years. He found a way for me to give up smoking.

I was a dedicated smoker, and had been for sixteen years. In most of the photographs taken since I was sixteen, I was holding a packet of cigarettes and a box of matches in one hand, and a book in the other. Cigarettes were the only uncomplicated comforts I knew, little friends who were always available, never answered back, and didn't object to being trodden on. By the time I was thirty-three I was smoking at least sixty cigarettes a day; one every twenty minutes; one thousand pounds worth every year. I smoked when I got into bed, and I smoked before I got up in the morning. I lit up as I walked out of the door, and again as I waited for the bus. I smoked before, during and after a bath. Often I would leave a church service or an important meeting halfway through, ostensibly to visit the toilet, but actually to snatch a few reassuring drags before returning to the smokeless zone. Most delicious of all – oh ecstasy! – I smoked after a meal.

My smoking was conducted with a curious underlying intensity. I protected my addiction fiercely, realising, perhaps, that I was using it as a weapon in the battle to postpone real involvement with a world that was never quite satisfactory. At the same time, I had always felt guilty about being a smoker. It was one of the things a Christian *ought* to feel guilty about, wasn't it?

Nowadays, I believe that God is, in fact, quite nice, but for years I retained the image of something between a headmaster and a bank manager, before whom I played the role of a naughty boy with an overdraft. Now that I no longer smoke, I am quite sure that smoking, in itself, is no more of a sin than anything else, but I was a slave to the habit, and it was costing a fortune. I performed every spiritual gymnastic in the book. I made decisions at meetings, I went forward at rallies, I repented and pleaded and argued with the rigidly austere God that my heart had created. The only thing these experiences had in common was the pleasure with which I lit up the cigarette that invariably followed each decision to give up. Money, health, guilt – nothing was a strong enough motive to stop. For a couple of years now, I hadn't bothered to try.

Then, one day, as Bridget wrestled grimly with our dilapidated top-loading washing machine, something happened. She burst into tears of frustration as the appliance forced her, yet again, into a losing submission. She said just ten words.

'If you didn't smoke, I could have a new machine!'

She had never complained before. I walked round to the electricity showrooms and bought a washing machine on hire purchase. I calculated that if I cut down my daily ration of cigarettes to twenty, the money saved would cover the repayments. I decided to smoke one cigarette each hour, on the hour. I lived for the moment when, as my youngest son put it, the big hand was on the twelve. Each hour lasted several months. Each cigarette seemed to last a few seconds. My family hid. After a month of this, I knew that the moment of final decision had come. It was now or never. Give up altogether or go back to sixty a day. I decided to give up. The difference this time, was that I knew how to put a much more effective armlock on myself than at any time in the past. A few days later I talked at the Company table about how I no longer smoked. My heart sank as I burned my boats so finally. Relatively small though the Company audience might be, I knew that it was large enough for me to be 'leapt on' by regular viewers if they saw me smoking in the street. But it was my pride that would do the trick in the end. I had said I no longer smoked, and I hadn't the humility to fail. So much for sharing weakness!

The next few months were horrific. Each morning I woke, to remember, with a stab of horror, that I'd given up. I saw little point in getting up – in working – in doing anything. Like someone who has been bereaved, and that's how I felt, I could not be consoled. I resigned myself to suffering. Prayer? God? Don't ask!

Then, one afternoon, six months later, I could stand it no longer. By then I had moved over to work in the secure unit for violent and absconding children, and for once, everyone else was out. On the desk in front of me as I sat in the small staff office, lay a single cigarette, white and alluring, firm with tobacco – beautiful. It had been a hard day. I was tense and nervous. I had had enough. Company or no Company, pride or no pride, I was going to smoke that cigarette. I hunted feverishly through the desk drawer where the lighter was usually kept. As I searched, a small, feeble voice at the back of my mind repeated the same desperate prayer over and over again.

'Don't let it be there – don't let it be there . . .'.

It *was* there. The cigarette was in my mouth. I flicked the lighter. It didn't work. I flicked it again. It still didn't work. The stupid thing was out of petrol. I wanted that cigarette . . . !

Of course! Matches! Some of the children kept matches in the little pigeon-holes set against the wall on my right. I leaned over and started to pull out the contents of the little square wooden boxes.

'Don't let there be any . . . please don't let there be any . . .'

There were no matches in the pigeon-holes. Not a single, solitary match. Never mind. I was going to smoke that cigarette. The bin! The rubbish bin! You always found the odd live match among the rubbish. I had no dignity left. I emptied the metal container onto the floor and scrabbled through the messy heap of papers, orange peel, and general stickiness.

'Please, don't let . . .'.

Nothing! No live matches. I got up and almost ran down the corridor, out of the unit and down towards the kitchen that supplied meals for the entire children's centre. I knew I could get a light there. I stopped on the threshold of the large, busy kitchen, and looked around. On my right a gas flame burned brightly beneath the water heater. In front of me a huge, yellow box of matches sat fatly on a shelf. To my left, one of the cooks worked over the stoves. She was a smoker. I knew that she carried cigarettes and a lighter in her apron pocket. I took a step forward, then stopped. Quite suddenly, the madness left me. I slipped the crumpled cigarette into my side pocket, and trailed wearily back to the unit. Since that day I have not smoked a cigarette, but it was a year before it became easy.

So why was it so difficult? Why couldn't the desire to smoke have been taken away by some sort of divine surgery? That certainly seems to happen to some people. Why not me? I think there were three things I needed to learn.

First, there is no real sacrifice without suffering. I had known that, but only in my head.

Secondly, when you have reached the end of your own resources, God does help – even if it involves 'fixing' lighters and removing matches. Sometimes a miracle is just the tiny puff of wind that makes it possible to go on toiling at the oars.

Thirdly, it allowed me to believe in change. It is not an exaggeration to say that, in my view, if weak-willed old me can give up smoking, then anybody can do almost anything.

So, stage one in the divine plan was completed. One of my most deeply rooted defence systems had been removed, and if it hadn't been for my 'declaration' on Company, it just wouldn't have been possible.

But that was only the beginning. From the start of my involvement with Company, I was meeting people who forced me to re-examine and overhaul my whole understanding of spirituality, Christianity and organised religion. The first and certainly one of the most influential of these was Peter Ball, the Bishop of Lewes.

Chapter Six

'I could sit and watch that man all day.'

As I sat behind the cameras in Studio two watching the three Company participants chatting quietly as they waited for the programme to begin, I became aware that the technician sitting next to me was gazing with a peculiar intensity at the still figure in the monk's habit, seated at the end of the kitchen table.

'What do you mean?' I knew what he meant.

'Well . . .' He leaned back in his chair slightly embarrassed by his own remark.

'It's like sitting on the edge of a lake. He doesn't even have to talk. It's just sort of relaxing to watch him.'

I knew exactly what he meant. Since the day when I first met him in February 1982, I had been intrigued and fascinated by the phenomenon that was Peter Ball, the Bishop of Lewes. I had never known a bishop before, and I had a vague and totally uninformed prejudice against ambitious prelates – princes of the church – that sort of thing. So too, I was soon to discover, had Peter Ball. I think I was fortunate in that I had never heard of him before we met as Company colleagues. When he drew up in his rather battered blue car outside our house in Hailsham, to drive Bridget and me up to the TVS studio in Maidstone, I felt under no obligation to be impressed or overawed by this man who, I later learned, is regarded by many as one of the wisest and most godly men in the Christian church. This was just as well, as his first words to me were, 'Hello Adrian, have a Mars bar.'

As I climbed into the front passenger seat, I registered various obvious pieces of information. Middle aged, healthy looking but tired, dressed in a full length dark grey habit, rather charming boyish smile, perhaps a hint of toughness in the eyes. As we travelled northwards towards Maidstone, the three of us chatted very easily together. Peter didn't seem much like a prince of the church. He seemed more like a normal, but oddly happy human being who had somehow managed to achieve maturity without losing the excitement and playfulness of childhood.

'I expected you to talk about God all the time,' said I, rather crassly, as he negotiated the very busy Tunbridge High Street.

'You being a bishop I mean . . .'

Peter's smile lit up the car.

'People do seem to think that I ought to have a view on God all the time, and of course I have, but I do find it difficult when people assume that God is my sort of hobby. They talk to me about religion in the same way that you would talk to a philatelist about stamps, or a photographer about developing or something. Basically, they are not seeing me as a real human being.'

I was sure Peter meant what he was saying but his manner belied his words. I sensed that he had spent many many hours indulging the belief of others that he should talk to them about God.

Bridget leaned forward and spoke.

'But why is that Peter? Why don't people want you to be a real human being?'

'Ah, well . . .' Peter became serious. 'I think, Bridget, the problem is that we have got this attitude in the church at the moment, that the good Christians are those that spend a lot of time with religion. That's a load of junk! In fact there's too much religion.'

Listening to Peter was beginning to feel like a beautiful but unexpected cool shower on an oppressively hot day. As we turned onto the Hadlow road and headed out across the Kent countryside, the world seemed to me a slightly better place than usual.

'When you say "religion" . . . ?'

'I mean religious exercises. The more time you spend in church, the more Bible studies you go to, the more prayer meetings you attend, the better Christian you'll be. That's a load of junk. We're here for the transfiguration of the world, not to form a little cosy club of Christians who are all constantly involved in religious exercises. Of course we must pray – of course we must worship; those are at the centre of our lives, but then we need to live as fully as we can in a sort of joyful unselfishness, caring about people, and transfiguring ordinary life. We hope that we can touch everything and see it sparkle.'

Oddly enough, I didn't find Peter's use of the pronouns 'we' and 'our' discomforting or guilt-inducing. I couldn't honestly say that prayer and worship were at the centre of my life, and as for things sparkling when I touched them, well – they didn't seem to. Joyful unselfishness? Not a lot!

The curious thing was, though, that there seemed to be a power in Peter's words and presence that made me feel I could become all the things he had described; something that caused me to think that perhaps I wasn't such a bad chap after all.

This was quite new for me. Most of my Christian experience seemed to have emphasised the vast gap between the perfection of God and my own sin-ridden, worm-like existence. Often there had seemed to be some kind of ban on feeling 'liked' by God. It was all right to be loved, because that was *despite* everything you were. The atmosphere around Peter, however, contained a sort of rich encouragement that gave permission to relax and be warmed by something that is better described as fondness than anything else. This principle has held good with many people I have met since then. The nearer they are to God, the better they make you feel, without in any way suggesting that you should minimise or ignore your faults or weaknesses. I find this very encouraging. Presumably, God himself is the source and ultimate example of this quality. God is nice, and he likes me. What a thought!

When we arrived at the Gillingham Studio, we were able to witness the 'sparkling' principle, as Peter greeted cameramen, make-up ladies and security men in a way that suggested each one was vitally important to him. As he moved around the large studio building, he seemed to carry his own shining atmosphere with him. Later, in the course of the Company programme, I asked him about this.

'Peter, do you enjoy meeting people – all of them . . . ?'

He patted his flat hand gently on the table and nodded slowly.

'I do, Adrian. I honestly do enjoy people enormously. I am absolutely scintillating with excitement when I meet anyone; but it can cause problems.'

Bridget and I must have both looked puzzled.

'Well, you see, there are only two things that I am really any good at. One is squash, and the other is making people feel that they are special to me, and of course they are; but I meet so many people and you simply can't give yourself totally to everyone all the time. It gets very complicated, and I think sometimes its dangerous because people get very angry when I don't telephone them or write letters . . .'

He shook his head in dismay at the thought.

'Obviously,' said Bridget, 'they see something in you that's different, like I do; but you've only got twenty-four hours in your day, like everyone else. Do you think that what they're actually seeing in you, is Jesus?'

Peter's face shone again.

'I do hope so, I do hope so. I'm sure it doesn't happen all the time with me, but I wish it happened every minute of the day. We've all got a personality, and I believe that it can be transfigured by Jesus. We each must be a tiny little diamond in the kaleidoscope of the glory which is Jesus.'

Suddenly I felt personally involved in what was being said. The lights and the cameras drifted away from my awareness as I asked another question.

'The thing is, Peter, that diamonds are valuable, and one of the problems a lot of Christians have, is how to go on being valuable when they know what kind of people they really are. How should they go about learning to appreciate their value in God's eyes?'

I tried to sound detached, and interested in an academic sort of way. It wasn't easy, as I was actually hungry for his reply. Peter thought for a moment, his brows knitted. Then his face cleared.

'You see, the church has gone round saying that all humility means is that you think yourself a load of junk, a load of "garbage" as the Americans call it. In Lent, for instance, we all have to regard ourselves as garbage cans for forty days. We need to realise that, actually, God is totally fascinated by us. He took five thousand million years to, in a sense, evolve and create us. That's quite a long time even in terms of eternity – it's a second or two, isn't it? He is absolutely entranced by us. I love it! When I kneel down to pray in the morning, I don't say to begin with, "God, you're really great, you're wonderful." What I do feel at that moment, is that I am coming home. I know that he *is* really great, but I am coming home, and he is saying, "Oh, it's great to have you!" I don't understand it. You see – I know that I am very, very sinful, but I know something else as well ...'

I was too much of an expert in controlling my emotions to actually cry, but I could feel tears swimming in my eyes as Peter's gentle voice continued, warmly enthusiastic about this God that I had difficulty in recognising.

'You see ... I know that if I was to go out today and commit the foulest crime possible with every single person in the village where I live, and then went to prison as a result, then repented, and said sincerely to God, "God, I am so very, very sorry", he would say ... well, what do you think he would say?'

We were like little children listening to a bedtime story. We shook our heads, wide-eyed.

'He would say, "Great! This prison is full of people who you can love with me, and I love you, even more than I did before!" So I would get on with loving where I was, and a whole new world would happen in that prison. God is all right! I really do believe that with all my heart, and I can't really understand why everyone doesn't.'

'God is absolutely real to you?' A statement of fact rather than a question. Peter leaned back, his hands disappearing into the sleeves of his habit as he folded his arms.

'Ever since I can remember, Adrian, I have never known a time when God has not been the realest presence in the world to me, more real even than human, touchable presences.'

'So when ... I mean ...'

Bridget paused, her hands outstretched as though testing for rain, while she searched for the right words.

'You wouldn't say then, that you have had what is usually called a conversion experience in the evangelical church? A point where you asked Jesus into your life, and then the Holy Spirit came into your life, and then you started to walk the Christian path – that sort of experience?'

'No.' Peter continued carefully. 'Not one in which I would be able to say, as evangelicals do say sometimes, "Before it I wasn't a real Christian and after it I was.' I find that way round difficult. I mean, I haven't any doubt that these are real experiences, given to them by Jesus Christ, and when I hear about it I rejoice. I haven't any inhibitions about it; but I believe that rather than me inviting Jesus into my life, Jesus is actually, very sweetly, taking me into his life. There have been very special times of course. I remember when I first realised that I hadn't got to try to "make-it" with God. There he was, and he accepted me totally. There was nothing I could do to work for my own salvation. I was just totally assured by him. It was a great *release* to know that I never needed to earn approval with God. I could totally relax. That was a big experience.'

After the programme had finished, we drank coffee in the canteen up on the first floor. I was beginning to see why people wanted to talk to Peter about God. Guilty as all the rest, I took up the conversation where it had ended a few minutes ago.

'Peter, why do you think people get so screwed up about whether God loves them or not? What goes wrong?' Another casual, disinterested question! Peter stirred his coffee rather absentmindedly as he replied.

'God doesn't just *love* us. He loves us extravagantly. I want to use the word extravagantly because people sometimes use the phrase "God loves us" in a way that puts me off entirely. Sometimes it sounds like a sort of pressurised love. "He loves yer, an' he's gonna get yer!" Or, he loves you and you are going to become someone totally not yourself. These testimonies you hear sometimes ...'

He grinned wickedly.

'Sometimes I think people were far more attractive in their old unredeemed state. No – I want to use the word "extravagantly", because that's how God loves. After all, that's how lovers love, isn't it? They don't love moderately, or if they do there's not much point in getting married.'

He finished stirring at last, and took a sip of coffee, then replaced the cup on its saucer and beamed at us.

'Extravagantly – profusely – outrageously – that's how God loves us!'

It was extraordinary. After that first meeting I seemed to hear about Peter Ball everywhere. So many people seemed to have seen him or been confirmed by him, or been changed by something he said, or simply impressed by an encounter with him. The interesting thing was that these were not just Church of England worshippers. He seemed to have appeal for a wide variety of folk, including nonbelievers, who were attracted by his informal style and the sheer sparkle of the man. He related easily to people of all classes, and to a wide selection of church denominations, including the extreme evangelical ones, where even those who weren't quite sure if Mother Teresa was 'saved' or not, couldn't help but sense in him the spirit of a very loving God. Peter himself, clearly did not enjoy some of these occasions. I have never known a man in whom nervousness and effectiveness were so strongly present together, as in Peter when he addressed the monthly 'Growmore' meeting at the Congress Theatre in Eastbourne one Sunday evening. After the worship session, consisting largely of choruses led from the front, Peter, who finds that type of worship a little difficult, grey in habit and face, plodded from the back of the hall to the front to deliver an address remarkable for its humour, humility and insight, in contrast to the obvious feelings of woeful inadequacy in the speaker.

Impressed as I was by this unusual person, I wanted to find out what fuelled or energised him. How had he become the man he was? How did he remain the man he was? Was it the result of some kind of religious trick, or had God decided to smile on Peter for a particular reason? One day I visited Peter at his home in Littlington, a little Sussex village tucked away in the Downs, not far from the famous Long Man of Wilmington. There, in the homely sitting room of the rectory he talked about himself and his work.

Peter told me that he had been a monk for more than twenty years, as has his twin brother, Michael, who is the Bishop of Jarrow. Eight years ago, somewhat against his personal inclinations, Peter was installed as the suffragan Bishop of Lewes, and is now based at the old rectory in Littlington. Here he lives with a group of young people who are participants in the scheme that he devised to enable school leavers to spend two months at the rectory in work and spiritual training, followed by ten months in the community in teams of two or three, actively occupied in such areas as youth and voluntary work, while supporting themselves by part-time paid work.

Clearly, Peter's years as a monk under vows of poverty, chastity and obedience must have had a lot to do with the quality and steadfastness of his present life, but I wanted to know what kept him going now that he was a monk who was also a bishop, closely involved with all aspects of the real world. How did he cope with it? Peter settled back in the comfortable settee opposite me and talked about his daily routine.

'The first thing that happens each day, is my alarm clock going off at 4.15 am . . .'

He noticed my wince of horror.

'We get through a lot of alarm clocks in the monastic life, because the temptation is to throw them straight out of the window. But usually I manage to get up and the first thing I do is to make an act of devotion, saying, "Lord, this is the *best* day there's ever going to be in my life," and I mean it too, although I don't always say it with conviction . . .'

Peter chuckled reflectively.

'I want it to be – I really do. Every day I ask God that I shall go out to love and praise him with all my whole being, and over the last thirty years I must have managed that for . . . oh, at least five minutes.'

I was still wrestling inwardly with the idea of rising at 4.15 every morning.

'So, that takes you to – let's say, 4.30 am. I still don't see why you need to be up quite so early.'

Peter's eyebrows rose.

'Oh, well, the next thing I do is rush downstairs, do one or two ordinary things, then take the dog for a walk. That's the most beautiful part of the day really, walking down the lanes in the early morning. The shapes in the winter, the freshness in the summer. Then, usually at about a quarter to five, I hurry down to our little chapel in the cellar for about an hour and three-quarters of – hopefully – uninterrupted prayer or meditation, whatever you like to call it. I hope it is adoration. God embraces me in that time. I think he is always very pleased to see me.'

I was silent for a moment, thinking of my own fragmentary, undisciplined prayer life. By 6.30 each morning, Peter had already spent at least two hours being with, and being embraced by God. That was before the day got going. I sighed rather ruefully.

'Right, so what happens at 6.30?'

'We say ordinary morning prayer ...'

Good heavens. More prayer!

' ... then we hold our daily celebration of the eucharist and then it's time for breakfast.'

Breakfast – common ground at last. I had breakfast too!

'We have our very simple breakfast in silence, always in silence, because the devil likes to get at people after they have prayed, especially at the beginning of the day, in order to spoil the rest of the day. The silence means that you can only *think* a person is horrid rather than say it.'

'Is it all right to think it?'

'Well, it's only half a sin.' Peter burst into laughter at the expression on my face. Still smiling he went on.

'After breakfast we wash up, and then we clean the house from top to bottom every day, and we do it with a feeling of absolute urgency because we are on the border line between heaven and hell, where we believe we have been called to be the mouthpiece of creation in a big way. Every Christian is, but in the monastic life perhaps more so. In Christian prayer and service we are at the centre of life. Not the periphery as many think.

'We are here to stand between the world and the devil, to fight him before he corrupts and destroys, and sometimes it's a real old struggle against his infernal majesty.'

I was out of my depth. Breakfast, cleaning and the devil?

'Why is the cleaning so important, Peter?'

'In all things, Adrian, we aim to do a perfect job. Each one of us must be super-Harpic round every bend. You see, the Lord is here. His spirit is with us, and we know that we want to do it as perfectly as we can because the king of kings arrives every minute of the day – even in you, the king of kings has arrived.'

'Even in me?'

Through the sitting room window I could just see the top of the Downs in the distance. For some reason I found Peter's comment, light though it was, profoundly comforting. Even in me, the king of kings had arrived ...

I wanted to pursue Peter's comment about not being on the periphery of life.

'How can a monk be at the centre of life?'

Peter suddenly looked very serious.

'Adrian, I have got to say honestly, and I mean it most sincerely, I am not a holy man, but if you spend hours and hours with God, you may very well see things more clearly and with more real knowledge than the person who lives on what I would call the periphery. That's why people go to holy men for help even if they've been shut up in a monastery for twenty years, because they sense that here is a chap who lives in the middle of life, and is able to, for instance, discern right and wrong, in a quite different way. Why, I've known people go to a monk who has been closed away for years just to ask him what kind of petrol they should use.'

'And would he have known the answer to that?'

Peter smiled. 'I don't know about that, but there is no doubt that one does get communications about things.'

I was intrigued. I tried not to sound too interested.

'Like . . . ?'

His voice was very quiet as he replied.

'On two occasions when I have been talking to someone, I have known that they were going to die.'

'Really?' I said foolishly, and probably a little nervously.

'Oh, yes, I could see death around them. I remember one chap – he wasn't particularly ill – I went back to the brothers and said, "He'll be dead in six months," and he was. I saw death around him.'

'And this is part of seeing the world from the centre?'

'Yes – and I recall another time.'

Peter sat forward as he suddenly remembered.

'There was a lady. Doreen was her name and she was very pregnant. One night I woke up at a quarter to twelve, and something – "within me or without me, I know not which" as Paul would say – said I should get out of bed and pray for Mrs Flag because she was just having her child. So out I got. Later, I heard that her baby had been born at just that time.'

'Was that in the form of a thought that came into your head, or . . . ?'

He clasped his hand thoughtfully.

'To quote Paul again, "In the flesh, or out of the flesh, I know not." But I do know that there wasn't any doubt about it.'

What a meal some Christians would have made out of these experiences. It didn't seem to bother Peter whether they were labelled or classified. They were just a natural feature of this vision from the centre that he was talking about. I wondered how Peter viewed the way in which other churches dealt with spiritual gifts.

'You hear a lot nowadays about things like prophecy and speaking in tongues. Word of knowledge is another gift that seems to be "in vogue" as it were. How do you feel about these things, Peter? The idea that God can zoom in on a service and say, "I've got a message for Fred, and this is it . . . "'

For the first time I felt the bishop was not altogether easy in his reply. His words were slow and carefully considered.

'Yes ... I am happy. Paul makes it quite plain that everything must be done decently and in order and it's very difficult to get this balance. The Catholic Church, on the whole, has made the liturgy so frameworked and stereotyped, that it's actually very difficult to get these bits of informality in. On the other hand, some of the evangelicals have made it such a "hats in the air affair", that it's difficult for people to be able to concentrate on God, on giving themselves to him in sacrament, and in his word. It's very difficult to get it right. On the whole I think we need eucharistic worship and we need informal worship, but we probably ought to keep them distinct.'

It was a very careful reply.

'And the gifts themselves ... ?'

'I am sure that there are people who have gifts of knowledge or prophecy. I've been to a lot of churches where it happens ...'

His voice took on a more definite note.

'What worries me about prophecy is that it always seems to be jejune.'

I didn't know what he meant.

'Well, here we are, living in a world which could be on the edge of a nuclear war, where the wealth of the West is absolutely gross compared with the starving world, and you don't hear people saying any of the real strong stuff which I believe we should expect from prophets. It amazes me. Most of the prophecies I hear are saying that God is love and he loves you a lot. Well, of course he does, but is that what prophecy is for?' He paused, gazing into the distance, then smiled and relaxed back into his chair with a bump, his feet see-sawing into the air as he landed.

'I like tongues! I like to hear people singing in tongues. I've always said that if you have a special friend then there are two things which you must be able to do. You must be able to be silent with them and you must be able to talk nonsense with them ...'

I laughed, remembering how, when John Hall and I met, we often talked complete but enjoyable rubbish for hours on end.

' ... and the nonsense is not nonsense. It's because the love is so big, it bubbles out, and tongues is that freedom of bubbling out in love. It's lovely, you just go on and on.'

There was a short pause as I watched this bishop giggling with his legs in the air. No one who got up at 4.15 every morning had the right to be this happy.

'Have you ever doubted the existence of God, Peter?' He became quiet and serious again.

'Not doubts about the existence of God, no. Times when holding on was very difficult though, times when there was a great temptation to disobey, or seemingly disobey God.' Peter became very still, his voice so low that I had to lean forward to make sure I didn't miss what he said.

'I very much wanted to be married once ... when I was about twenty-three. And God seemed to be saying, "Become a monk." I remember the whole time over that Christmas – they were very very black days.

'The balance was so fine. I only had to pick up a pen, and in thirty seconds write to this girl and say, "OK, it's on again. When shall we meet?" Just a thirty second job it would have been, and it would have made all the difference between two totally different lives.' There was an expression of wonder on his face.

'When I think of Jesus calling Matthew "as he passed by". Amazing isn't it? Fifteen seconds to decide. Jesus looked over his shoulder and said, "Hi, Matthew. Come on – follow me!" Then he just walked on. He probably didn't even look behind him to see whether this geezer was coming. . . . Amazing!'

'Who made that choice about your future? Was it you, or was it God?'

'We made it between us, I think – together . . .'

He raised his voice in mock anger.

'He suggested it and I agreed, and I've got a bone to pick with him about it too!'

Suddenly he was laughing helplessly.

'I'm not a resentful creature,' he said, his mirth subsiding, 'but I get close to it.'

'So you've come to terms with celibacy then Peter?' I queried.

He looked at me for a moment, his eyes twinkling.

'Adrian, as I've already told you, God loves me extravagantly. I'm not just a celibate. I'm an extravagant celibate!'

Peter often returned, and still does return to the twin themes of extravagance and transfiguration. He is fond of quoting the story of Jesus feeding the five thousand, and points out that twelve basketsful of food were collected after the meal. A sign, he says, of God's extravagant giving.

He maintains that the church has a responsibility to transfigure the community instead of just forming a holy huddle once a week. For instance, he says, local churches should be as interested in producing a good football team, as in organising a good Bible study group. He is an inspiration to many, a puzzle to some.

As for me, he was the initiator of my understanding that Christianity is not about *systems* and God, but about individual people, and the relationship they build through raw, prolonged contact with a creator who is genuinely and warmly interested in them. Peter is a man who has real discipline, a real prayer life and a real joy. He is one of the small group of people I know, who has gained his experience of God from God.

Unfortunately, Peter was involved with Company for a relatively short time before pressure of work and other responsibilities made it impossible for him to continue, other than for very occasional guest appearances. Three years later I was still meeting people who remembered things that he said in those early programmes. Peter is just the same today. Whatever he touches seems to sparkle. He even makes me fizz a bit.

Chapter Seven

One of the problems about saying that you're a Christian through a public medium like television, is that people have an awkward tendency to believe you, and neat organised expressions of faith seem to wilt rather, in the heat of real human need.

My friend and colleague, Ian, was really going through it. His father, who over the years had been loving parent, first-choice fishing companion and close friend, was dead. Cancer. For the last few months, Ian and I had worked together in a locked treatment unit, dealing with violent or chronically absconding teenagers from all over East Sussex. I had grown very fond of Ian; a warm, vulnerable, complex character, for whom pipe-smoking was a rich and absorbing activity, well suited to a nature that swung from deep contentment to heavy depression. He had a great talent for expressing affection, and real gifts with difficult and distressed children. I hurt for him when I saw his grief. I wished there was something I could do or say to help. There was something; but when I learned what it was, I felt quite frightened.

It appeared that in the seven months since Company had first come on the air, Ian's mother, Mrs Figg, had seen Bridget and me on a number of occasions as she sat up late watching the television, and was able to identify with much of what we said. Ian and I had only rarely talked about such things, but he asked me if I would deliver the address on the day of his father's cremation. He wanted me to do it, he said, first because I was his friend, and secondly, because, although I was a Christian I wasn't very religious. (I think this was intended to be a compliment, though it made me think at the time.) I agreed of course, but it was from that moment that I began to feel uneasy. I'd given talks before, but never on occasions like this. It was all very well to sit in that little island of light in the TV studio throwing out my views on God, left, right and centre, but this was going to be a real human event, full of pain and tears and the fear of death. What did I really know about God? What, for that matter, did I know about Ian's dad? Was he a Christian? If not, what would I say? Something vague but comforting perhaps. That would be the easy option; but would it be right? Or should I scratch the old evangelical itch, preach the 'hard line' gospel, and let people make their own minds up? It seemed to me that in a peculiar way I was neither humble nor arrogant enough to say very much at all.

As the day of the cremation drew nearer I felt more and more troubled. On the day before the service, I travelled down to Brighton to meet Ian's mum and stay the night with Ian and his wife, Sue.

Mrs Figg was nearly broken by her husband's death. I took her hand as we sat side by side on the settee in her sadly cheerful little sitting room.

'Tell me about Frank,' I said firmly. 'I want to know what he was really like.'

'He was the first person who really loved me,' she replied.

She told me that as a child she'd had a very strict religious upbringing. A lot of ritual, a lot of meetings, a great deal of church attendance and no love at all – no softness. Then, as a young adult she met Frank. He was the first person to offer her real affection and warmth. They fell in love and were married. Frank, a carpenter by trade, had always been popular at work and in the local community, especially as he had a great gift for settling arguments and disputes. She pointed to photographs of the smart, pleasant-featured man who had meant so much to her, and wept a little. She said that Frank would not have described himself as a Christian, and Ian, who had been listening quietly while his mother spoke, added that he might well have resented anyone attempting to stick that label on him after his death. I sighed inwardly. It wasn't going to be easy . . .

That night, I lay awake on my bed in Ian and Sue's spare room, gazing up at the ceiling and wishing that God would write the end of my talk for me. On the little table beside me lay the sheet of paper on which I'd jotted down headings and notes for tomorrow's address. But I couldn't write the ending. Lying there in the darkness I realised what a jumble of half-formed beliefs, feelings and thoughts still made up what I so easily described as my Christian faith. I just didn't know what I could say to all those people tomorrow without compromising God, or Frank, or myself or ... I was still asking God for ideas when I fell asleep.

Sleep is a strange thing. The mind seems to go on working while the body takes a few hours off. In my case, the 'night shift' often seems more efficient and effective than the daytime one. Or perhaps God is more easily able to introduce ideas and suggestions when I am less defended and aggressively conscious. Whatever the reason, when I woke the next morning I *knew* how to end that address. The words were printed clearly on a sort of mental ticker-tape; all I had to do was transfer them to the sheet of paper beside me.

I was still nervous about the unfamiliar task awaiting me, but the central truth, the kernel of the event, was in my grasp, and as I stood in front of the mirror that morning, knotting, unknotting and reknotting the necktie that always seemed to half throttle me on these formal occasions, I knew that everything would be all right. My natural nervousness was not helped, however, by an absurd interval just outside the chapel of rest, when the undertaker asked where the minister was, as it was he who would lead the procession into the building. We had all spent a few minutes gazing around tensely, waiting for him to appear, when it suddenly occurred to someone – clearly brighter than the rest of us – that I was the minister on this occasion. Sweating slightly with embarrassment, I led the mourners into the cool interior of the chapel and after a hymn and a prayer, I began speaking to the fifty or so people who seemed to completely fill the available space. For a few minutes I spoke about the things I had learned about Frank from his wife and son. How very much they loved him, how he had many friends, how much he would be missed, how significant it was that Ian, in his thirties, would still rather go fishing with his old dad than with anyone else. I didn't have to make any of it up. It was all true. As I neared the end of the address, I lowered my notes to the table beside me. The last paragraph was still printed in my mind – I didn't need to read it. I spoke directly to Ian and his mum as they sat opposite me like two lost children, hands interlinked, eyes wet with tears.

'I am not sure what Frank thought about Jesus,' I said, 'but I am sure about one thing. They'll have met by now. And I'd guess that Jesus looked straight into his eyes, and smiled, and said, "Frank, you brought love into someone's loveless world, you were a peace-maker, and you were a carpenter. That's three things we've got in common. I reckon we've got plenty to talk about."'

On the following Wednesday night I described this event to Company viewers, pointing out how vulnerable I had felt when Ian first asked me to take the service. I had feared failure of some kind, failure to deliver the Christian 'goods', failure to make the event memorable and meaningful, failure, as well, if I'm honest, to impress. It occurred to me after the programme was finished that I was still playing games about honesty and openness. I had often said to people that I was quite happy to lay myself open at the Company table; to be truly vulnerable; but was I really? Later, as I settled comfortably back into my seat on the southbound train from Victoria, I frowned through the murky glass of the window and conducted an inner dialogue with myself.

'What do you mean when you say I'm not vulnerable on Company? I've just told goodness knows how many people about my rotten selfish feelings when Ian asked me to ...'

'Ah yes. So you have. Did you tell Ian that at the time?'

'Well, no – but ...'

'And isn't it a fact that you rather enjoy running yourself down about things that have already happened? It makes you feel good, and it protects you from real criticism.'

'Well ...'

'Doesn't it?'

'I suppose so – but, look. What about the way I've talked about the arguments and problems Bridget and I sometimes have. They're real enough.'

My internal inquisitor chuckled. 'Oh, yes. I know what you mean. You mean when you and she sit there full of confidence and looking crackers about each other, and talk about the terrible problems you have.'

'But we do have problems! Surely it must be worthwhile to talk about things like that.'

'Oh, yes. I've no doubt it is. But that's not what we're talking about. We're talking about your claim that you're vulnerable sometimes. Let me ask you a question.'

'Yes?'

'Has it ever really cost you anything, mentally or emotionally to say the things you say round the kitchen table?'

East Croydon flashed by. I sighed.

'No – it hasn't.'

'Aren't you actually determined not to show your real feelings to anybody, let alone television cameras?'

I inadvertently vocalised the irritable 'Yes!' with which I answered this question, slightly shocking a precise looking elderly lady on the other side of the carriage. Perhaps she thought that I was practising being positive.

The next day I described this conversation to Bridget, and we decided to raise the question of 'being vulnerable' with the rest of the Company participants as soon as possible. We had our opportunity very shortly after this when the whole team, including Frances, Angus and Maurice met to discuss all aspects of the programme and its development so far. By now the team had changed and grown significantly. Peter Ball was no longer with us, but we had a 'replacement' bishop in the form of George Reindorp, a very sprightly seventy-year-old, who had recently retired as the Bishop of Salisbury. He was now looking forward to an active retirement with his doctor wife, Alix. Other newcomers included Steve Flashman, an unusual combination of Baptist minister and highly talented rock musician, Robert Pearce, who worked for Christian Aid, Shirly Allan, an actress living in the Maidstone area, and Ann Warren, already well known as a Christian writer and broadcaster. At an appropriate point in the agenda Bridget brought up the subject of openness and vulnerability, and there was a general discussion about the advantages and difficulties of the expression of genuine feelings on television. It was finally agreed that the programme could only benefit from real communication, especially as the whole team had recently fallen into the trap of merely expressing agreement about rather unexciting truths. We all solemnly nodded our heads and vowed to be *really* vulnerable in the future. I, of course, nodded my head with all the rest, as one does in large meetings of that kind but I seriously doubted that, after all my years of being so well defended, I would really be able to open up. Less than two years later I was to be surprised by the extent to which I did reveal myself at my very lowest, but back at the beginning of 1983 it was George Reindorp who took the first step, when he told viewers about a tragic event that had happened many years earlier.

George Reindorp seems to have been in training all his life to become a grandfather. After only one encounter with this slim, white haired, vivacious character, Bridget and I knew that here was a man in whom children would delight, and there are few higher compliments than that. George, in his own way – and although it's not the same way as Peter Ball it is just as valuable – was able to make events and people sparkle with his infectious brightness and impish sense of humour. When I first knew George however, although I thought him very charming and competent, I also, rather arrogantly, suspected that he was more Anglican than Christian. He appeared to have responses and comments about all aspects of the Christian faith neatly labelled and filed in his mind for easy reference when required. Indeed, it appeared to me that, in his scheme of things, the Church of England was God's outer office, scrupulously tidied and cleaned, and presided over by highly organised receptionists like George, who were employed to ensure that things ran smoothly; not to create problems where there were none, by asking unnecessary questions or exploring alternative ways of operating.

In my great wisdom I decided that George had never really been exposed to suffering and was effectively cushioned from real life by the privileges of high office in the church. Little did I know that George had already experienced one major tragedy in his life.

One night, soon after we had first met, George and I enjoyed an evening meal together at a hotel in Rochester, prior to a Company programme the following day. We ate and drank well, talked quite a lot (George is very good company), and then moved over to more comfortable seats for coffee. It was then that he told me about the death, in 1947, of his beloved baby daughter, Veronica Jane.

George was a parish priest at the time. He had married Alix in South Africa during the war and they were now living in Vincent Square near Victoria, with their small son Julian, in a house only three doors away from the flat which he later occupied in his retirement. Life seemed very full and good then. George was more than ready to tackle parish work after a long and eventful period as a navy chaplain during the war years. His was a large parish, including twelve thousand tenement dwellers, as well as the idle or industrious rich. There was ample scope for the use and development of those delicate skills of communication which he is able to use like a magician at times. George has always maintained that if David Jenkins, the controversial Bishop of Durham, had been able to experience life as a parish priest earlier in his life, the knowledge and understanding of ordinary people thus gained, would have balanced his academic training, and perhaps resulted in a more careful and caring expression of his views on events such as the virgin birth and the resurrection. George felt, as a working vicar, that it was necessary to get really involved with such issues as the flower-arranging rota, and the debate about whose turn it was to clean the pews, for it was in these apparently trivial, day-to-day concerns that one could meet and learn about people, and perhaps earn the right to stand six feet above contradiction to preach to them. He is the same today. Somehow he learns about the personal lives and problems of many people who others hardly notice. Often as we have walked through the TVS building together, he has called out a cheery greeting to a cleaner or cafeteria assistant and added a query about the health or progress of a friend or child or parent.

In addition to the stimulation of his work, George was deeply in love with his blue-eyed, attractive wife, who as well as being a successful doctor was an ideal clergyman's wife, although she never allowed herself to occupy a stereotyped role.

Her only fault in George's eyes was her inability to give up cigarettes. He estimated that she smoked 'half a curate a year'. In all other ways though, she was perfect for him, being – by his own admission – less self-centred, and more controlled than he ever was.

Their joy was made complete by the arrival of a second child, Veronica Jane, a beautiful baby girl, in 1947. George adored her. Four hundred people were present for the christening of this special 'Parish Baby', none prouder than little Julian who thought his tiny sister quite wonderful.

Up to now, George had chatted lightly and easily as he recalled those first, pleasant, post-war years, but now a pattern of pain, like a much-used map, spread over his face, and he stared past my shoulder into the far distance as he spoke quietly about the death of his daughter.

'She was lying in her pram, just as she often did. I was in the drawing-room talking to another clergyman, when the door suddenly opened, and Alix came in. She's a very unexcitable person, and she simply said, "Get a doctor quickly!", which struck me as being a very odd thing, because of course she's a doctor herself. Anyway, I went and got a doctor who lived close by. I knew by then that there was something wrong with Veronica Jane, but I took it for granted that everything was going to be all right. They both went upstairs, and after hanging around in the hall for a while I followed them . . .'

George's eyes misted slightly as he went on.

'When I first saw her I thought she was moving. I realised later that she wasn't really. It was just the effect of the artificial respiration they were doing on her. Alix knew in fact, as soon as she picked her up, that the little one was dead. Alix wept. I was just stunned. I cry a lot about all sorts of things, but that was ... I don't know ...'

He shook his head slowly from side to side, reliving the shock of that moment.

'She was a blue-baby you see. Nowadays, of course, they could have done something, but then ... well ...'

Dear George. As I looked at him I felt ashamed. I thought I knew about people, but I knew nothing. Never suffered? I thought of my own children and experienced just a hint of the pain that the death of any one of them would cause Bridget and me, and their brothers, of course.

'What about Julian, George? How did he cope?'

He smiled and relaxed into the warmth of the memory.

'Veronica Jane went on being very real to Julian. I remember he had a little friend round to play with him one day, about three months after the death. They disappeared up to the bedroom, and a little later we heard Julian screaming at his friend, so we rushed upstairs and it turned out that this other boy had picked up a little woolly toy, and Julian was screaming, "You can't have that! You can't have that! It belongs to Veronica Jane!" In the mind of that little five-year-old, you see, she was still very much alive. And, in fact, very much later, when we had had three more children, I recall somebody saying to Alix and me one day, "How many children do you have?", and when I replied that we had four, Julian, who was of course much older then, interrupted quickly and said, "No! Five! You're forgetting Veronica Jane!" And he was right of course.'

'And how about you? Was she still there for you?'

George took a folded sheet of paper from his inside jacket pocket, unfolded it and passed it across to me.

'When she died we were devastated, naturally, and for a while I found it difficult to see where God fitted into what had happened.

Then a dear friend – a saint really – wrote this to me.' He pointed at the paper in my hand. 'That's a copy of the letter. It brought peace to me, and since then it's been amazingly helpful to lots of others to whom I've given copies.'

I read the letter.

It was with great sorrow that I heard today of the death of your child. The religion of Christ was always sincere and clear-sighted. He refused to obscure the fact that tragedy was tragedy; and wept at the grave of Lazarus. It must therefore be in the circumference of His love that we recognise our torn hearts when we part with a child who has held all that was best in us in fee.

The fact that He could weep over the death of a loved one when He knew that in so short a time He was going to supply the answer which made hope the sequel to every tragedy, even the tragedy of sin, surely shows that here in time and space, grief and hope can come to us side by side.

Thus I pray it may be with you and your wife.

It has been given to me to see our progress to God as a road divided in the middle by a low wall, which we call death. Whatever our age or stage of development, or relationship with other human beings, there is no real change involved in crossing the low wall. We simply continue in a parallel course with those who loved us in our development and relationship. I do not believe that God has altered one whit your responsibility or service for your child.

I do believe that she will grow side by side with you, in spirit, as she would have done on earth; and that your prayer and love will serve her development as they would have done on earth. There is nothing static about the other life.

The difficulty is that our spiritual sight is so little developed compared with our earthly sight. We cannot watch the development and growth as we could on earth. Yet much can be done by faith, by the realisation that what we hope is true, and that we can train our minds and imaginations to think in terms of truths, even if they are pictured in earthly forms. The companionship which was given you, you still have. The growth to which you look forward will still be yours to watch over and care for.

You will be much in my prayers at this time. What I have written I know to be true and I pray that you may be enabled to live in that truth and to find the answer to your tragedy.

When I had finished reading, I refolded the paper and handed it back to George.

'Thank you,' I said. 'Thank you for telling me about what happened to your daughter and for letting me see that.' I paused.

'Are you going to talk about Veronica Jane on the programme tomorrow, George?'

'Yes,' he replied brightly, 'I thought I would. It may help others who have lost someone they love very much.'

The following evening George repeated the story of Veronica Jane as we sat around the kitchen table in the Gillingham studio. It clearly cost him a lot to go through the whole thing again, and I felt glad that there was a cushion of thirty-five years between him and the tragedy. There was an unusual stillness about the studio as the programme came to an end. Those working on the studio floor and in the control room had been deeply moved by George's story, and so, presumably, had viewers at home. It had been an event rather than a performance. Bishop Reindorp had undoubtedly pioneered the vulnerability that we all thought to be necessary, but suppose, I reflected, one wanted to talk about a tragedy that was happening in the present, and not thirty-five years ago. Would that be possible, or even desirable? Not very many weeks later we had a chance to find out, when George talked in a Company programme about the second major disaster in his life. This time we were quite unprepared for what he said, and it was not an incident from the past. It was happening to him right now.

We didn't associate George with tragedy. It was fun preparing and making programmes with him. He had a fund of stories that were very amusing and always well told. What was more, he never seemed to mind being stopped in the middle of his attempts to repeat them for the second or third time. His ability to switch from being avuncular to being like an excited small boy was very endearing and enriched our gatherings greatly, especially when we all felt rather limp and formless. George stacked untidy bits of the world very neatly when necessary. We indulged in a little playful sniping at times. I noticed that George had developed a very effective conversational ploy which he used in argument or debate. He would state his point of view with great force and panache, then, thrusting his chin aggressively towards the person he was addressing, say, in a tone implying that any attempt to put forward an alternative view would indicate advanced mental decay, 'Don't you agree?' I kindly pointed this out to George who was as grateful as one might expect, but I did notice that he modified the query thereafter to '*Do* you agree?', which does at least have the virtue of sounding like a real question. He bided his time, awaiting an opportunity for revenge. It came one day when I started a Saturday night programme by describing a thought that had occurred to me while I sat in the local pub on the previous evening.

'I was well into my second pint,' said I, 'when I really saw what Jesus meant when ...'

George's sense of humour was so tickled by the idea of divine revelations beginning to occur at the two pint mark that he never allowed me to forget those few words.

'You know, Adrian,' he said one day. 'You're very fortunate. Most people have to drink all evening before they start to see things.' He paused, then stuck his chin out, his eyes glinted. 'Don't you agree?'

It was so enjoyable working with George, and he seemed such a happy man that the revelation of his great sadness was a real shock. We had decided to make a programme about the year that had just finished, and although we hadn't discussed the content in detail, Bridget and I assumed that most of the conversation would be about events that had made news in 1982; politics, sport, significant social change – that sort of thing. George was due to start the ball rolling, and sure enough, when the floor manager cued him he began to speak. But it wasn't what we'd expected.

'The most important thing to happen in my year never got into the newspapers or onto television,' he said. 'As you know, my wife Alix and I were hoping to retire into the country when I finished full-time work, but it is not going to happen now because Alix is suffering from Pik's disease, and she's going to move into a nursing home.' George's voice broke slightly as he went on. 'The thing is, you see, that the disease involves progressive deterioration of the brain, so ... so she will need to be there for the rest of her life.'

Bridget and I sat in stunned silence, temporarily incapable of taking in what he was saying. We had never met his wife, but we had heard so much about her. Alix. The girl with the vivid blue eyes; the lover of flowers, the marvellous mother, wife and friend, full of inner sympathy and strength, the hostess who had entertained a thousand people a year. George's 'thought-mate', and an eye to catch across the room when someone said something ridiculous and you wanted to share your secret laughter with the only other person who would really understand ... She was not to be with George in his final years.

He went on to describe how Alix had become more and more withdrawn over a long period until it became clear at last that something was terribly wrong. When the illness was diagnosed, George's first concerns were practical ones. Where would she live for the rest of her life? Fortunately (George said that it was like Christian losing his burden in *Pilgrim's Progress*), someone presented him with an anonymous gift at this point, and through the generosity of that unknown person it was possible to arrange first-class care for Alix for an indefinite period. The next, and greatest task facing George was learning to live alone and face his retirement years without the steady, loving support of his wife.

'It's not the big things, you understand. You've had a good day – you've maybe had a bad day. You go home and she says, "How did it go?", and you say what happened and who said what, and she says, "How do you feel about it . . . ?" That's what you miss, that sort of ordinary, comfortable chat. And then you miss having someone to hold in your arms; and quite apart from that, you were such good friends . . . such good friends.'

At the close of the programme, Bridget and I and Frances, the producer, were in tears. But behind my tears all the old anger flared up again. I found myself saying silently to God, 'Well? Explain that one then!'

Over the following weeks, George came to terms with his situation quite remarkably, although a basic level of sadness remained of course. He seemed to have gained a new understanding of God's love for him as a son and a friend, quite apart from the official and ceremonial relationship that had existed over the years.

I probably had more difficulty accepting what had happened than George did. Perhaps this wasn't so surprising when one considered the fact that he had been pursuing a clear path of duty for more than half a century, and had good reason to trust God. Much later, over lunch one day in his Vincent Square flat, I told George how I had felt on hearing about Alix, and asked him the question I had wanted to ask at the time.

'Where is God in this, George? Has he allowed it? Has he got a point to make in it? What's going on?'

'I did ask a lot of questions like that,' he replied slowly. 'You go all through the possibilities. Is it because I have to learn something? Is God saying, "You've talked a lot about faith, now – what about it?" You ask yourself all those questions.'

For a few moments he studied the end of his fork, then laid it gently down on the table.

'In the end I simply have to say the same as old Polycarp, the Bishop of Smyrna, who was a holy man – rather different from me! They said to him, "Now, we really don't want to have to put you to death, so be a good chap and throw a few grains of incense on the altar for the emperor just to make it all right, then he'll let you live." And he said, "Lo, these eighty and six years have I served God. Shall I cast him off in my old age?" Well, now, God has been marvellous to me. We've got wonderful children and we're a very happy family. We've got nine and four-eighths grandchildren! So, although at first I did ask all those questions, and I still don't really understand it, I know that in it somewhere – God knows where – and I mean that literally, God IS, and I hold on to those words from scripture: "God has prepared for those who love him, such good things as pass man's understanding, that we loving thee *above all* things ... " I've said that – talked about it a thousand times. I have to go on trusting.' He stopped for a second. 'Good heavens. It sounds as though I'm saying it's so *easy*. I get very very lonely still, especially as Alix is so out of character now, and when I do visit her each week, she quite often seems to lack interest in me, and draws the visit to a close after a very short time. It's hard sometimes when I go down there, longing to see her and then ...' George straightened his cutlery neatly on his plate.

'Do you believe that you'll meet Alix, as she was, in another place, after death perhaps?'

There was more passion and certainty in George's voice when he replied, than I think I had ever heard before.

'Oh, Adrian ...' For a moment he was lost for words. 'Somehow – if Christ is what I'm convinced he is, and believe and know him in my heart to be, so far as my little mind can take it in, I'm absolutely certain that all will be well. Shall we see again those whom we love? Yes! What will they be like? We do not know! When I wake up after thy likeness I shall be satisfied!'

Each sentence that George quoted, sounded like a girder that strengthened him. I realised that these words had a meaning for him that brought far more than intellectual reassurance.

'A bond of love like the one between Alix and me could never be completely shattered,' he continued. 'My God is not capable of such a capricious whim. We shall somehow be together again, not as husband and wife but in some other, better way. For the present I can only live a day at a time, but for what I've had, I give thanks.'

I had one more question. 'If Jesus was sitting here in this chair beside you now, and you wanted to say one thing to him about all this, what would it be?'

Through the big front window of George's sitting room we could see on the other side of the road, two of the masters from the famous nearby public school, hitting golf balls across the school sports field. One of them gave his ball a mighty crack, and I watched it sail into the blue, and disappear, to land somewhere on the far side of the grassy expanse. George's voice, as he spoke, was very gentle.

'I think I'd say, "For the past – thank you *very* much." Why?'

The 'Why?' was not a demand, just a simple question. George trusted God. I knew that now. And could it be, I wondered, the reason he had been able to be vulnerable on Company, was that he was accustomed to being vulnerable to God? An interesting question.

And what about me? Would I ever be able to let people see *me* broken and bruised? Never!

Chapter Eight

Peter Ball, George Reindorp, and other Company regulars and guests all shed their own particular light on the truth. Father Tony Cashman, for instance, brought my understanding of the Roman Catholic faith right up-to-date when he described how spiritual gifts such as tongues and prophecy are increasingly common among Catholic Christians nowadays. Robert Pearce, a regional secretary for Christian Aid, has broadened my understanding of international issues, especially when describing his trips abroad and his personal reaction to the sight of people in acute need. I particularly enjoyed meeting Mother Frances, an Anglican nun who runs Helen House in Oxford, the only children's hospice in the country. She was a delightful mixture of strength and freedom, with a sense of humour that seemed, somehow, to invigorate the air around her. Another welcome guest was the Roman Catholic Bishop of Arundel, Cormac Murphy O'Connor, an ex-rugby player and a man with a deep commitment to the building of bridges from denomination to denomination. I'm sure Cormac won't forget Bridget and me in a hurry. After we had made our programmes on that Tuesday, he kindly offered to give us a lift home to Hailsham on his way to Arundel. Unfortunately my navigating skills deserted me when we were about halfway home, and we wandered through endless Sussex lanes for what seemed an eternity. We did get home in the end, and Cormac was very patient!

When Vishal Mangalwadi joined us as a guest, I was determined to get his name right first time. Vishal works on behalf of

111

the poor people in his part of India, and has suffered imprisonment and violence because of his quiet determination to be a true
follower of Christ in that situation. As the run-up to the first programme began, I repeated Vishal's mouthful of a second name
over and over in my mind, to make sure it came out smoothly.
'Mangalwadi – Mangalwadi – Mangal . . .' The floor-manager
cued me and I spoke confidently to camera three.

'Hello. It's nice to have a special guest with us tonight, and it's
. . .' My mouth opened and shut like a fish. I'd forgotten his *first*
name!

All of these people were Christians of one variety or another,
of course, but the time came when Frances announced that there
was to be a new member of the team who was not a Christian,
but a Jewish Rabbi. His name was Hugo Gryn.

Hugo turned out to be a bundle of fizzing activity, a short,
physically dynamic, clean-shaven man with a crackling sense of
humour, enormous energy, and a gravelly voice with an attractive
combination of transatlantic and Central European accents. Like
me in the past, he smokes incessantly, and with something akin to
dedication, as though each fresh cigarette wards off the resolu-
tion of some fearful issue. With others he is rarely still, always
watchful, studying and learning from eyes, adapting a little here
and there in his responses, still employing, perhaps, in a modified
form, the survival skills he learned in the harsh schools of
Auschwitz and other camps during the war. Highly educated,
multi-talented, a fascinating speaker and supreme teller of stories,
Hugo is a congregational rabbi in the West London Synagogue,
which has a full membership of thousands, and is a constituent of
the Reform Synagogues of Great Britain. He seems to have been
to most places and met most people. He is always on the move
around the city, the country, the world. A skilful user of the
media, he is familiar with both television and radio broadcasting,
and he has brought a new dimension of interest and entertainment to many many Company discussions. Hugo always 'deliv-
ers'. He is not a man who would find it easy to be at a loss, and
I have only very occasionally seen him display anything but

buzzing competence. I don't think Hugo believes that many people would be interested in his sadness when it occurs, and, as he said to me once, when he does get hurt, he tends to go inside himself, rather than turn to others.

I had often wondered, before meeting Hugo, where all the Jewish jokes came from. I now believe that, even if he doesn't make them all up, Hugo is largely responsible for giving them currency. Whenever we meet nowadays, I look forward with relish to the latest story. I don't interrupt, but I recall that, when I first met him, I stopped a joke after half a sentence.

'These two Jews were on a bus . . .'

I interrupted pompously. 'Do they have to be Jews, Hugo?' What a wonderful non-racist person I was.

Hugo's expressive face twisted into concentrated thought, then relaxed, one eyebrow raised humorously. 'Okay, I'll start again. There were these two Chinamen on their way to a Barmitzvah . . .'

I collapsed.

A story that was much appreciated by Company viewers was Hugo's account of the elderly Jew who desperately wanted to win the weekly lottery that was organised in his community. This man stood before the open ark in the synagogue and called out with a loud voice.

'God! Let me win the lottery this week. I need the money. Please let me win!'

To his dismay there was no reply, and someone else won the cash that week. On the following week he came back to the synagogue, and stood before the ark once more, beating his breast and calling out in an even louder voice.

'Oh, God! You must hear me! I've been a good Jew all my life. I've done what you've told me to do. I've been in the synagogue every week. Now I'm asking you to help me. Please! Please, let me win the lottery this week!'

Again there was only silence, and again the prize-money went to another man a couple of days later.

The next week he prostrated himself before the open ark, pleading and begging God to answer his prayer, and let him win the lottery, just once. After a few minutes of this, he lay exhausted and speechless on the floor of the synagogue. Suddenly a voice came from the open ark. It was the voice of God.

'Look, meet me halfway, will you? Buy a ticket!'

My mother, well into her sixties by the time Hugo joined Company, and a very reliable barometer for the programme generally, took a real shine to the rabbi. She thought him kind, good-looking and original; very high praise from her.

On a more serious level, I wondered how we would handle the gap between Hugo's beliefs and those of the rest of the team. Most of us were Christians of one denominational shade or another. He was a Jew. Should we confront? Should we compromise? Should we ignore the differences and talk about something else? Generally speaking, discussions tended to be very polite and non-controversial when we did talk about our contrasting faiths. Hugo was asked on one occasion to say something about the enormous variety of faiths that exist in the world. Were they all misguided, or perhaps, all true in their own way? Hugo subscribed to the latter view. Just as a crystal will throw out different facets of the same light, so, he maintained, each religion or like-minded group receives a facet of the single, central truth, which is God.

It was a good answer, and a diplomatic answer, but I couldn't make up my mind when I saw that programme, whether Hugo really did believe what he was saying. What would I have said if I had been involved in that discussion? I would have been polite I expect. I'd have nodded, and said, 'How interesting'. What did I believe? Did I go for the crystal idea? Or did I believe that, unless they turned to Jesus, all Jews would be rejected from God's presence on the day of judgement? I imagined Hugo and me walking side by side into the presence of God. I tried to picture myself being accepted and the rabbi rejected. My mind wouldn't do it – the other way round, perhaps, but not that way. I could sense a piece of the love of God in Hugo – nothing to do with his religion. It was just there. God would surely welcome home that piece of himself. Who was I to judge after all? There was little to show for my faith. Hugo's had survived experiences that I could only guess at. What did I know about suffering, compared with this man who had not long been a teenager when he first entered a Nazi death camp, and saw his younger brother taken away to be executed because he had no useful function for the Germans? Why was Hugo not only still a believing Jew, but a rabbi, after coming through experiences that might be thought to deny rather than affirm the existence of a loving God? There was never enough time or an appropriate opportunity to explore these areas with Hugo during the Company broadcasts, but I really wanted to know the answer to that question in particular. Also, what was the difference between Hugo and George in relation to the way they coped with personal tragedy? Or Peter Ball for that matter, who had given up the warmth and fulfilment of marriage and family life for the sake of serving the same God as Hugo. Why did they all continue to follow him whatever happened? The only way to ask Hugo these questions was to actually book time with him. His diary was always packed, but he named a date and on that day, a strangely significant one as I learned later, I met him at his London office.

Hugo was oddly ill at ease that morning, partly because he had been following what was, even for him, a very rigorous and demanding schedule, but also for another reason which I was to learn as we talked. People were clamouring for his attention in person and via the phone up to and beyond the point where we finally sat down. He fumbled with the telephone as he replaced it on its rest at last, half-dropping then retrieving it, glancing up quickly to see if I had noticed his uncharacteristic clumsiness.

Finally he was settled, with the inevitable cigarette safely lit, leaning back in his chair and narrowing his eyes as the smoke rose in front of his face like a thin grey screen.

I had with me a book called *Returning,* a collection of exercises in repentance by past and present Jewish writers and poets. One poem in particular had moved me more than anything I had read for a very long time. I knew Hugo was familiar with it, because he had chaired the RSGB Prayer Book Committee which had assisted Jonathon Magonet, its editor in his compilation of the anthology. I read the poem out loud.

> The house of God will never close to them that yearn,
> Nor will the wicks die out that in the branches turn;
> And all the pathways to God's house will be
>   converging,
> In quest of nests the migrant pigeons will come surging.
>
> And when at close of crimson nights and frenzied days,
> You'll writhe in darkness and will struggle in a maze
> Of demons' toils, with ashes strewn upon your head,
> And lead-shot blood, and quicksand for your feet to
>   tread.
> The silent house of God will stand in silent glade.
> It will not chide, or blame, or scoff, will not upbraid,
> The door will be wide open and the light will burn,
> And none will beckon you and none repel with stern
> Rebuke. For upon the threshold Love will wait to bless
> And heal your bleeding wound and soothe your
>   sore distress. . . .

I finished reading and looked up. Hugo was nodding vigorously.

'Yes, I know that piece well. Actually, it's about abandonment – the kind of abandonment that we experienced in the camps. It reminds me of . . . did I ever tell you about the postcards?'

I shook my head.

'It was in a relatively small camp in Silesia. About four thousand prisoners I think. It must have been in . . .' Hugo frowned as he tried to remember, then stabbed the air with his cigarette in triumph. 'It was the summer of forty-four! We were made to work from dawn to dusk for six and a half days a week. I think it was Sunday afternoon we were allowed off, and then, absurdly, sometimes the camp orchestra would play. Can you imagine that, in the middle of death? Anyway, one day, to our great amazement we were all supplied with a postcard each, and some pencils, and told that we could write to *anyone* we liked, *anywhere,* and they would be delivered via the Red Cross.

'So, there I was, standing with my pencil and my postcard, and gradually I realised I had no one to write to. My father was there in the camp with me, but I had no idea where my mother was. The rest of the family had all died in Auschwitz. Everybody dead. Grandparents, brother, cousins, aunts, uncles, everybody from my part of the world, by that time they were already dead. I knew I had some relatives somewhere in America, but I didn't know their names, and I certainly didn't know any addresses. I really tried to think of someone, but, in the end, I was one of many who handed in a blank card. I had no one to write to, and I didn't think there was anyone in the world to whom it mattered if I wrote, or didn't write, if I lived or died. There was a sense of being totally abandoned.'

'Was that very hurtful?' Another great 'Plass' question.

'It was *so* painful. I came face to face with the fact that I didn't matter to anyone outside that camp. Thank goodness I mattered to me, because plenty of people around me soon stopped mattering to themselves, and then, well ... the suicide rate was very high.'

'But you did have your father there with you?'

Hugo stubbed out his cigarette.

'Yes, I did, and it was really because of him that I managed to avoid the excesses that many other prisoners were driven to. He was a very sane, very intelligent, very good man and he kept me from doing really bizarre or shameful things. I don't mean that I was particularly good. I just had that peculiar dimension of luck in having him with me. He kept hope alive, you see. I remember he once saved the margarine ration for weeks, and he made a little bowl out of clay, and a wick from strands of cloth, just so that he could light a candle to celebrate the festival of Hannukah. "One way or another," he said, "we *are* going to celebrate!" And he got all the people together to light the Menorah.'

'Did you understand why he did that?'

Hugo threw his hands out and opened his eyes wide. 'No! I thought it was a waste of margarine. I said so. Especially as the

117

candle didn't even light when it came to it. It just sputtered and died. But he took me on one side – I was about thirteen or fourteen then – and he said, "Understand this. You and I have gone through a lot. A long, forced march with next to no food, and once we lived for a couple of days with no water. You can live for quite a long time without food. You can even live without water for a day or two, but I am telling you that you cannot live for three minutes without *hope*. You've got to have hope!" And he was right. As long as people were taking that much trouble to make a single candle to use for a religious ceremony – well, there must be hope, even in the middle of suffering. He taught me that.'

'Did your father die in the camps?' I flinched inwardly as I waited for Hugo's reply.

'Actually, he survived the whole war, but … you see, we ended up at this camp in Austria, a really vicious place, just a few days before the end of the war. We had been on a forced march to get there – more than half of the march died on the way – and in this camp there was not just hunger, but raging typhoid. Everybody had it. When the Americans liberated the camp on May the fifth, there were unburied corpses everywhere, and those who were alive were all sick. All those still living – and my father was living – were taken to a kind of makeshift hospital, although I'm not sure that they really knew how to treat us. And my father and I shared a bed in this place … It was then that he died.'

'So he died after …'

'Yes! After liberation! When they came to take him away, and I knew for sure he was dead – I wouldn't let 'em! I was hysterical – beside myself. It was the ultimate in being cheated, you see. He'd actually survived … the sight of him being taken away was very bad. I had typhoid too, and everything seemed blurred and confused. I do know though, because they told me afterwards, that at that moment I attacked one of the German SS men that they were using as orderlies. I mean … I really wanted to kill him. I was completely out of control. And after that … it was just oblivion. I wasn't even able to be there when they buried him, presumably in some sort of mass grave …'

Hugo selected another cigarette from the packet beside him, and flicked his lighter expertly. He was in control, but there had been a glimpse of a very young and desperate Jewish boy for just a moment.

'Do you know the date of his death?' I asked.

He thrust a hand towards me, palm downwards, fingers outstretched, patting the air, a characteristic gesture. 'Adrian, you're catching me on a very, very, peculiar day. After I came to, some pious Jews who had been there when my father died, gave me the date and told me not to forget that my Yahrzeit – that's the anniversary of my father's death – was the fourth day of the Hebrew month of Sivan. Whether they were right or not, I'm not sure, but that's the date I've got.'

'And that day is . . . ?'

Hugo nodded energetically. 'Today!'

No wonder he had looked distracted – less together than usual. Time heals, but scars can ache terribly. Should I go on?

'So . . . is this a bad day to talk about . . . ?'

Hugo interrupted, leaning forward and smiling. 'Peculiar! Not bad, just peculiar.'

I took the plunge again. 'What happened to your mother, Hugo?'

'She survived. She went through Auschwitz, just as we did, and then on to another camp, where she not only survived, but helped to organise an escape group of women.'

'She wasn't with you when your father died, then?'

Hugo's response to this question was a strange, gentle, sweetly-growled 'No-o-o-o.'

'When was she freed?'

'She was released a few months earlier – in March I think, so she had already made her way back to our home town, and eventually, I made my way there as well.'

'Do you remember your first meeting with her when you got back?'

He replied vehemently. 'I remember it very, very, *very* well!' He settled back in his chair. 'I had a very complicated journey home

119

from the camps. Transport in Europe was all over the place at the time, and you just had to travel as best you could. It was a very odd time. I went by train, I went by boat, I walked, I even stole a horse and cart with a couple of other people once, and used it for three days then abandoned it in some town. Eventually, I came to Budapest. I wasn't home yet, but I suddenly remembered that I had relatives in that city. I managed to find out where they lived and presented myself at their door.'

Hugo paused for a few moments, his hand arrested in mid-gesture, his eyes focused on the image in his mind. It didn't look like a happy memory. He went on in tones that sought to excuse the people who had opened that door to him.

'I must have looked very peculiar . . . and I think they felt very ill at ease with me. They never even invited me in. . . .'

Hugo threw the last sentence away, but I caught it, because it triggered the memory in me of that doorway in Bristol, and the abject misery of being turned away when I most needed to be taken in. That had been bad enough. How must Hugo have felt after so many years of desperate survival, so much loss and death, when people who might have laughed and wept with him, however distantly they were related, didn't even ask him in? I didn't know how deeply that had hurt him, and for some reason I couldn't face asking him. For my own sake, I think.

I realised that Hugo was going on.

' . . . and this train went and went and went until we reached a point about three or four stops from my home town in Russia. Before the war it had been in Czechoslovakia, but now the borders had changed, and suddenly I lived in Russia. No matter! Wherever it was, it was home, and I was nearly there. Anyway – the train stopped at this station a few miles from my destination, and a man got on and sat in the same carriage as me. We got into conversation, and after a while it turned out that he knew my family.

'"Did you know," he asked, "that your mother is at home?"'

'Well, I didn't know, of course. It was the first time I'd heard of it. I told him so.

"'Yes!" he said. "She's there and she's fine, and she's waiting for you, ... and your father. Where's your father?"

'He told me that someone had come back from the camp where my father and I ended up, just after it was liberated by the Americans, and given my mother the news that we had *both* survived. So I now knew that my mother was sitting at home waiting for me to walk through the door with my father. Well ...'

I stared at Hugo in silence, moistening dry lips with the tip of my tongue as I tried to imagine how he had felt. No fiction writer could have concocted a more tortuously dramatic situation.

'When the train stopped at my home town,' went on Hugo, 'I didn't want to get off. I said to this man, "Look, I'll just stay on for a couple more stops, and have a think about things, and then I'll come back." I was afraid to get off! But ... they wouldn't let me stay on the train. Whether they actually held the train up for a while I don't know, but somehow they persuaded me – conned me – into getting off the train, and I started to walk towards my house. Believe me, I didn't have much luggage! So, I'm walking down the road towards the house where this man said she was staying. It's a summer afternoon, and, you can imagine, I'm nervous. Then, I looked up, and there was my mother, watching me from an upstairs window as I trailed along the road towards her – alone. And when we were finally face to face, she didn't ask me anything. She looked at me and took it all in, then we embraced. And then ... you know, we have a tradition that when someone in the family dies, you sit Shivah. That means you sit on a low stool for seven days, and that's the formal mourning. But if the news of death is delayed, you still go through this ritual of mourning, but for just one hour. So my mother just looked around, found a low stool, and sat in silent mourning for an hour. At the end of the hour she got up – she still hadn't asked me anything – and she said to me, "Hugo, you're the son. You say Kaddish." That's a prayer of praise that we say, and it doesn't actually mention death at all. It starts "Magnified and hallowed be the name of God ... " So I said it. And then, when I'd finished – then, we started to talk. I didn't really understand it then, but I do now.

You see, the language of religion and ritual was, if you like, the mediating influence.'

'You mean that the ritual *was,* in a sense, the conversation between you and your mother?'

Hugo nodded. 'That's right, and we didn't need anything else. It wasn't until days later that she said "Now, what exactly happened?" There was too much to say at that first meeting, so we didn't try. The most important thing, she knew anyway, just by looking at me.'

Coffee arrived. After a little clinking and stirring we were settled again.

'Why, Hugo . . .' – it was the question I had wanted to ask – 'why, when you had seen so much suffering, so much misery, did you decide to become a rabbi?'

'Well, it's a good question, because, actually I always wanted to be a scientist – I *am* a scientist, I've got a degree in maths and bio-chemistry – but I agree with Emil Fakenheim when he said that Hitler mustn't be allowed a posthumous victory. He invented an eleventh commandment . . .'

'Which was . . . ?'

Hugo wrote the words in the air with his hand. 'Thou Shalt Survive! It wasn't enough to stay alive physically. It was just as important that Jewish values, and above all, Jewish learning should be preserved. And the thing is, Adrian, that in the Jewish tradition, learning and spirituality go hand in hand. Most of us come to spirituality through learning – not the other way round. I was very lucky to have a great teacher . . .' He pointed to a picture on the wall beside us. 'Leo Baeck. In the end, he and another rabbi who was coaching me, sensing that I was beginning to believe I was the only person in the world who was still seriously interested in Jewish studies said, "All right, if it's so important, then go ahead and devote yourself to Jewish learning!" So I did.'

Hugo chuckled richly. 'I was bluffed – dared into it, and I was lucky really. They stopped my bitching just like that. It just shows how important it is to fall into the right teachers' hands at the right time.'

'So you became a rabbi?'

'I became a rabbi.'

'But you didn't feel a call from God in the sense that Christian priests talk about it sometimes?'

'I might have been *sent*, but I don't think I was called.' Hugo was laughing again. 'I don't really know . . . I believe that God actually rules all our destinies, so, in that very general sense, perhaps he sent me. More specific than that I wouldn't like to say. I don't quite see God picking me out and saying, "Now, Gryn, I think you ought to do so and so . . . " No, it's not my notion of God.'

'But if . . .'

Hugo interrupted. 'We have free will! I have it, you have it. If you abuse yours you might well diminish mine. That's where it all goes wrong. But . . .' He leaned forward, one hand raised, but flat, to separate heaven from earth. 'I can't blame God for *my* getting it right *or* wrong. For me, that equation just doesn't work. The things that I saw in the camps, the suffering I experienced can be wasted or not, according to how I exercise my will. I am able to know more accurately than some, perhaps, what hurts, causes pain in others. My aim is to simply *not* do that which is hurtful.' He waved his cigarette as if to attract my innermost attention. 'The Golden Rule is different in the Christian and Jewish traditions. The Christian tradition says "Do unto others as you would have them do unto you." But the Jewish tradition says "Don't do unto others what is hateful to you." There's a difference, and it's a difference that I learned through suffering.'

'And God is involved with suffering.'

'I think that God wept with the Jews in the camps. I think that God weeps with all who suffer, and I mean *with*, not just *for!*'

I was still having great difficulty in understanding Hugo's relationship with God. I felt I had grasped the importance and significance of learning and the need to preserve tradition and ritual, but there was so much in him, and in the stories he had told, that spoke of a God who did take a personal, caring interest in this person who had been 'lucky' enough to find a teacher like Leo

Baeck, whose influence had changed the course of his life, and 'lucky' enough to have his father with him through the camps.

Perhaps it was just the conditioned Protestant in me, but I couldn't dismiss the strong impression that at some point in his life Hugo must have encountered God in a very close and profound way. Was it I wondered, that I simply needed to have my own image of God reinforced?

'Has God ever spoken to you, Hugo?'

'In so many words?'

I adapted hastily. 'Not necessarily, but has there ever been an occasion when God gave you a nudge, or a push?'

'Yes there was. Yes. Quite clearly.' No hesitation at all. I sat very still and listened as Hugo went on.

'It was Yom Kippur, and I was in prison, and I had a kind of bolt-hole in this place I worked in. I knew that if I worked the twelve to fourteen hours a day they demanded I wouldn't last. There just weren't enough calories coming in to keep me going. By that time I was a cunning, experienced prisoner – I knew the ways of the prison world anyway. So, I used to disappear for a few hours at a time, and just sit in this bolt-hole of mine. It was in a builder's yard. You can do things in a builder's yard. Well, it was Day of Atonement, and all the Jews in this camp knew that, and I knew it, so I got in there – into my hiding place. Well . . . I didn't have a prayer book, but I remembered some of the prayers, and I . . . I decided I'd pray. So I did.' Hugo's voice was a soft growl. 'Half-remembered prayers . . . bits and pieces, and I ended up really crying. I just cried and cried . . .'

It was a vivid picture. Hugo, already forced to be old beyond his years, sitting in the darkness, weeping for Judaism, for his family, for himself.

He went on, his voice low but very firm. 'I was convinced then, and I remain convinced to this day, that my cry was heard. I'm not saying it saved me, because that was a chance thing, but I *know* I was heard, and I in turn also heard . . . understood that the ways in which we hurt each other, these are not God. Actually, that's when I became religious, in that bolt-hole that day. It never left me. I could draw a picture of that place now. It's that clear. On that day, I understood, for the first time, the reality of God; understood that he is not just an extension of me – that he is wholly "other". And, yes, I can communicate, and it's not a one-way thing . . .'

'And that principle continues?'

'All the time.'

I felt surer than ever that there was something that Peter and George and Hugo had in common. Something about trusting, despite not really knowing. Something about not claiming more than was actually true . . . I couldn't quite put my finger on it. I glanced up at the clock – nearly time to go. One more question.

'Hugo, you said that today might be the anniversary of your father's death. What would he think of you if he was here now?'

For a moment I witnessed a rare sight – Hugo at a loss.

'I want notice of that question!' He considered for a moment. 'Well, first of all he would be surprised that I was a rabbi, and not a scientist. He would say I have reverted – my grandfather and his father before him were both rabbis. He wouldn't be displeased about it, just surprised.' He blew a long stream of smoke towards the ceiling. 'Then I'd set out to show him he could be pleased. I think we'd get on well. I don't think he would be particularly ashamed.'

I didn't think he would either. In fact, I thought that he would probably be very proud of the way in which this son of his had kept the eleventh commandment.

Chapter Nine

As 1983 got under way I was feeling rather shell-shocked. So many things had been happening in all areas of my life. I had given up smoking more than a year ago, something I had always thought impossible. Then there was the television programme which seemed to fill up a large proportion of my free time.

The bulk of my time and energy, however, was spent on the work I was doing in the newly opened locked unit at the Children's Centre in Hailsham. Planning and running this treatment facility had proved to be an intense and often stressful experience for all concerned, as we were dealing with extremely difficult teenagers in a very small and restricted environment. One child in particular was very disturbed. She had been with us for many months, a fifteen-year-old girl who, after a disastrous early life had been unable to settle for very long in any of the county establishments or foster homes that had been tried over the years. Placement after placement had failed, and now Meryl was an expert in institutional disruption, unwanted by her family, and unsuited to any but our small physically secure wing catering for no more than five children at the most. Meryl was able to wind up and manipulate adults to screaming pitch. On more than one occasion I arrived at work to find a staff member alone in the office, shaking with tension and anger after a few hours with Meryl, who seemed to feed on this kind of response.

Generally speaking there was a relatively peaceful atmosphere when she and I were together but there were times when she tested my self-control almost to breaking point with her finely judged, spiralling hysteria, and constant attention-seeking ploys. I was no longer the very immature personality who had hit out at that boy in the middle of a field ten years ago, but that was really only because I had learned more techniques and knew how to stack tension away in some inner space that, although I didn't realise it at the time, was already dangerously overpacked.

A typical incident occured one autumn afternoon, when Meryl and I were the only two people in the unit. I was ensconced in an armchair in one corner of the multifunctional dayroom while she, rather moodily, pushed snooker balls around the half-size table that stood in the centre.

Meryl desperately wanted to find foster parents who she could live with, but, predictably, the search for these 'super-humans' was taking rather a long time.

Already, that day, she and I had talked about how much progress had – or rather, had not – been made and I knew that she was feeling angry and frustrated. Poor Meryl, despite a succession of horrendous failures, always managed to whip up a froth of optimism and excitement about 'The Next Place'. Everything would be different! Oh, yes it would! She would change! Why couldn't it happen tomorrow? It wasn't usual for her to use aggressive tactics with me, but today was different. Her mind and body were aching with the strain of containing such heavy, jagged emotions, and I was the only available means of off-loading some of this intense feeling.

Sitting comfortably in my chair, absorbed in a newspaper, I was suddenly aware of Meryl's voice, filled with a sneering challenge.

'What would you do if I put this effing cue through that effing window?'

I knew how essential it was to think very quickly in these situations. Indeed, it was the extra half-second's thought that often made the difference between a successful outcome and disaster at times like this. I had been the author of enough calamities in the past to know that. In the moment after Meryl's question, the following thoughts flashed through my mind. Firstly, she was quite capable of doing what she threatened, and there was a real danger of injury, leaving aside the less important matter of damage to the building. She was on the far side of the snooker table, and therefore out of grabbing range, even if I came out of my chair like a rocket. Also she would expect me to react angrily, or nervously, or to reason with her. Any of these responses would have suited her well, offering as they did, the possibility of tension-filled dialogue, culminating in an emotional 'splurge' of some kind. I had learned to avoid predictable responses. And lastly my stomach was knotting up, as it always did when 'aggro' loomed, no matter how confident I might feel about the outcome.

The pause before my reply must have been imperceptible. As I spoke, I didn't move my eyes for even a fraction of a second from the open newspaper that I was holding.

'Just a minute.'

It was hardly a response at all. There was a short pause. Meryl must have decided that I couldn't really have heard what she said. She repeated her threat in a slightly louder voice.

'I *said*, I'm going to put this effing cue through that effing window!'

Still without looking up I answered her, trying to put into my voice the mild, abstracted irritation with which one reacts to an annoying, but trivial interruption.

'Look, Meryl, I just want to finish this little bit in the paper, then I'll be with you. Okay?'

The newsprint swam before my eyes as I waited for her next move. There was another, longer silence. When Meryl spoke finally, it was with a rather pathetic, baffled wistfulness. I wasn't keeping to the rules!

'Yeah, but I said I was going to put the effing cue through the …'

My raised hand interrupted her. I folded the newspaper, placed it neatly on the magazine rack beneath the coffee table, then turned deliberately in my chair to face her, crossed my legs, folded my arms and demonstrated my readiness to give her my full attention.

'Now, Meryl, I'm listening. What can I do for you?' It was the polite bank clerk with his next customer.

Meryl was a little muddled by now. She held the snooker cue up and replied quite quietly and politely, 'I'm going to put this effing cue through the window.'

'Yes ... and?'

Meryl looked blank. I was supposed to supply the 'and'. She collected herself a little. 'Well, I'm going to do it! I am!'

I nodded soberly. 'I'm sorry, Meryl. I don't quite see what you want me to do. If you've decided to break a window with that cue, then I expect that's what you'll do. You must make your own decision about whether it's a good idea, or not. I'd like to be able to help, but ...' I spread my hands in a helpless gesture. 'What can I do ...?'

Meryl raised the cue, her eyes fixed on mine. Was I bluffing? 'I am gonna do it!'

I looked up at the clock above the sink over on my left. 'Look, Meryl, I really have got to make some phone calls. I'd better go and get on with it. You stay here and decide what to do, and I'll be in the office.'

I stood up and strolled casually past the end of the snooker table, down the passage on my left, and into the little unit office a few yards along the corridor. As I passed within 'striking' distance of Meryl, I sensed her sudden increase of tension. I knew that it would happen now if it happened at all. I waited for the sound of smashing glass ... but it didn't come. Instead, the disconsolate figure of Meryl appeared in the office doorway, the long wooden cue now dangling loosely in her hand. I snatched the redundant weapon from her, and shouted loudly into her face as all the pent up emotion of the last few minutes burst out.

'Don't ever do that to me again!'

After this explosion, we sat and reviewed what had happened, looking for ways in which Meryl might have expressed her feelings more appropriately.

Meryl had many difficulties after her placement at Lansdowne but Bridget and I became very fond of her and she continued to visit and stay with us as a friend in the years that followed.

Work with children like Meryl was very stimulating and exciting – you never knew what would happen next – but it was also rather wearing.

Nowhere was the God who came, and comes down in the person of Jesus, more needed than in the lives of these children I was working with. Children like Meryl, and many others, were already emotionally crippled before they reached their first or second birthdays. Theoretical compassion was useless to them. Their experiences did not generally make for an attractive presentation and success in caring for them demanded a carefully balanced mixture of warmth and firmness. This could occasionally take extreme forms, as in the case of Miranda, another long-term resident in the secure unit, a very powerful girl, full of passion and chaos. On more than one occasion I was able to defuse the violence in her, only by putting my arms lovingly around her and whispering bloodcurdling threats into her ear at the same time. It worked because she knew I was sincere about both. I suppose – on reflection – that God operates in a similar way. The Bible has always struck me as being largely made up of God's love on the one hand, and his blood-curdling threats on the other.

Both Meryl and Miranda were victims of cruelty and mismanagement. I have always strenuously resisted the argument that says people cannot be held accountable for their crimes because of difficult childhood experiences, but there are notable exceptions, who, by the time they have struggled through and arrived wild-eyed at the age of sixteen, deserve a full apology and a pension for life.

Many people, however, do not actually commit crimes or anti-social acts as a result of early problems. They do, however, often end up with an emotional limp, an inadequacy in one area or another. Perhaps Jesus' statement that people need to be 'born again' has a special meaning for those who would welcome the opportunity to start life again and get it right this time round.

I was interested to see, as the months went by and people started to be more open, how many of the Company team had suffered as young children, and had seen, or wanted to see, God coming down into their lives to change the consequences of early trauma. Ann Warren, for instance, lost both of her parents at a very early age, and has been a refugee from her past ever since. It is her insight into her own situation, and her determination – with God's help – to overcome the darkness inside her that has enabled her to help so many others through her books and counselling. Peter Timms, the prison governor who made headlines when he left the prison service to become a Methodist minister, lived with the conviction that he was unloved for years, after his mother's early death, and formative years spent with a family who, although very caring, never really succeeded in making him feel that he belonged. Sue Flashman, one of the brightest contributors to the programme, has been very open and honest about the fear and insecurity that has dogged her all her life, and that is only now beginning to ease after much expert Christian counselling. Again, the roots of her problem lie in childhood, and any attempt to find a solution without reference to that fact would fail before it began. Frances Tulloch, Company's producer, has much in common with these folk. She also sustained a lot of inward injury as the result of her parents' broken marriage, and has had to slowly and painstakingly reassemble a shattered self-image over the years.

Does God come down and help? How does he do it? I'm sure he does it in many ways, but one of the most striking examples that I have seen is in the case of Jo Williams, my good friend and Company colleague. Of all the team, she is the one whose background most reminds me of the children I have worked with.

When Jo was 'discovered' as the newspapers put it, she was working as a cleaner in the TVS studios in Southampton and running a local scheme offering help and friendship to old, sick and desperate people. She called it Neighbourly Care and appeared one day on the TVS community services programme PO Box 13 to describe her work. Angus Wright immediately asked Jo if she would like to join the Company team and, slightly bewildered, but willing to have a go, she agreed. She became even more bewildered when the national press ran a story about her elevation from cleaner to TV star, especially as there was no question of her giving up her cleaning job to live on the 'huge' income she would receive from her television appearances. Whoever wrote that story clearly knew nothing about the kind of budget usually allowed for late-night religious programmes.

On the day Jo was due to make her first trip to the studio as a broadcaster, there was a ring on the doorbell, and on opening her front door she discovered a uniformed chauffeur standing smartly to attention beside a vast white limousine looking oddly out of place in the very ordinary little Southampton back street where she lives. With great ceremony she was ushered into the cool interior of the sleek vehicle and soon found herself gliding smoothly across the South East of England in the direction of Maidstone. Feeling very apprehensive, Jo leaned forward eventually to timidly ask her charioteer if it was 'all right to smoke'. Sensing her unease the driver abandoned his air of respectful detachment and suggested she ''op in the front with 'im', an invitation which she gratefully accepted. On the outskirts of Maidstone, however, he stopped the car, and insisted that she returned to the back seat in order that her arrival should be suitably regal. As the car purred to a halt outside the big glass doors of the TVS building, Jo reached out with her hand to pull the door lever and felt her heart suddenly leap into her mouth as the driver hissed violently out of the side of his mouth, 'Don't touch that handle.' Jo, suitably chastened, sat like a pudding while the chauffeur stepped smartly out of the car, marched smoothly round to the side and released her with the dignified servility peculiar to his profession. From there, she ascended to the press-room, where interviews and photographs awaited her. That was the end of that kind of super-star treatment, but it was the beginning of something much more valuable for

Jo's very first memory is a violent one. She was three years old at the time, sitting on the kitchen table at home in the middle of being washed by her mum. An argument sprang up between her parents, increasing in intensity as the little girl, in her birthday suit, forgotten for the moment, watched and listened nervously hoping that things would soon be all right again.

Eventually, her mother picked up an alarm clock and flung it at Jo's dad. Jo doesn't remember whether it hit him or not, but she does know that following that argument, she was sent to live with an aunt in Wales for a time, completely bewildered about what was going on, and more importantly, about whose fault it was. From Wales she moved to another aunt in Portsmouth, and from there back to her mother in Southampton only to be evacuated to Bournemouth almost immediately because of the war.

When the war ended, Jo, aged nine, was at last able to come back home, and she must have hoped against hope that she would never have to leave again. About a year later, however, her hopes were dashed when, as a ten-year-old, she arrived home from school one day to find that her mother had left for good. On the table was a brief letter, telling her to go with her younger brother and sister to another member of the family, and a pound note, presumably for bus fares. Jo had no idea where this other person lived, so pocketing the letter and the money, she led her brother, aged six, and sister, aged nine, round to the lady next door, who took them in and called the police. When a very kindly policeman and policewoman arrived, Jo was taken to a local reception centre, where she lived for about six months as one of a group of children in the charge of a house-mother, before being transferred to a Doctor Barnardo's Home, far away in Liverpool, where she stayed until she was fifteen.

Jo's memories of life as a child 'in a home', are not good ones. She already had the idea firmly fixed in her mind that she was a 'horrible' little girl. She must be. If she had been a nice little girl her mummy would never have sent her away when she was three, or at least she would have got her back as soon as she could. And then, later on, that note on the table had been the final proof. Her mummy didn't want her, and in that case, how could anyone else ever want her? She was *horrible!* Her experiences in children's homes did nothing to dispel this lack of self-value. As a twelve-year-old, Jo used to assemble with the other children in the home every weekend to await the arrival of local people who would 'select' a child to invite to their homes for tea on the Saturday or

Sunday. Each time, Jo presented herself, scrubbed pink, and wearing her very best clothes, longing to be the one who was picked for this treat. 'Let it be me!' she would say silently to herself, 'Oh, please! let it be me!' But, for some reason she never was picked. Not that she ever really expected to be. After all, what else could a horrible little girl expect?

At school there was a different kind of problem. Jo was sent off each day from her children's home, wearing the regulation issue black gymslip and stockings to mix with girls from ordinary families who seemed to have an enormous variety of clothes in all sorts of lovely colours. Noticing the curious glances directed at her sombre attire, which remained clean but unvaried as the days went by, Jo decided that something had to be said. Unwilling to confess to the shameful crime of not having a family, she invented a baby, tragically lost before birth by her mother, and explained that she wore black because she was in mourning. This very sad tale attracted quite a lot of sympathy, but two months later someone became curious about the fact that the period of mourning seemed inordinately long. Poor Jo, remembering how well the story had been received the first time, and having only the scantiest understanding of the facts of life, invented a *second* lost baby which, on this occasion, did not go down at all well. Jo laughs now when she tells this story, but it requires little imagination to see how excruciatingly embarrassing it was at the time.

At fifteen, Jo was transferred yet again, this time to Didcot in Kent, where, as a quite unreligious attender at the local Anglican church, she found herself rather fancying a good looking young curate, whose name was David Shepherd. From there she was moved to a hostel in Reigate, where she was taught housecraft, followed by yet another move to a working girls' hostel in Norwich, where she found a job selling fruit for a firm called Sexton Brothers. The effect of all these moves should not be underestimated. Each one involved breaking bonds with friends, with a distinct locality, with an environment which, even if not particularly pleasant in itself, offered the security of familiar sights and sounds from day to day. By the time she was sixteen, Jo had moved at least ten times.

One of the regular customers at the shop where Jo worked was a 'little old lady' who lived nearby. They got on very well and it wasn't long before Jo left the hostel to move in with her new friend, who became not only her foster mother, but a little later, her mother-in-law, when Jo married Netta's son, Joseph, a sailor in the Merchant Navy. Jo was blissfully happy for the first time in her life. Her husband was sixteen years older than her, and she didn't actually love him at first, but she had a home. She was wanted by nice, good people. She had married for security, and found it. Later she did fall in love with Joseph, experiencing what she calls 'tummy feelings' when he was due to return home from sea after a trip.

Joseph turned out to be a very good husband. He looked after Jo, made all the important decisions for her, and even cured her of the worst effects of her bad temper. She used to break things when she got angry. One day Joseph carried a complete china tea-set out into the garden and very calmly and methodically smashed every piece. When Jo, puzzled and aghast, asked him what he was doing, he replied quietly and reasonably that if she could do it, then so could he. She stopped breaking things.

In 1957 their daughter, Karen, was born. Jo was twenty-one and determined that Karen would not suffer the kind of neglect that she had. She admits she overdid it. Karen became a spoiled and difficult teenager. It was a problem, but Jo also had Netta and Joseph who continued to provide a place where she really belonged, where she could feel secure.

In August, 1978, Jo was in hospital having treatment for back problems. At 10.30 one night, as she lay in the ward, unable to sleep, someone brought the news that Netta had died that day. Netta was dead! Jo could hardly believe it. Thank goodness Joseph was all right. She knew he was at home feeling rather poorly, but it couldn't be anything very serious. It couldn't be! She needed him to be all right, to go on looking after her.

Less than two months later, on Sunday, October the first, Jo knew that her husband was about to die of cancer. Suddenly she was filled with overwhelming panic. She phoned the local Roman

Catholic priest, and begged him to come to the house. As she waited for him to arrive she feverishly hunted out every candle, every holy statue, every religious emblem she could find and placed them on a table in the same room as the dying man. When the priest arrived at last, she dragged him into the house, up the stairs and into the bedroom, crying and screaming for him to pray for a miracle to save Joseph. They both prayed, but there was no miracle. At 2.55 on the following Sunday, Jo's husband died. His last words to his wife were simple but true. 'We've had twenty-five good years.'

The only emotion that Jo could feel was anger; deep bitter anger. She was angry with Netta for dying, angry with Netta for taking Joseph with her, angry – so very, very angry with Joseph for going with his mother when Jo needed him so desperately. The people she loved had done it all again – gone away, leaving her lost and alone. They didn't care – they'd never cared! She'd known it all along, and she was stupid to think it could ever really change. She *was* horrible! She was a horrible little girl . . .

Jo sat down one evening soon after Joseph's death with a half bottle of whisky and more than a hundred codeine and aspirin tablets. Carefully, she crushed the tablets between two sheets of paper and poured the powder into a tumbler. She then poured whisky into the tumbler, stirred the powder in with a spoon, and swallowed the mixture straight down. She wanted to be dead. Fortunately, her attempt to swallow such a huge quantity of tablets all at once resulted in vomiting, and instead of dying she lay unconscious and undiscovered for the next forty-eight hours. When she eventually came to, the impetus to die had diminished, and over the following month, a month in which she was virtually deaf as a result of the suicide attempt, Jo did a great deal of thinking about her situation. She realised that the only way out of her darkness and depression was through offering help and support to others, and it was out of this realisation that the Neighbourly Care Scheme was born, a scheme that resulted in enormous benefits to many sick and troubled people in the Southampton area.

Jo worked hard and found it easier to live with her own grief as she became involved with the lives and problems of others.

In 1980 she married again, somewhat on the rebound, but her new husband, Don, was a very charming and intelligent man, and it was good to feel secure again. Three weeks later, she arrived home one afternoon to find Don hopelessly drunk and very abusive. He was a chronic alcoholic. Jo was horrified: there had been no hint of the problem before their marriage. Now she was confronted with a situation that was as frightening as it was unfamiliar. There followed a dreadful year of conflict and despair. Jo, terrified by the intensity of the hatred she now felt for Don, but relieved to hear from others in the same situation that her feelings were not abnormal, decided that, for the sake of her own sanity, Don must leave.

Alone again, Jo threw herself with even greater energy into her Neighbourly Care work, and the studio cleaning job. Then, came the appearance on PO Box 13, followed by Angus' invitation, and, in a little flurry of publicity, Jo became one of the Company team.

By the time Jo joined us we had moved from the Gillingham studio to the brand new TVS building at Vinters Park near Maidstone. Here we shared a studio with the news and current affairs programme, Coast To Coast. At one end was the news desk, at the other, the Company kitchen.

Frances had managed to find a flat in the country, out at Harrietsham, where the four participants for each week were able to catch up on news, discuss programme topics for the coming week, and generally relax together. Sometimes there would be a special guest joining us for a few programmes, and he or she would usually stay at the flat with the regulars, helping out with domestic tasks like everyone else, regardless of rank or status. This was very useful as it helped to create a closeness between members of the group, which resulted in a more natural interaction in the studio itself.

We had some good evenings at the flat. Bridget and I particularly enjoyed being there when George was staying. He always entered into the occasion with tremendous zest and good humour, invariably teasing Frances about what he described as her 'posh Islington life-style', and christening her 'Black Rod' at an early stage in the proceedings. We grew very fond of many of our fellow kitchen-dwellers as we came to know them better through time spent in that informal environment. The friendships we have established with some of our colleagues will last long after Company is gone and forgotten. Certainly, we shall never want to lose contact with Jo Williams.

We liked Jo as soon as we met her, although she tells me that I 'put the fear of God into her' when she came up to Maidstone for an audition. She remembers thinking that I was very aggressive in the programmes she had seen in the past. She soon realised that I was a softy really, and once we were able to get to know each other in the relaxed atmosphere of the Harrietsham flat, we became good friends. Jo is a very motherly type, and I must confess that I do enjoy being mothered, especially in the mornings. Jo shares with George Reindorp and Peter Timms, one supreme virtue that probably gives them the edge in the race to heaven. They all get up early in the morning to take tea to everyone else. It is a mark of my greatness that I am happy to lie in bed and let these three store up riches in heaven through this charitable act. It is a sacrifice, but I do it.

During Jo's first evening in the flat, she told us about some of the events in her past, concluding with an account of her second, disastrous marriage. Later that same evening, after our production meeting was over, and we had eaten together, she talked in more depth with Ann-Marie, who is a very sensitive listener. Ann-Marie listened quietly as Jo told her that she could never have Don back again, then promised to pray for both of them. This was quite a new idea for Jo, who had always believed that prayer was for emergencies and special occasions.

That week's programmes went well. It was clear that Jo was going to be a valuable member of the team. She was quite unselfconscious about asking the 'obvious question', unlike one or two of us who had perfected the art of looking as if we knew the answer really but were generously allowing others the chance to talk!

A few weeks later Jo received a phone call at home. It was from a hospital in Bristol. Don had jumped from a bridge in an attempt to kill himself. Obviously it was a genuine attempt; his body was wrecked by the impact of the fall and there was a strong chance that, if he lived, he would be confined to a wheelchair. Did Jo want to see him? Everything in her wanted to say 'Never!' but she didn't. She said 'Yes.' Later, seeing him broken and helpless in his hospital bed, she felt pity for Don, but not forgiveness. That year of misery was too clear in her memory for that. Nevertheless, she agreed that he could come home when he left hospital. The day before Don's return, Jo remembered her conversation with Ann-Marie, and said a prayer about the future. The next day, standing on the platform at Southampton railway station, she watched Don as he alighted from the Bristol train, and felt a wave of forgiveness and compassion flood through her, washing away – for the time being at any rate – all the anger and bitterness she had been feeling. She took Don home.

That was far from being the end of Jo's troubles. Don was still an alcoholic, and he was still drinking. Jo herself was ill much of the time, and often very depressed as the old bitterness began to creep back in and poison her efforts to find peace. In addition there were problems in Jo's relationship with her daughter who now had a lovely little boy called Joseph.

But something else was happening as well. Both inside the studio, and at the Harrietsham flat, Jo was asking a lot of searching questions – desperate questions, not for the sake of theological debate, but because she wanted and needed to know.

She had never read the Bible. What was it like? She read it in a modern translation and understood it for the first time.

She asked on the programme one evening why no vicars or priests had visited when Joseph died. Over the next few days she was inundated by ministers of various kinds.

What was all this about healing? Could Don walk again if she prayed for him? She did pray, and gradually he did walk again.

Did God listen to all our prayers? What about all the suffering? Jo wanted to know everything. They weren't unusual questions, but there was a childlike quality in the way she asked them, and in the way that she received the answers, that I frankly envied. George was wonderful with Jo, but she seemed to attract great warmth from everybody, including James Blomfield and Roy Millard, two young men who had become very much part of the team. They developed a very soft spot for Jo – James once zooming across country from Dover to Southampton at a moment's notice when Jo hit a really bad spot.

Once, she phoned Bridget at home, when she was feeling suicidal, and said, 'Give me one reason for staying alive.' Bridget could think of nothing very logical to say, but what she did say was enough. 'I love you, Jo. As long as I love you, you just can't die.'

It was clear that Jo was beginning to see the Company team as a sort of extended family; her trips to Harrietsham and the studios were a refuge from the storms of everyday life. Whether this was desirable or appropriate, I really don't know. I think that many viewers enjoyed becoming part of this 'family' of Jo's. Over the months she had shared the whole of her life story with people at home.

There came a day when Jo had simply reached the end of her tether. The doctors had just examined Don in hospital after yet another drinking bout. Their verdict was chilling. There wasn't much of his liver left to function. He was unlikely to live for very much longer, especially as he was still drinking. Not only that, but Jo was ill herself. That was how she felt – ill, lonely and useless. That night the Company participants were Jo, myself, and Prabhu Guptara, a freelance writer and journalist and a man for whom I have a great liking and respect. Jo wept openly as she told Prabhu and myself how close she was to giving up altogether. She couldn't pray, she said. God was angry with her. I reached across the table to take her hand, and Prabhu joined his hand with ours as I prayed for Jo and Don, for their peace and health – for some deeper kind of healing in both of them. I don't think I felt much faith in my prayer being answered, but I said the words, and we all said 'Amen'. After the programme, Prabhu put his arms round Jo who was still crying, while I stood by with a heavy heart. I'd said so many prayers in my time, often for children whose lives were just like Jo's and Don's – a mess. How many of those prayers had been answered?

I shook my head and compressed my lips as I watched Jo regain her composure. I prayed again silently. 'Please, God! Please do something for Jo! For Don!'

Had he heard? Was he going to do something? I couldn't have guessed at that moment, how much was to happen to me before I knew the answers to those questions.

chapter Ten

I knew why I felt so hopeless about praying for Jo. It wasn't just the memory of children in care who had stumbled from disaster to disaster, regardless of what I did or prayed, although that was certainly part of it. It was something else – something that had happened earlier in the year, to someone I hardly knew.

Just after I was converted at the age of sixteen, I travelled to Bakewell in Derbyshire with the other young people of St John's Church, for their annual weekend house-party, organised by Clive Sampson, the curate, and featuring a very impressive guest speaker, a young Anglican curate whose name was Ross Patterson. We arrived in the conference room for our first meeting, to find that Ross had rigged up a system of strings across the top of the room to support a very large, and very vicious-looking kitchen knife in such a way that, if it should fall, the point would plunge straight into the top of his head as he stood talking to us from the platform. We liked that. After all, it *might* fall. It was a powerful visual aid in his talk about the need for salvation, and he was a good speaker, strong and humorous. He was also a good tennis player and all-round sportsman. One of those people, in fact, who seem to have a magic touch in everything they do, and a vivid illustration of the truth that not all Christian men are effete.

During the course of the weekend Ross invited as many of us as were interested to come to a mission meeting a few miles away, where his vicar who had travelled down from York for the occasion, was due to speak. I was quite intrigued. I suppose I reckoned that if Ross was only the curate, then his boss must be

Patterson cubed; some kind of superman. It was with great interest, therefore that I filed into that church hall somewhere in Derbyshire to see and hear David Watson for the first time.

He wasn't like Ross. He wasn't like anybody. There was something in his speech and delivery that was quite unique. I was fascinated. Most of us keep words and sentences stacked carelessly in untidy piles in our minds ready to throw around haphazardly. There was a bespoke quality about every word and phrase that this man used. It was as if each tiny component of his speech had been carefully cut and polished by hand before being inserted into sentences that seemed to shine with a sort of translucent purity of intention. I had never heard anything like it before, and although I soon forgot the content of that particular talk, I never forgot as the years went by, the feeling that I had listened to someone who not only *believed* what he was saying, but was able to translate his thoughts into words of crystal clarity.

Over the following nineteen years, David Watson became known all over the world as one of the most effective communicators in the Christian church, through books, television appearances and missions. The unusual combination of a strong simple faith and an ability to show clear and cogent reasons for his beliefs, meant that he could appeal to people on all levels including those who might previously have felt that the Christian faith required an abandonment of intellectual integrity. Personally, I found his books much less appealing than the man himself, although they have obviously been very helpful to many many people. For me, he was a reminder, sometimes irritating, and sometimes reassuring, that there were Christians around who meant what they said for reasons other than that they had some personal emotional or psychological axe to grind.

At the beginning of 1983 it was announced that David Watson had cancer. The prognosis was poor. Unless a miracle happened he would die. All round the world people prayed for that miracle. I think some people would have jettisoned God and kept David if that had been an option. Perhaps that was the problem. Friends from a church in America, where many healings have reportedly occurred, flew specially to England to pray for him. David spoke in interviews about how he felt a strange warmth pass through his body when they laid hands on him for healing, but neither he nor they ever claimed to *know* that he would be healed, only that God could, and might make him better.

One night we asked Company viewers to join us as we prayed, like thousands of others, for David's peace and recovery. Later on that year, in July, Frances invited him to join Bridget and myself and George Reindorp in Company for seven evenings to talk about how those prayers had, or had not been answered, and how he viewed the future.

George had met David on a number of previous occasions, but for me it was rather strange to encounter a distant memory in the flesh. I was not disappointed. There was that same clarity of expression and delivery, and a much greater depth of peace and confidence. I marvelled once again at the differences in people who followed God closely. David was very much himself, however much he might have in common with other Christians. He didn't look or behave as if he was terminally ill, and during the evening that we spent in the flat out at Harrietsham, there was no visible sign of his energy flagging.

As we left the flat on the following morning, the owners of the property, Lord and Lady Monckton, appeared from the main house, and were introduced to David, who shook hands warmly with them. As we were about to move off, Lord Monckton, who is a Roman Catholic convert and an endearingly lordish sort of Lord, took a small transparent paper packet from his pocket and held it out towards David.

'Like you to have this,' he said with a gruff cheerfulness.

David looked at the little envelope. Peering over his shoulder I could see that it contained a small square of cloth of quite unremarkable design.

'Relic of Padre Pio,' went on Lord Monckton.

I had heard of Padre Pio, an Italian priest and mystic, now dead, who was said to bear on his body the marks or wounds of the crucifixion. Others had experienced the same strange phenomenon –

Saint Paul, Francis of Assisi, Dorothy Kerin and others. Presumably this little piece of cloth was a fragment of some part of the old priest's clothing.

'That's extremely kind of you,' responded David. 'Thank you very much.'

Lord Monckton smiled happily, pleased with the way his gift had been received.

'He's very active in Kent and Sussex y'know.'

I was a little taken aback by this. The Roman Catholic belief in the significance and influence of the dead on our day-to-day lives was not something that I could identify with at all. I was pretty sure that David would feel the same way. I wonder why it is that the way in which he reacted to this last comment of Lord Monckton's has been my most abiding and personally helpful memory of David. It wasn't *what* he said, it was the way that he said it.

'Really! How *very* interesting.'

Those few commonplace words conveyed an enthusiastic respect for the other man's point of view, and were not followed by one of those words like 'but', or 'however', or 'nevertheless', which usually lead quietly into total disagreement. It may seem rather trivial, but I learned something quite new at that moment about meeting people where they are, and not dragging them crudely into the arena of my own beliefs in order to club theirs to death.

We recorded seven programmes in the studio that morning, watched by Michael Harper, who was a close friend of David's and a religious adviser to TVS. Most of the programmes were indirectly or specifically connected with the illness and its effect on David's faith and family, and attitude to God. The atmosphere in the studio and the control room was one of hushed concentration as he spoke about the panic of waking at midnight, drenched with sweat, wondering if there was a God after all; of examining his faith to find out what remained when all else was shaken away, and of finally reaching the point where he wanted to go to God, but was willing to stay if necessary, instead of the other way round. He spoke of his present conviction that the best was yet to be, and grinned, like a child on Christmas Eve, when he said it.

'God's love,' he said, 'will not necessarily transform the situation – the sickness itself, but it will transform our reaction to it, and that's what really counts. I am responsible for either giving way to self-pity, which actually becomes a problem for other people as well as myself, or letting God's love and peace transfigure my reaction.'

We asked David what his central message to people would be at this stage in his life. He didn't hesitate.

'The most important thing is that people really need to *know* that God *loves* them. An awful lot of people are hurting for one reason or another. Down at the roots you find that they are not *sure* that they are loved and accepted – by anyone. To know that God loves them, that's the important thing.'

At the end, David prayed aloud.

'Father, we thank you that you have shown yourself to be a God of love. Help us, and all those in pain and need, to realise how *much* you love us, and to trust you whether we understand or not, for Jesus' sake, amen.'

As we left the studio that day, David was looking so well, and sounding so strong and optimistic that it was difficult to imagine that the cancer existed in his body, let alone that he could be dead in the near future.

Later in the year Bridget and I met David again, when we visited him and his wife Anne at their house in London with Frances Tulloch, to discuss a Sunday morning worship programme scheduled for the following spring. It was interesting to meet Anne. She struck us as being very real, and refreshingly practical about spiritual matters. Our discussion went well, although David didn't seem as well as he had done earlier in the year. We were quite excited about the prospect of making a programme that would last for an hour instead of less than ten minutes, and I think that I had developed a rather unreal expectation about the way in which personal spiritual problems might be resolved through frequent contact with David.

When I arrived at the TVS studios one evening, early in 1984, to learn that David Watson had died, it was as though some kind of heartless trick had been played on me. I know it seems childish and selfish but I felt cheated. Of course I felt for Anne Watson and her children as well, but they were strangers to me. I just wondered why God had, apparently, snatched away the man who could have solved my problems. Rational or irrational, that was how I felt, and the little fire of anger that had always burned deep inside me, flared up dangerously as this fresh fuel was added to it.

We went ahead with 'Meeting Place', as the Palm Sunday programme was called, and we were fortunate to have David MacInnes, a close friend of David Watson's, to take over the task of leading the service, but it was not a happy occasion for any of us, including little David, our youngest son, who was also taking part in the programme, and developed German measles on the day of the recording. I don't know who was more unhappy, him or me!

The period from Easter to autumn that year, I remember as a series of manic highs and miserable lows. Everything was losing its worth before my eyes, so it didn't really matter what I did or thought, or said. I was heading for some kind of crisis, but on the way to it there were two 'moments' that were to seem very significant in the future.

The first happened as I sat in church one Sunday morning. A picture started to form in my mind of a huge lake surrounded by plots of land, each one occupied by a single person. Behind the plots that gave access to the lake were more plots, again occupied by individual people. As I explored the picture mentally, I saw that the lakeside dwellers were made up of two kinds of people. The first kind rushed to and fro from the edge of the lake to the boundary between their own plot and the one behind, carrying cups of water to their landlocked neighbours. Most of the water got spilled in the process, but they worked on frantically, doing their best. The other kind were not working frantically at all. They were simply digging steadily on their plots of land, with no apparent interest in the fate of the waterless tenants whose land adjoined theirs. One of the cup-carriers stopped, red-faced and breathless, and spoke with some annoyance to one of the diggers.

'Why don't you do as we do? Why don't you get a cup and carry water to those who have none? It is selfish to work only on your own land as you do.'

The digger leaned on his spade for a moment and smiled. 'You don't understand,' he said, 'I'm digging a trench.'

The second moment was a moment of prayer. Like most people I had always had great difficulty about talking to God. It was all right sometimes, but more often than not my prayers bounced off the ceiling and the walls like a badly hit ping-pong ball, rolling to a halt eventually at my feet. On certain rare occasions though, a particular prayer seemed to pierce the barrier between myself and God with the kind of sweet certainty that one experiences on hitting the perfect off-drive in a cricket match (equally rare in my case). This prayer was like that. Bridget and I, realising that the kind of Christianity we were living out fell very short of the picture painted by Jesus, decided to say a very risky prayer.

'Father, we know that we haven't done very well with anything much up to now, but we really want to go all the way with you. We realise that we don't even understand what that means, but, whatever it costs, and however much it hurts, please let it happen. Amen.'

If I could have grabbed that prayer back as it zoomed off to its heavenly destination, I think I would have done. But I couldn't, and it wasn't long before God started to answer it in an unexpected and alarming way.

Chapter Eleven

'The police are here.'

My head was spinning as the nurse put yet another stitch into my injured wrist, but the words penetrated my brain with needle-sharp clarity. I was going to be arrested. After years of collecting children from police stations, and countless discussions about how to avoid getting there in the first place, I was about to find out how it felt to be 'nicked'. I relaxed my head back onto the pillow, and tried again to make some sense of what was happening to me. What had the doctor put on my sick note three weeks ago? 'Severe stress reaction.' They were just words. What had really happened?

When my three sons were all 'little' children, I used to wake in the morning sometimes to find that there were five people in our king-size double bed. Matthew, long and well-built, would be draped across the foot of the bed, forcing me to take up a near-foetal position, while Joseph was usually jammed firmly into my back, thus causing me to throw my head back and create space just under my chin for little David, who, during the night, was little more than a heat-seeking device. I ended up lying in exactly the same posture as a long-jumper in mid-leap; arms stretched above my head, back arched, legs bent, the classical position for gaining maximum distance. Poor Bridget would just be a shape-less form, crushed against the far wall by this living jigsaw of human bodies. In the morning I had to painfully ease and straighten out all those parts of me that had been adapting for most of the night to the unyielding bodies of my three small but solid night visitors. Being very tall, the pain could sometimes be intense, and on occasions I would abandon my own territory and either get up very early, or seek refuge of a sort on a vacated, two-foot-six wide bunkbed in the children's room. Anything to ease my aching bones.

This is the best way I can think of to describe what was happening to me in the summer of 1984. My mind and emotions were cramped and strained by the constant need to adapt to the varying demands and expectations of people, situations and attitudes that never seemed to allow me to stretch and relax, to be unashamedly myself, whatever 'myself' turned out to be. Whether I was under more pressure than others in similar situations I don't know. I only know that the 'act', the ability to go on playing all these complex games that normal life seemed to involve, was using up all my inner resources.

Even as my faith and belief in God and myself was draining away from me, there seemed to be an increase in what was wanted from me as a social worker, as a father and husband, as a Christian, and as someone who appeared often on television talking about God as though I had something worthwhile to say.

I was tired of locking children up for a start. Ironically, in the two years that I'd worked in the secure unit, I had finally begun to accept that it was safe to relax and be genuinely concerned about the people I was caring for. I enjoyed the challenge that each child's needs presented, and I began to believe that I might be on the verge of becoming real in my dealings with them. But real people are vulnerable, and for years I had disallowed, repressed, and postponed the expression of feelings that were too deep for words. Now, I cared desperately about the fate and future of these children, and although we did have some success, it became increasingly difficult to live with the failures, especially as I, like the other staff in the unit, was turning the key on them daily. By then, Meryl had gone to a psychiatric hospital, and Miranda had gone to prison. So many children had passed through the 'sad-mad-bad' cycle even before reaching us, and all too often a custodial sentence seemed to be society's relieved response to a conveniently concrete crime. The whole exercise began to appear a vastly expensive, cynical game, and I, who had pretended so much in the past, simply could not pretend any more. At work, in the six months before I finally broke down, I had felt mounting inner hysteria, and detachment from an institution which, although excellent in comparison with other places I had known, now seemed ridiculous; a place where we supervised the disposal of social rejects and colluded with social-service higher management in playing the 'professional and caring people game'. No doubt my vision was distorted by tension and role-play fatigue, but now, as I view things more calmly and objectively I see it in the same way. There were some good people working in a system that was top-heavy with bureaucracy, and too often expedient rather than caring.

The other game that I had become very bad at was being-a-Christian-and-going-to-church. I didn't seem able to keep to the rules any more. I wanted to say that I was sad when I was sad, happy when I was happy, non-believing when God didn't seem to exist, angry when I was angry, and bad when I was bad. I wanted the freedom to be all of me, and not a little, spineless, spiritually arthritic version of myself. I wanted to break away from the awful, simpering, Christianese language that seemed to obscure and stifle passion and human-ness whenever it threatened to break through the carefully organised spontaneity of meetings, services and conversations.

I wanted to shake off the arid virtue which had taken the place of real goodness for so many years, and force a full-frontal collision with reality; to dive naked into the dark waters of the risk-infested non-religious world, from which God – if he was God – would rescue me because he loved me, and not because I strained to conform to precious group norms that depended for their maintenance on unspoken agreements that nobody would mess things up by telling the whole truth. These were not clearly specified or dignified needs at the time. They were ragged, wild longings to find the reality of God that had been promised all those years ago on a Sunday evening in St John's Church. No more systems, no more pretence, no more props. I had been conned and compromised for long enough. Let the props snap, and let God do whatever he was going to do – if he was there!

For more than thirty years a great shout had been building up in me, a shout of tearful protest that I couldn't manage, that people *didn't* seem to mean what they said, that I felt like a small person trapped in a large actor's body, that all I wanted was to collapse, and be allowed to be useless. As for God, and most of those who claimed to represent him, they – in my mind – were the arch-offenders, the 'smiling' ones who had deceived themselves just sufficiently to be able to deceive others. I hated and despised the neat middle-classness that allowed them to pose as Christians without significant effort or cost. It was my turn to do, be and say what I liked, and the rest of the false, smiling, stupid, bloody world could go hang!

One night I returned home late after going out for a drink with friends. As I walked through the front door, something snapped. I started to scream and shout, punch the walls with both hands, and sob uncontrollably. My wife, who, with a friend, wrestled through the whole thing with me for hours, tells me that I shouted the same phrases over and over again.

'I can't lock them up any more! I can't lock them up any more! I've tried to be good – I've tried to be good! I want to be me! I want to be me! I can't lock them up any more!'

And indeed I couldn't. Children, feelings, hurts from the distant past, agonies I'd never shared, bitter anger against God, the church, and everything connected with it – I couldn't lock them up any more. Down went all my defences for the first time since I was a little boy, leaving me raw and vulnerable to whatever temptations and influences might be around.

The weeks that followed were a nightmare, not only for me, but for Bridget as well. No work, no church, no stability, no reason for me to do or not to do anything other than what was immediately stimulating or sense-dulling. The darkness had a thick, sweet attraction difficult to resist. I would disappear for hours at a time, returning home late at night, usually drunk, still wanting only to drown thought and feeling in loud, powerful rock music, or more drink. And the anger continued to rage in me, making it impossible to meet most of the people I knew, especially those who wanted to tell me I had 'stepped outside the Lord's will' and could step back in again by applying some formula or other.

There are aspects of that period that are very difficult and painful to remember. For some reason I seemed to need to abdicate completely from commitment to previous close relationships. My family, more important to me than anything else in the past, suffered and watched, and waited for some light to appear in the darkness. Every day offered new potential for disaster as I wrestled with the strangeness of a world that, in some ways I was seeing for the first time. I would stand on the pavement in the High Street, watching people as they passed to and fro, and wonder with genuine amazement how they could possibly have discovered a strong enough motive for moving in such a purposeful way. I recall sneering sceptically at the girl in the Chinese take-away when she responded to my order in a normal, pleasant way, 'You almost sound as if you really care!' The whole world felt like the setting for a wearisome game in which everyone cheated.

One day, I arranged to meet a friend, someone who I could still communicate with, in a pub in Eastbourne. I arrived late to find that he'd gone. I boiled. Disproportionately angry and tense, I slammed out of the pub and crossed the road, intending to call Bridget from the phone box and unload some of the blackness that was building up in me. As I stepped into the kiosk, a hot wave of anger surged through me. Part of me, oddly detached, watched, hypnotised, as my fist arched towards one of the small square glass panes, and smashed through. I drew my hand back, all the anger gone now, and gazed disbelievingly at a long and sickeningly deep gash in my wrist. Oddly enough, at that moment, I felt only relief as I watched the blood drip onto the floor of the box. It was so good to see some external evidence of the gaping wounds inside. Fear followed immediately. Why had

I done it? Was I really going mad? Suddenly I was very calm. In a nearby shop I got someone to call a taxi for me, and a few minutes later, I wrapped a piece of cloth round my wrist and climbed in. Before long I was in the accident and emergency ward of the local hospital.

The nurse put a final tape on the dressing, and grimaced sympathetically at me as I swung my feet onto the floor. I realised that the old, tired coping mechanism was grinding slowly into action, just as it had in so many difficult situations over the past years. But this was different. I was the one in trouble, not some desperate teenager needing me to get them out of a fix. My 'crime' was not a major one by any standards, but the situation was a completely new one for me. How was I going to handle this encounter with the law? I automatically selected and rejected options. 'Sullen and disturbed', maybe? Or perhaps 'weary and resigned' would be more effective. I finally settled on 'surprisingly calm and pleasantly co-operative'. The receptionist led me to a small side room where two young policemen were waiting. Politely, and with a hint of embarrassment (it turned out that both of them were Company viewers) they informed me that I was arrested on a charge of criminal damage, and that anything I said would be taken down and might be used in evidence against me. Later, in the bowels of the police station, I was fingerprinted, photographed, and left to sit in the corner of a small room containing nothing but a table, a bench, and a couple of posters on the wall. For some reason, this bleak little room seemed familiar. Then I remembered. This was exactly the same room in which I had found Miranda on the last occasion that I had been called to collect her from a police station. I was a rank amateur in crime and violence in comparison with her, but as I sat on the same bench as she had, waiting for someone to return, I felt the sting of tears in my eyes as I realised for the first time, why she, and other children I'd known, had shown such violence in similar situations. Why were two young, pink people in blue uniforms, so obsessed with a piece of glass? Didn't they know about the last thirty years? Didn't they *want* to know? I wanted to ask them, to argue with them, to *make* them understand, because they were the visible, official representatives of punishment without passion, the hard words without the loving arms. By now, if it had been Miranda, the place would have been in uproar. I was lucky. I had been around longer, and back home I had four pairs of loving arms to balance the inclination I suddenly felt to shout and punch and kick and swear at the mechanicalness of justice. I was thirty-five; not fifteen. I held my tongue, and smiled, and wasn't charged, and went home.

Richard Wurmbrand tells of a judge, placed in the cell next to him in an underground communist prison, who spent much time asking forgiveness for the way in which he had passed sentence on so many convicted criminals without any genuine understanding of what imprisonment really meant. For any arrogance or self-righteousness that I have shown towards children in trouble in the past, I also ask pardon, realising that we all stand together in the need for mercy and compassion. God help us all.

The difficulty and despair of this time is well illustrated by two pieces of writing that have survived the turmoil somehow. The first is a poem, written at the point where I realised that the particular kind of Christianity I had tried to embrace, was more likely to prolong the agony than cure it.

> Who made these poison pools
> In desert lands
> So sweet and cool?
> A welcome lie;
> The chance to die with water on my lips.
> I've seen how others try to die unpoisoned in the sun,
> I do not think that I can do as they have done.

The second, and far more graphic illustration is provided by an extract from a letter written by Bridget to a very close friend at the time. I include it here, with her blessing, in the hope that others who find themselves in the same position, will see that theirs is not a unique experience, nor a hopeless one.

. . . if anyone else asks me how he is, I think I'll scream. I don't know how he is. I don't know *him* any more. He keeps saying this is the real him, and only my memories of fourteen years keep me from believing him. He is still lovely to the children, and they, thank God, seem by their cuddles and hugs to be able to reach him in a way I can't. All I seem able to do is wait and pray, and I seem to do an awful lot of both!!! I just keep on and on at God all the time, it feels like bashing on his door until he finally answers, and every now and then I get a total feeling of peace, as if he has done just that. When Adrian is out, and I don't know where he is, I just beg and beg God to just hold on to him and keep him safe and bring him home – Whatever state he's in.

I'm living one day at a time now. I only wish everyone else could. They seem to want instant recovery, and I feel a ludicrous sense of failure when I have to say, 'He's about the same, really . . .'

. . . Sometimes I just feel hurt and angry that it's happening. I love him so much, and it's my life he's wrecking as well as his. – I know that's horrible, and I hate myself, but I do feel it, especially when he says he's glad it happened. I wish to heck that *I* understood what's happening to us all. I can't see any future at all at the moment . . .

. . . sometimes all I can do is hold him like a child, and I can feel the agony in him. I must try not to keep crying – it makes everything ten times worse, because he feels so guilty about what's happened – so sorry for all of us. I wish God would hurry up and *do* something, anything! . . .

Bridget was quite right when she said that some people wanted my instant recovery. They fell into two groups. The first was made up of those who had used *me* as a prop until now. There was almost an air of annoyance in their response to the news that I could no longer offer support. I understand that now, but it hurt me then. The second group, not large, but significant, was composed of those Christians for whom non-recovery seemed to constitute an attack on their faith.

God knows, I was a million miles from being as innocent as Job, but there was no doubt that as far as one section of the church was concerned, I was 'spoiling the game' by not recovering quickly and testifying to the healing power of God. I had shared their creed, and now I was threatening the theology of that creed by stubbornly refusing to get better, and protect their religious confidence. One or two were visibly angry, not just with me, but with others in a similar situation, who were letting the side down by being chronically unwell. Rightly or wrongly, I felt that such people had what Oswald Chambers calls 'The ban of finality' on them, the result of theology – albeit lively, active, theology – being put before God. After one or two very negative encounters of this kind, Bridget deflected approaches from people who wanted to tidy me up spiritually, not least because I had abandoned politeness, and was quite likely to say exactly what I thought in strongly unreligious terms.

On the positive side, I look back with enormous pleasure at the wide and sometimes surprising variety of folk who supported and loved and put up with me, not because they had a particular axe to grind, but simply because they cared. Some were Christians from our own church, some were from others. Some were not Christians at all. There were friends from the past and the present, one or two from work, others who, previously, I had felt I hardly knew. They had one thing in common. They gave something of themselves to me, and asked for nothing back. They were glimpses of God in the desert.

The image of the desert is particularly appropriate as, shortly after I stopped work, my perception of myself in relation to the church was crystallised in my mind by a daydream, or mental picture in which I found myself in a vast desert, standing on the edge of an oasis full of excited, cheering people. They were all facing inwards towards the centre of the oasis, and, try as I might, I just couldn't break through the tightly packed bodies, to see what was causing all this noise and activity. In the end I asked someone on the edge of the crowd to tell me what it was he was trying to see, and why everyone was pushing and shoving and jumping up and down so excitedly.

'The king!' he said. 'It's the king! He's there in the centre!'

'Have you seen him?' I asked. 'Have you actually seen him?'

'No,' he replied. 'I haven't seen him, but we all know he's there! Isn't it exciting!' And he went back to his calling and waving.

Disheartened, I turned my back on the oasis and walked slowly away into the desert. As the commotion gradually faded behind me, I became aware of a dot in the distance, which, as I came closer, seemed to be a heap of rags, piled untidily on the sand. At last, I was near enough to see that it was a man, his eyes large and dark with suffering, his clothes in tatters.

'Who are you?' I asked.

The man smiled a smile of deep, sweet sadness, and spoke softly. 'I am the king. I couldn't get in either.'

There were other glimpses of God. A friend suggested I should visit the Anglican vicar of a small, nearby country church, a man who might be regarded by many people I knew as 'unsaved', or 'uncommitted'. At one time I might have thought him so.

So why, I wondered, as he and I walked his dogs along the old disused railway track, and took shelter from the soft autumn rain under one of the tall, brick bridges, did I feel a relaxation and a peace that I had not found elsewhere?

'What do you think of God, then?' I was still rather graceless.

Frank smiled imperturbably. 'I've never met him,' he said quietly, 'but,' gesturing around him with his stick, 'if he made all this, and was the one who gave me my talents, I think I would love him if we met.'

What was all this? If we met? Was this any way for a Christian to talk? Not where I came from! And yet, on the two occasions that I walked through the countryside with this gentle, peaceful man, I sensed, even in the midst of my confusion, that Jesus walked with us, and that he and Frank were old friends.

I saw God, too, in the support of my fellow Company participants, when I arrived in Maidstone for the first programmes I had made since the night I had lost my 'props'. In many ways this attempt to continue with Company was an experiment. Just about everything else had fallen apart, and neither Bridget nor I were very confident about my ability to hold things together enough to cope with production meetings, studios and cameras. It was providential that my colleagues on this 'test run' were Hugo Gryn and Prabhu Guptara, a rabbi and a 'Hindu follower of Christ', but, more importantly, two compassionate and warm human beings who, with their own kindness and control, held me in a stable frame of mind, and enabled me to get through the meeting and programmes without too many problems. Some have thought it strange that I should have been able to go on making television programmes throughout this period. I can only say that it was the best anchor I had for a time. The flat in Harrietsham, and the kitchen table in its little pool of studio light, were familiar, safe environments, that were detached from the rest of my life, and always had been. My visits there provided an ongoing reassurance to me that I wasn't going completely round the bend, and that I was still – if only minimally – useful to someone. I soon realised though, that I could only carry on with Company if I was prepared to be honest about what was happening to me. It wasn't a welcome prospect. I had never exposed or shared pain and hurt before, and in my present fragmented condition, I couldn't be sure that I would control my emotions.

On the occasion when I did first describe what was happening to me I very nearly ended up in tears, but I managed to get through it somehow, and I was very glad I did. The response from viewers to that programme, and subsequent ones in which I talked about what was happening to me, was so warm and supportive, that it was like having a whole other family behind the cameras. Letters and messages from people 'out there' offered prayers, hugs, shared experiences, and constructive advice. It isn't easy to put into words how much the concern shown by those letters meant to me during this time.

Meanwhile, what about God? For a quite lengthy period, the answer to that question was very simple. There *was* no God, and if by any chance it turned out that I was wrong and he did exist, then I hated him with all the newly released passion in me. Other people, like George Reindorp and Peter Ball believed that he had been with them, helping and directing them, throughout their lives. Not me! With me, God had really screwed up, and I preferred the simple conclusion that he didn't exist, to the impossible task of reconciling my situation with the active concern of a loving, omnipotent presence.

Now here, as some comedian used to say, is a funny thing. I had dismissed God. He wasn't there. I was doing all sorts of things that my dry morality had woodenly prevented in the past. I was feeling and choosing and sinking and rising without any reference to any religious rule-book or its author. But, try as I might, there was one thing, or rather, one person, who I just couldn't shake off. No matter how far I penetrated the darkness, no matter how low I went, no matter how much I drank, there was Jesus.

One day, I was sitting in a pub with a man I had known in the past. He had moved away, and was back just to visit. He can't have known anything of what had happened to me, and we had met by accident that day. He was a farmer, and his name was Bill. He'd always had the disconcerting ability to see through lies and insincerity. He was about as tactful as an avalanche, but he had a sort of rich agricultural charm, and I liked him. Bill knew that I was a Christian. When he was resident in the TVS region, he'd often watched me attempting to put the world to rights at midnight on TV. Now, there was something about the way he was gazing into his beer with knitted brows and pursed lips, that suggested he had something to say about it.

After a sudden swift gulp from his pint glass, he banged it back down beside him, rested his elbows on the table, and pointed both forefingers in the direction of my eyes, unconsciously indicating that in them he would read the truth, whatever I might say.

'You still doing that programme?'

I nodded.

'I don't understand you,' he said. 'I can't understand why a bloke like you wants to be a Christian. You always seemed quite sensible – normal. I don't see how you can believe it.'

He watched me closely – waiting. Our eyes seemed so rigidly locked together, that I had the absurd fantasy that if he leaned back quickly he would pull my eyeballs out. Had he complimented me, or was it an insult? A bloke like me? For a moment I felt the old tension grow in me, the tension that invariably preceded my regurgitation of the undigested lump of evangelicalism that I'd swallowed in my teens; a congealed mass of guilt, half-remembered scriptures, and fear, that until recently had neither nourished me, nor passed out of my system. It was different now. In the old days I would have searched for words to keep me in the good books of both Bill and God. Quoted John 3:16 perhaps, like a magic charm, to ward off real communication. I realised that, now, I could answer truthfully. I was not bound to produce either a bon mot, or the paralysed jargon that had clogged the arteries of my spirit for so long.

'I just don't see how you can be a Christian,' repeated Bill, doggedly.

'Nor do I, actually.' I seemed to hear bells ringing, people cheering.

Bill's gaze relaxed a little. He looked more puzzled than accusative now. The fingers drooped.

'I mean – what about the church? I mean – surely you can't think the church is much good the way it is – surely?'

'The church is a mess,' said I, remembering my old set speech about it depending what you meant by 'the church'. I was beginning to enjoy myself. Realising that I wasn't going to enlarge on what I'd said, Bill ploughed on.

'Some of the people who say they're Christians – don't you find it embarrassing – people thinking you're like them, I mean?'

'Yes.'

'On that programme you do – Company. That bloke who seems to think everything's evil – I mean, do you agree with that?'

'No.'

Bill had almost reached the end of his furrow.

'Some Christians,' – the fingers were up again – 'some Christians believe the whole Bible is one hundred per cent historically accurate, every word. I mean – how can they?' He paused. 'Well, is it?'

'I don't know.' I wasn't sure. I realised that I never had been sure.

Bill was leaning back in his chair, rubbing the small bald patch on top of his head, (the one that had never bothered him at all) his face contorted by the search for comprehension.

'But in that case, if that's all true ... what's left? Why *are* you a Christian? Why bother?'

My euphoria faded suddenly. Why bother, indeed? Bill didn't know it, but he'd got the question wrong. Not – *why* was I a Christian, but *was* I a Christian at all? Was anything left? I suddenly remembered a rather frightening thought that had occurred to me one day, not long before I broke down, as I sat in church watching people come in before the start of the service. Supposing, I thought, each person came to church with a regulation black briefcase containing, in some impossible way, their personal evidence that the Christian faith was true. Every Sunday, we would nod and smile at each other, indicating our briefcases with genial confidence as if to say, 'Lots in mine, brother. No problem here!' One awful Sunday, though, the minister would announce that, today, we were all going to open our cases in front of each other, and examine this mass of evidence. One by one, in a heavy silence, the cases are opened. They are all empty ...

I had opened my 'case' in front of Bill. Was anything left in it? Could there be anything real and truthful tucked away in a dark corner somewhere? To my surprise, there was; but it was such a raw, indefensible, insubstantial piece of truth, that neither cleverness nor jargon could express it. It embarrassed me to say it, and Bill reacted as though I was some kind of spiritual flasher.

'I don't bother at the moment, Bill, but if I ever bother again, it'll be because I love Jesus. Do you want another drink?'

And it was true. Even in the deepest darkness, like the faintest of nightlights, he was there, not trying to make me do, or believe, or feel anything in particular, not even causing me to believe in God, absurd as that may sound, but simply 'being there'. It is not rational. It is a humble fact. Much later, I wrote some words to a friend's tune in an attempt to capture the essence of this experience. The title is simply 'Song to Jesus'.

I didn't have to see you,
In the darkness, there by the side of me,
I knew it had to be you,
Knew you loved the child inside of me.
You smiled in the darkness,
It seemed to blind and burn.
But when my eyes were opened,
I smiled in return,
For you were there.

I didn't have to hear you,
In the silence, you were a part of me,
I knew that I was near you,
Knew your love was deep in the heart of me,
I knew that you were saying,
'Our happiness has grown,
For prayer is only friendship,
You never were alone,
For I was there.'

I didn't have to hold you,
Tried to trust you, trust in your care for me,
The secrets I had told you,
Hoping you would always be there for me,
So let the darkness gather,
And let the silence roll,
The love that made you suffer,
Is burning in my soul,
And you are there.

In one sense it was this constant, unbidden awareness of Jesus, that led to the activity that was instrumental in my regaining stability, and an interest in relatively normal living. I started to write; and the first thing I wrote was a series of six stories called *The*

Visit. They chronicled the experiences of a fairly ordinary church member, confronted with Jesus, in person, paying an extended visit to a church of vague denomination in 1984. Not surprisingly, the stories are littered with allusions to my own experience, although the central character is quite unlike me.

Writing helped. It was a discipline and a therapy. The love of my family helped. They never stopped supporting me. Friends helped, especially perhaps, Ben Ecclestone, an elder at the Frenchgate Chapel in Eastbourne. He never preached at me once, and was – and is – refreshingly honest about his own faith and life. Company helped. It sustained a faint belief in me that I might not be totally useless. All these things contributed to a gradual process of rebuilding, or, more accurately, reassembling. I became calmer, more disciplined, readier to accept that I had to fit into the world as it was, albeit with a much freer outlook and a far greater flexibility in my view of myself and others. But I didn't know what to think about God. God, the father? He wasn't my father, and never had been. Despite the strange reality of Jesus, I still felt far removed from accepting the reality, let alone the concern of the senior member of the Trinity. Until, that is, one day when I took a very expensive taxi ride, all the way from Polegate to Haywards Heath.

Chapter Twelve

'Damn and blast!'

I cursed loudly as the London train disappeared infuriatingly into the distance, then flopped down on to the wooden bench behind me, rubbing my bruised knee and sucking air through my teeth as the pain started to make itself felt. I'd missed the train! Only by seconds, but that made it worse somehow. Anger and frustration crashed crazily around inside me, looking for an outlet. Perhaps I could throttle the ticket inspector, sitting inoffensively over there in his little box at the top of the steps. As long as the jury at my trial was made up of twelve people who had at some time in their lives missed a train by a hair's-breadth, I had no doubt that they would bring in a verdict of justifiable homicide. As I passed him on my way out of the station, my imagined victim nearly hastened his own end by calling out genially, 'Missed it then?'

'Yes,' I replied, baring my teeth, 'that sums it up nicely.'

As I limped off down the steps, he called after me, encouragingly, 'Never mind, there'll be another one along in an hour.'

In an hour? That was no good. I was supposed to be in Haywards Heath by four o'clock, and I'd just missed the last train that could get me there in time. As I stood outside the station, still fuming inwardly, it seemed to me that someone or something was doing everything in its power to stop me reaching my destination that day. Well, whoever it was, they seemed to have succeeded. I wasn't going to make it. I leaned against the wall, gloomily watching people arriving and departing from the taxi rank on the station forecourt, and wondered why this particular trip had come to seem so very important.

It had started a couple of weeks ago when I was thumbing through the dog-eared little volume in which Bridget and I recorded addresses and phone numbers. For some reason I had written down Michael Harper's address in Haywards Heath a long time ago, but had never had cause to contact him either by letter or phone. In fact, that meeting in the TVS studios during the recording of the David Watson Company programmes, was the only occasion on which I had met or spoken to him. Now, as my eye caught his name on the 'H' page of the little book, I remembered how impressed I had been by the depth and sensitivity that I sensed in his personality. Was it possible that he might have something to say to me that would assist, or speed up, or perhaps just encourage the process of reintegration that had already started?

Following the impulse before it had a chance to escape, I took the book over to the phone and dialled Michael's number. When I finally got through to him, all I could think of to say was, simply, 'I've had a sort of breakdown. Would you mind if I came to see you?' He responded warmly, suggesting a date and a time that happened to suit both of us. As the days passed, I looked forward to this meeting, although I had no idea just how crucial it was going to be.

The day of my trip started well. I didn't have to be at Polegate station until about ten past three, so there was plenty of time to relax and organise myself. After drawing some money from the bank after lunch for the coming weekend, I walked slowly down to the precinct in the centre of Hailsham to catch the 2.55 bus, which I knew from experience would arrive at Polegate in plenty of time for me to get the London train.

The bus arrived late. Not very late, but enough to set up a sort of nervous ticking in my stomach as we lumbered out of Hailsham and turned heavily on to the south-bound dual carriageway towards Eastbourne. The ticking increased to a frenetic whirr, as the bus breasted a slight hill and I saw the lines of stationary traffic before us. Of course – roadworks! I'd forgotten that they were taking the road up just before the Polegate turn-off. It put another five minutes on the journey, and by the time I got off near the Horse and Groom pub, I was almost whimpering with frustration. I still had quite a distance to walk – or rather sprint. I flew along the path towards the station, so panic-stricken at the thought of losing my train, that I lost my footing and fell heavily onto the ground, cracking my knee against the kerb, and shaking my innards into a jelly. With hardly a pause, I hauled myself up, and staggered onto the station, only to see my train standing tantalisingly by the platform, passengers boarding and alighting with impossible casualness. I could still make it! Unfortunately, the man at the ticket office refused to let me through without a ticket, and I had made the fatal mistake of letting him see that I was in a tearing hurry. With excruciating, deliberate slowness, he gave me my return ticket, took my money, and counted out my change. By the time I reached the platform the train was pulling out of the station, and all I could do was swear.

Now, as I watched taxis come and go on the forecourt, I felt miserable and defeated. There was nothing left but to find a telephone and let Michael know I wouldn't be coming. I knew that he had only an hour to spare, as he was going away the following morning. There would be no point in getting a later train. I trudged slowly up the road towards the centre of the town, knowing that there was a nest of phone kiosks just outside the Post Office.

As I walked, though, a wild thought occurred to me. Why shouldn't I go to Haywards Heath by taxi? Well, why not? I counted the money in my jacket pocket. There was twenty pounds exactly. Would that be enough? I didn't know, but I could find out. I hovered, undecided for a moment, imagining Bridget's reaction if she knew that I was contemplating using a sizeable chunk of our available cash for a taxi fare. I decided to take a chance. Turning round, I hurried back to the taxi rank, and asked one of the drivers if he could get to Haywards Heath by four o'clock. Yes, he thought he probably could. How much would it cost? He wasn't sure. About twenty pounds perhaps. I climbed in, and away we went.

I can remember only two things about that journey. One was the fare meter, displaying the cost of the journey as the miles rolled away beneath us. After a while I saw nothing but the red-lit numbers beneath the dash board, changing alarmingly every few minutes as another ten pence was added to the total.

The other thing was what seemed like an endless monologue by the driver on the subject of how he dealt with people who were sick in the back of his taxi.

By the time we reached Haywards Heath I felt as if I was going mad. My mind was in a surrealistic whirl of red lights and vomit. We stopped outside Michael's house. It was five minutes past four, and the meter showed eighteen pounds, fifty pence. I gave the driver the whole twenty pounds, and hurried up to the front door. My feelings as I rang the front door bell were rather similar, if I'm honest, to the way I had felt all those years ago when I stopped my bicycle next to the Cowden sign, and asked myself what on earth I thought I was doing. What was I doing *now*? Was it really going to be worth all that money and effort, just to spend an hour with a man I hardly knew?

Someone who I took to be Mrs Harper answered the door, and showed me through to a study at the back of the house, where Michael sat working at a pleasantly cluttered desk. He greeted me very warmly, and seemed genuinely concerned about the difficulties I had been experiencing. His depth and gentleness had an oddly softening effect on me, but it wasn't until we prayed together at the end of the hour, that I realised why it was so necessary to be at that place, at that time, with that person. God wanted to speak to me. After praying quietly for a little while, Michael was silent for a moment. Then he spoke again.

'The Holy Spirit is showing me a picture of a field, Adrian. The field is your life. It's going to be a bigger and more beautiful meadow one day, but at the moment it's being cleared. There are rocks and brambles and bushes that are being shifted and uprooted to make space for useful things to grow. But I'll tell you something ...'

'Yes,' I thought, 'please *do* tell me something.'

'Nothing has been wasted – nothing! The soil underneath all these things is rich; richer than it would have been if they hadn't been there. It's going to be a *beautiful* meadow.'

As Michael opened his eyes and looked up, he must have sensed that his words had reached me on a level that had been untouched for years. I was fighting back tears as I said over and over in my mind the words that had meant most to me. 'Nothing has been wasted – *nothing* has been wasted.'

He smiled. 'Dear Adrian.' The words were from God, care of Michael Harper, and they conveyed the love of a father.

I left, and as I walked through the darkness towards the railway station, all the tears I had been holding back were released. God had spoken to me. He cared about me. He was *nice*. How did I know it had really been God speaking? I can't say, but believe me – I knew.

As a matter of history, Bridget reckoned it was a pretty good twenty pounds worth too.

That day marked the beginning of a new kind of hope, and was the first in a series of events and encounters that led me, slowly but surely, into a quite different understanding of what a relationship with God might mean. Some were quite dramatic, while others, apparently, were too trivial to be worth noticing. There was my bike, for instance.

I hadn't had a bicycle for years, not one of my own. As a kid I'd had several, including the shiny blue one on which I had set out to find and captivate Hayley Mills back in the sixties. Since my teens, though, I had hardly ridden one at all, apart from an old boneshaker belonging to John Hall, which, I seem to remember, I lost, somewhere in Bromley. Perhaps I thought they were one of the less dignified modes of transport, I don't really know.

Now, in 1985, at the age of thirty-six, my mother was quite convinced that what I really needed was a bike. A nice big bicycle would offer more relaxation and therapy than a hundred books, or a thousand conversations, in her view. I knew better of course. Every time we spoke on the telephone, and she said for the umpteenth time, 'Have you got a bike yet?', I would smile indulgently to myself and make vague promises that I *would* get one eventually.

Then, one day as I was glancing through the local advertising journal, I noticed an ad in the 'For Sale' section.

> Gent's blue bicycle for sale.
> Large frame. Very good condition.
> Used only six times. £50.

I think it was the 'blue' that did it. A shiny blue bike of my very own. The years fell away, and I was an excited teenager again. I'd almost forgotten what innocent excitement felt like. I rang the number at the bottom of the advert, walked round to the bank to draw the money out, and within an hour I was the proud possessor of a large Raleigh bicycle; not, admittedly, with seventy-five derailleur gears, or however many they have nowadays, but nevertheless a 'good bike'. How nostalgic the words 'Sturmey Archer' seemed as I read them on the gear-lever housing attached to the handlebars. How strange to be back in the world of tyre-levers, cotter pins, saddle bags, chain guards, brake-blocks and, of course, puncture repair outfits. How satisfying to recapture the feeling of relish when negotiating the narrow gap between the kerb and the lines of cars doing the rush-hour crawl, or waiting for the lights to change. But most of all I just liked riding around like a kid or enjoying the whiz and swoosh that usually rewarded a bit of grinding uphill work. I had always hated the A-to-Bness of life. Now, I could go where I liked. I could start at A, head for M, and stop off for a while at F if it took my fancy. If I changed my mind at F, then I might forget M and pay a little visit to Q, which, as we all know, is only just down the road from R. It was lovely, and I loved it. I felt about as sophisticated as Pooh Bear on my bike, but I didn't really mind. In the course of just riding easily to and fro, I made real contact with the child inside myself, and in the process learned a simple but profound truth about contact with God. I discovered that prayer didn't have to start at A and end at B either. I learned or started to learn, that it's quite legitimate, and – dare I say – enjoyable, to meander aimlessly around, just enjoying the nearness of God, in the same way that you don't have to arrange special activities in order to enjoy being with a friend or a parent. God sat quite happily on his back doorstep, watching me as I pedalled happily around in my prayers, looking up occasionally to smile at him, and feel reassured by the way in which he smiled back. It was a new experience, and a very pleasant one, despite the occasions when I fell off my metaphorical bike and bawled like a kid with a bruised knee.

It's odd how different things affect different people. I talked about my bicycle in a Company programme a few weeks after I got it, and as I left the studio one of the cameramen stopped me to talk about *his* bike. Like me, he had at first felt rather foolishly adolescent just cycling to and fro, purely for the fun of it. He experienced the same nostalgic sensations of youth and innocence, and now, as he described the difficulty of confiding this to anybody without feeling a complete idiot, an expression of real pain contracted his features.

'What happens to us? Why do we lose all that? I was happier then than I am now that I reckon I know what's what.'

I knew exactly what he meant. One of the most moving aspects of parenthood is watching your children as they discover for the first time, things that have become so familiar that you hardly notice them. I had often prayed that the spirit of excited discovery would not die in my children, as it had in me for so long. When the oldest, Matthew, was five, he and I had taken a walk through the January streets one morning, to get to the park. When we came back, I tried to preserve part of that experience in the following lines.

> I wish I was my son again,
> The first in all the world to know,
> The cornflake crunch of frosted grass,
> Beside the polar paving stones,
> Beneath the drip of liquid light,
> From water-colour, winter suns.

Now, I was recapturing my own sense of discovery and excitement, especially in connection with natural things; flowers, skies, textures, the seasons. For some years I had been saddened by the loss of my ability to experience first-hand enjoyment of these things. A walk through a flaming autumn wood, for instance, produced only memories of the feeling I had once known of being right in the centre of a passionate, tragic symphony, full of sadness and hope. All seasons had their own character and poetry, but the spiritual vasectomy I had performed on myself a long time ago, had somehow prevented creative involvement with the world around me. It gave me real joy to discover that sense of wonder once more; to find, for instance, that I could gaze, astonished and enraptured, at a single daffodil bloom for several minutes, just absorbing the beauty of its shape and colour.

> Daffodils are not flowers
> They are natural neon from the dark earth,
> Precious metal grown impatient,
> Beaten, shaped and dipped in pools
> Of ancient, sunken light.
> Folded, packed and parachuted through,
> To stand and dumbly trumpet out,
> The twice triumphant sun.

It was my growing appreciation of natural things, and in particular perhaps, things connected with the season of autumn, that provided an almost immediate bond with a new member of the Company team, who first appeared on the programme at the turn of the year, and has since become a dear friend and valued adviser.

I know that the idea of the Christian life being a kind of journey, is an old and rather hackneyed one, but sometimes the metaphor is refreshed by encounters with fellow-explorers, who really seem to know where they are going. My new friend, Philip Illot, was one of these. My own journey had always been more of an undignified safari than an organised tour, and until now I had been hopelessly ill-equipped for the expedition. Like many Christians, I had tended to crash through the spiritual undergrowth, stubbornly clothed in my strange denominational and temperamental costume, refusing to discard the tools and weapons that seemed so essential. Now, most of my props had gone, but I was still physically fit. I still had the ability to stand and walk and move about freely. Philip had lost even that.

As a young man of eighteen, newly come into the Christian faith, and working in post-war Germany, Philip had a very strange dream one night. In his dream he was travelling across Germany in a train, when, unexpectedly the locomotive was halted by Russian soldiers who were searching for a particular man. Suddenly, Philip knew with total certainty that he was the one they wanted. Terrified, he hid by the window, hoping to be passed by. It was no use. He was aware of his fellow-passengers looking on helplessly through the windows of the train as soldiers forced him down onto a wooden cross lying on the grass. His hands and feet were nailed to the wood, and the cross was raised to a vertical position. Philip woke up screaming.

As the years passed, and he became an ordained minister in the Church of England, Philip never forgot that dream, assuming that one day in the future, he would be able to understand its meaning. He was a 'hyperactive' priest, always on the move, always busy, his life full of people and activities. There were many good, productive years, and a few very hard and difficult ones, but eventually, Philip, with his wife Margaret, and their two children, came to a parish in Bexhill, a seaside resort on the south coast, where, as usual, Philip threw himself into the life of the church, quickly earning the liking and respect of people throughout the town.

For some time Philip had been troubled by intermittent illness. At times it was so bad that he ended up in a Sunday service, lying across the altar, wondering if he was going to die there and then, and reflecting in the midst of his suffering that it wasn't a bad place to go! The symptoms continued, and became more frequent. Eventually, whilst in hospital, Philip learned that he was suffering from multiple sclerosis. He lost the use of all but his head and arms, and is now confined to a wheelchair.

That sounds like the end of a story, but it was actually the beginning of a completely new adventure in Philip's life. It was autumn when the illness was diagnosed, his favourite season. He sensed that, just as the natural world accepts change without panic or resistance in that season, so he was being called to be obedient to what was happening. To let it be. It was as though God was bringing him to a place that had been prepared from the beginning. He acquired an inner stillness that was the stillness of arrival. He was in the right place. The strange dream of many years ago seemed connected somehow with what was happening. But *why* was it happening? Philip dreamed again.

This time he dreamed that he found a key at the foot of the cross of Jesus. Choosing to pick up the key, he was then faced with a very low door, over which the word 'BEWARE' was written in large letters. Using the key, he unlocked the door and passing through in his wheelchair, discovered a vast crowd of troubled and broken people, waiting for the special kind of ministry that a man broken in body, but not in spirit, could offer. The dream is now a reality. Philip is constantly in demand as a counsellor, a speaker, and a leader of missions. What little strength he has is poured out for others, often in ordinary ministry, but sometimes with strange and amazing effects, one of which, too private to record yet gave me a greater sense of the absolute reality of God than anything I had experienced before.

For me, Philip is the smile on God's face. His joy, in the midst of what must be terrible suffering at times, is absolutely genuine, perhaps because of a different kind of intimacy with God, that can only be experienced on the other side of pain. He tells me that 'the darker side of God is brighter than the light side', a knowledge gained through long sleepless nights, when God feels as close to his heart as the darkness is to his face. For some reason I have been able to tell things to Philip that I could tell to no one else, knowing that they (and I) are safe with him. Most of all, perhaps, I love his sudden laughter. My relationships with people who lack a sense of the absurd, are necessarily limited; but there is no such limitation with Philip. Laughter erupts out of him at times, and is invariably infectious. The combination of strength, tenderness and humour is irresistible.

I asked Philip once during a Company programme, a rather idiotic question. It was the kind of question that a lot of people would like to ask, but don't, for fear of giving offence. I knew he wouldn't mind.

'Supposing,' I said, 'you could choose to have the spiritual insights and growth that you've gained since you became ill – or – you could have your health back, and walk and move normally. Which would you choose?'

True man, and true Christian, Philip smiled as though he had asked himself the same question many times, and replied firmly, 'I would, without question, choose both!'

Another whole book could, and probably will, be written about Philip's life, but the important thing for Bridget and me is our contact, not just with Philip, but also with Margaret, who has also suffered, of course. She is pure gold. We have much in common with them, and at a time when we needed people who would really understand, God gave them to us for real, no-nonsense ministry, and for a very special kind of friendship. My visit to Michael Harper, my new bike, a new appreciation of natural things, and the ministry and friendship of Philip Illot; all of these things played their part in turning me gently towards the God that is, rather than the rather unpleasant image of the deity that I had strived with for so long. I had space to explore this new direction, as I took early retirement from my employment with Social Services, and I was not being confused or distracted by regular attendance of any one church. Each day I did little more than pray and write, and hope that the relative calm I had found would last. I really was beginning to feel that peace might be possible. I felt it even more after a surprise phone call from Jo Williams one day.

'Do you realise,' she said, 'that it's a year since you and Prabhu prayed for me and Don on that programme?'

I remembered my faithless prayer, and the feeling of hopelessness that had followed it.

'Yes, Jo. Of course I remember it. Why?'

'Well, do you realise what's happened since then?'

Jo went on to describe, over the phone and later when we met in Maidstone, how that prayer had been answered. Don, close to death a year ago, had been off the drink since that time. They say, 'Once an alcoholic, always an alcoholic', but for Don to stay away from alcohol for a year was a miracle in itself. Later, Bridget and I and the three children stayed in Southampton with Jo, and had the opportunity to meet Don for the first time. We found him to be a very charming and intelligent man, with a particular talent for getting on with our children, who thought Uncle Don was 'terrific!' That is high praise, believe me! It was a heart-warming weekend for everybody.

Then there was Jo, herself. Since the night on which we had said that prayer, something had happened to change her life. Jo decided to visit her auntie in Wales, the one she had stayed with as a very little girl all those years ago, after the big row between her mum and dad. She'd never thought of visiting her before, but now, for some reason, she and Don decided to make the long trip to Wales so that Jo could meet her mother's sister for the first time in over forty years. While they were there, Don asked a very important question.

'Was Jo difficult and horrible when she was a little girl?'

Jo's heart must have missed a beat as she waited for Auntie Vi's reply.

'No!' said the old lady without hesitation. 'No, she was a very caring little girl. When her baby cousin was ill with rheumatic fever, I remember Jo laying a nappy out on the floor, and saying that maybe if the baby stood in the middle of it, she'd get better. She was like that. Very quiet, but a really nice little girl.'

She turned to Jo. 'Don't you let people put you down, you hear? It was your mum's fault, what happened, not yours.'

In all important ways, Jo is very uncomplicated. This information from the past changed everything. All her life she had blamed herself for anything that went wrong. It was only right. What else could a horrible little girl expect? Now, suddenly she had discovered that all her guilt had been based on a lie. She

178

hadn't been a horrible little girl. It hadn't been her fault. She was a lovely little girl – a very caring child.

Auntie Vi had said so, and she should know. In a peculiarly real way, it was like being born again.

At the end of this year, Jo's attitude to God had changed radically. As far as she was concerned, the trip to Wales had been 'set up' by God, who had been trying for a long time to show Jo how much he loved and cared about her.

'Now,' she said to me late one night over coffee in the Harrietsham flat, 'it wouldn't matter to me deep down if nobody loved me, because I *know* that God does, and that's that!'

My faithless prayer had been answered, and so had that 'once for all' cry that Bridget and I had sent up to God in the summer of 1984. Trenches had been dug through our lives; it only remained to wait, and see the water flow.

Chapter Thirteen

Company has now completed its fourth year. Only Ann-Marie, Bridget and myself remain from the original team. George is no longer a contributor, but is very much alive and kicking at his flat in Vincent Square. Hugo is still with us, still telling stories, entertaining and educating. Jo Williams makes the trip from Southampton to Maidstone every month or so, and Peter Ball joined us quite recently to take part in a week's broadcasting. Peter Timms is a central figure for viewers nowadays, while Roy Millard has made it a real family affair by marrying James Blomfield's sister, Jane. There are new faces, including Ruth Soetendorp. Ruth and her rabbi husband, David, have become good friends of ours, especially as I no longer feel a neurotic need to switch on my evangelising machine every time I meet someone from a different faith. That man in the wheelchair still appears from time to time, and every now and then Bridget and I spend a very enjoyable half-day with Philip and Margaret at their house in Bexhill. Frances Tulloch, the major architect of Company, continues to produce the programme with the assistance of her hardworking secretary, Wynn Steer, who is beloved by all of us for her patience and good-humour. Angus Wright has now left TVS, and, at the time of writing, no one has been appointed to take his place.

Bridget and I calculate that between us, we have sat at the table in the Company kitchen on at least seven hundred separate occasions. So much has happened to us through the four years of the programme's life, and a great deal of it has been mentioned during those midnight chats. It has been a rich and productive experience – one we would not have missed for the world.

Company's fourth birthday sees me at a turning point, a point where I haven't the foggiest idea what's going to happen next. I don't know where I'm going, or how I'm going to get there; I don't know what I'm going to do or how I'm going to do it; but I feel an odd mixture of uneasiness and anticipation.

When I told my eldest son, Matthew, that I was about to write the final chapter of this book, he paused for a moment in his activity of transferring great wodges of dried mud from the bottom of his football boots to the kitchen floor, and nodded with all the wisdom of the modern twelve-year-old.

'Oh yes,' he said, 'that's the bit where you have to say everything's all right now, and you and God get on very well and all that.' Matthew has read his share of Christian paperbacks!

He was right of course. Many, if not most, of the huge number of testimonial books that exist nowadays, end with a tidying-up chapter in which God, man and the universe are slotted firmly into their proper places, and the reader is invited to submit himself to a simple process that will ensure spiritual growth or transformation.

I would *love* to be able to write a chapter like that. If only it was possible to pass on the information that Jesus lives at Number Ten, Gorringe Road, Luton: ring three times and say that Adrian sent you. I know that many people would like it to be that easy, and I know that some folk think it is that easy. I even know a few people for whom it really does seem to have been that easy, but they are very few. Nothing in my recent experience has made me any happier with simplistic formulas for spiritual living than I have ever been, nor, I'm afraid, am I much more patient with those who peddle such recipes.

Not very long ago, for instance, a Company viewer stopped me in the street and asked me why 'that man in the wheelchair doesn't say the prayer of faith and get up on his feet'. I was almost dumbstruck. Philip Illot believes in, and has had experience of miraculous healing, but God is using his physical situation in a particular way, just as St Paul's physical suffering was clearly part of his ministry. I'm glad that Jesus didn't say the prayer of faith, and come down from the cross to live out his life quietly in some Jewish suburb. Neither Philip Illot, nor St Paul, nor Jesus, for that matter, actually wanted to suffer physically; only loonies want that; but more important to them was discovering what God wanted of them and obeying him despite the suffering that obedience would bring. I told Philip what this lady had said one day, and asked him what he thought about it. He answered without any hesitation.

'If you should happen to see that lady again, I'd like you to tell her, with my best wishes, that I say the "prayer of faith" every single day!'

Of course we should pray for healing, anoint with oil and lay hands on the sick, but they won't always get better. They *don't* always get better. Everyone knows that they don't always get better, and it requires a peculiar form of corporate dishonesty to claim that they do. God will do what he will do, and sometimes we can only live in the mystery of that fact, waiting for it all to make sense when the right time has come.

The disciples had this problem of course; wanting to develop systems and rules to make life safer and easier to handle. Every now and then they really thought they'd got Jesus pinned down.

'She could have sold the ointment and given the money to the poor!'

He was always going on about the poor. Surely they'd got it right this time. Sorry lads – wrong again!

'Shall we call down fire from heaven on this village, Lord?'

Jesus told them not to be silly.

'I shall never let you be killed, Lord!'

Peter really got an earful for that.

'Tell Mary to help me, master, she's no use to anyone sitting there!'

Poor, likeable old Martha was wrong as well.

God cannot be reduced to a set of simple propositions, however simple his dealings with any individual person might be. This was, in hindsight, a large part of my problem in the sixties. When the church tried to compete with other 'instant cures', or means of establishing identity, it was, and still is, offering a version of Christianity that is, in one sense, too simplistic, and in another sense too difficult. The hippie movement tried to say that love is free, that it can be given away with a flower. This was no more true than that Jesus saves without cost or complication. I don't mean that he doesn't want to – far from it! But an honest and genuinely open reading of the four books that record what Jesus said, shows me that there are two essential parts to the message he wanted to put over.

First, I read that God is passionately committed to a world that he is absolutely crazy about, and there is no doubt that he would go, and has already gone, to the most extraordinary lengths to open up the channels between him and us, channels which are *so* blocked nowadays that only a very few people are genuinely and specifically hearing God talking to them. A lot are pretending or imagining (I've done so often), but very few really hearing.

The other part of what Jesus says is about counting the cost, keeping one's hand to the plough, loving your enemy, using talents properly, and being able to lose or give away all that you value most, if that's what is required of you. In other words – turning your own world upside down! I believe that these things need to be preached as part of the Christian message, instead of being the small print that you notice with dismay after committing yourself to receiving the free gift. I can't believe that Jesus said them all for fun. He must have meant them.

The problem for me, and for many others, was how to reconcile these two areas in my life from day to day. I was glad that God loved me – although I, in company with countless other Christians, probably never quite believed that he did – but I was quite unable to comply with, or even comprehend, the awesome demands that were being made on me. This is made even more difficult by the way in which God is all too often presented in evangelical and charismatic circles. He tends to come over as either a sentimental softy with such a pathological need for human affection that he doesn't really care what we get up to, or as a harsh, vindictive, austerely pure being, more concerned with narrow moral issues than people. I have seen so much fear and guilt transferred from speaker to listeners, disguised as 'conviction' and 'divine chastisement'. I recall one man who put an empty chair in the centre of the church, and invited us all to imagine that Jesus was sitting in it.

'Wouldn't you feel bad!' he said, 'wouldn't you want to hide your face and creep away, knowing the sin that's in you – the things that would make it impossible to meet his eyes!'

All I could think of as I stared at the empty chair, was how marvellous it would be to fling myself at him, like Peter dashing through the shallows to have an exciting breakfast with the risen Jesus. He didn't think of his own sin first, and remember, the denial business still hadn't been sorted out yet – he just wanted to get to Jesus because he loved him. Not want to see Jesus? I thought there must be something wrong with me!

I have begun to understand the way in which God is both loving and meticulously demanding by exploring an image used consistently by Jesus. He knew God as father. Now, as anyone who has read this book so far will know, that image presents problems for me, but there are good fathers around who I have been able to 'see in action', as it were, and I have been involved, directly or indirectly, with many children in care who needed to be fostered or adopted by families other than their own. Saint Paul says that Christians are the adopted children of God. God is their new father; so what does a really good father look like?

Well, first of all, joining a new family, adoption into a different kind of environment with different rules and different expectations, needs careful thought and preparation by all concerned. It isn't like joining a club; more a matter of deciding where to put down your deepest roots. The candidate for adoption will need to visit the home in which he has been offered a place so that he can see the head of the household in action, without the pressure of immediate decision or commitment. He will see this prospective father of his being very firm, punishing his children at times. He will see him being very loving and forgiving as well. He might well see him rolling on the floor with the kids, laughing and joking. He will see how he weeps when one of the family is hurt or lost, how everyone is encouraged to love and look after everyone else, and how all have direct access to their father, but show different degrees of trust and confidence depending on what kind of people they are and what their backgrounds have been. He will be intrigued by how different the children of the family are; some quietly, deeply affectionate, others loud and boisterous in the way they show love to their father, a few can manage only a small smile because they hurt too much to do anything else for a while. Some may just sit in the furthest corner of an empty room, paralysed with fear of rejection, but nursing the tiniest of tiny hopes that the smile they glimpsed on the face of the man in charge was meant for them as well as everyone else. They are all in the house. They all belong. The most fearful will be loved into happiness in the end.

If our candidate likes the place, and is happy to take the rough with the smooth, do what he's told when necessary, and accept his adoptive father's control and guidance as a sign of his care, then he'll probably move in. He doesn't have to be perfect, or even good, to qualify, and even after he's arrived, space will be allocated, allowances will be made, time will be spent and given. He'll be left in no doubt about what the house rules are, but everyone will be aware that it takes time to learn and adapt. Adopted children take ages to settle in sometimes. He'll be all right in the end. He might leave, but the offer of a home is forever; he will always be able to come back if he wants to; his new father will never stop loving him, however annoying he may be. Eventually, the spirit of the place will get right inside him; he will mature and learn that he really is wanted. The rules will suddenly seem much easier to keep, in fact they won't seem like rules at all. He will probably be given one or two responsible tasks to perform on behalf of his father. In the end, he will be so well tuned in to his dad's voice, that a single word will bring him flying to his father's side, saying excitedly, 'Yes! What do you want me to do?'

The family image is reinforced for me by what I see in those who really have learned to trust the head of the family. They don't become narrower and more condemnatory, they become broader and more loving. They show little interest in gifts, but are profoundly fascinated by the giver. Their spirituality does not seem loony, it feels real; it fits, on some crucial but undefinable level, with everything else that is real. They may be travelling on the hard road that Jesus said was the only road for his followers, but something makes them smile even when their feet hurt. They have usually paid dearly for their joy, and the price seems to be, quite simply, everything. They are convinced that they are the worst of sinners, but equally convinced that they are the most forgiven of men. As far as they are able, they organise their priorities so that God is at the top of the list, knowing that an honest reading of the gospels makes it quite clear that all other things begin from that starting point. And yet, as I've said in connection with Peter Ball, the effect is not to make someone like me despair, and study my sins in a misery of self-loathing, but to feel that the source of all this love and warmth must be able to do something, even with me. I catch sight of God's optimism and feel cheered and encouraged. I remember visiting Peter once with my friend James, whose Christian life has followed an agonised path, not unlike my own. The three of us talked for an hour or so, then, as James and I drove away towards Hailsham, he said with a sort of wistful puzzlement, 'He knows a different God to the one I do. His God's nice!'

He didn't mean soft, he meant 'nice'. Warm and caring and consistent and reliable and firm and forgiving and competent – like a father. That same sense of rich, compassionate, intelligent care can be found in the works of Paul Tournier, a Christian writer who, again and again, has preserved my spiritual sanity. His book, *The Adventure of Living,* is an invigorating invitation to get off the Circle Line of religion, and explore the mystery of *really* living as a follower of Jesus in the *real* world. Because we do live in a huge and thrilling mystery. Whatever I may say here, the things that happen to me are not the things that will happen to the next man, and I have no right to try to crush him into the little box of my own experience. It is so easy to be wrong, so easy to decide that because God did 'X' on Tuesday, he will do 'X' on Wednesday; so easy to preach our own salvation as the way things should be, instead of acknowledging the excitingly complex and creative nature of God's dealings with men. I know a lot of Christians, they're all different – gloriously different. I used to think, for some strange reason, that our ultimate goal was to be exactly alike, but now I don't. I love the differences, and so, I believe, does God. Despite the fundamental similarities in faith, who could be more Paulish than St Paul, more Peterish than St Peter, more Jesus-like than Jesus? I don't want to be like anyone else, nor do I want to force anyone into being like me – God knows I don't want that! I want a hair-raising adventure of cosmic proportions with this God whose aim is to make me the best possible 'Adrian' that I could be. In the process I might even become a useful member of the family, and be able to lend a hand with the newcomers. I'd like that.

Meanwhile my own adventure doesn't look much like an adventure from the outside. Each day, after sharing the arduous task of producing three reasonably dressed and equipped children out of the morning chaos, I settle down to do three things.

First, I read a chapter of the New Testament. I read it in the Jerusalem Bible because I like the print and the headings and the lay-out. I have never read the Bible in a disciplined way before. When I have tried to do so, I've usually taken a couple of verses only, and squeezed them pessimistically in my mind, hoping to extract a drop or two of meaning or significance. Now, I read in order to grasp the broad intention of a chapter, happy to stop and consider a point if it catches my interest. I am reading the gospels at present because I am suddenly fascinated to know what Jesus really said. With my mind still cluttered with prejudices and preconceived notions, this isn't easy, but even I can see that the full gospel of Jesus Christ wouldn't go down too well in most churches that I know. I can also see, though, that he himself would bring healing and tenderness to individuals in those same churches who carry inside themselves a deep-rooted conviction that they are too bad or too insignificant to enter what Jesus calls the Kingdom of God.

Interestingly, as I discover a new freedom to be disciplined in Bible-reading, a close friend has discovered a different kind of liberty through his conscious and careful decision to postpone, for a few months only, the daily study of scripture that has been his habit for many years. I relish the contrast between the ways in which our individual needs are being fulfilled.

Secondly, I pray. At last I have found a way of prayer that is not excruciatingly boring or meaningless, or hopelessly fragmented. On the desk in front of me as I write, lies a pile of about thirty long brown envelopes. On the outside of each is written one or more names. Inside each sealed envelope is a written prayer for the people concerned. Each day I pick up each envelope, hold it up to God, and ask him to do whatever is needed for them. If I am in a grumpy, or sulky mood, I flick through them quite quickly, saying, 'Bless him, and him, and her, and them ...' If I am feeling more peaceful, I try to be creative in my prayers. I might, for instance, imagine Jesus administering communion to each person, and try to see what happens in the encounter. I might, on another occasion, hold the hands of each one in my mind, and say a prayer for both of us. Sometimes I picture Jesus standing by an open door, greeting people individually, and inviting them in. They all respond to him differently. Sometimes I see strange things occurring in these 'mind-pictures'. Whether they are purely imagination or something else, I have no idea. I begin to feel, nowadays, a real sense of responsibility towards this little group of people, and I enjoy meeting them and God every day. I usually say a prayer of confession before doing anything else, and perhaps spend a few minutes after this trying to float in the warm sea of God's love for me. I try to do these things however I feel. In the old days I would have abandoned the attempt to make contact with God if I had been unpleasant since getting up, or if things seemed generally bleak, or if Bridget and I had gone through one of our monumental arguments over some trivial issue. I'm now much more aware of the difference between temperamental and spiritual failure, and far more conscious of the fact that God is as anxious – more anxious probably – to meet me when I've been a berk, as when I fancy I'm one of his little sunbeams!

Thirdly, I write – or try to. We have frequent visitors, and as others who work at home will know, this is a sweet-and-sour dish. I love seeing people – first, because I simply like people, and secondly, because they are a welcome addition to the long list of 'things that prevent you from getting started on filling up the horrific blank sheet of paper'. The list includes such essential activities as going to the lavatory, making coffee, answering the phone, scratching your ear, combing your hair, anything to avoid the moment when the pen first touches the paper.

As I've said, it doesn't look much of an adventure on the face of it, but I feel a growing excitement about the prospect of living in an upside-down world, presided over by a passionate, humorous God, who wants people to be as free and involved and creative and committed and tough as Jesus was. God forgive us for the way in which we have presented Jesus as a 'wet-willie' over the years; as an 'A-stream/doesn't play sports' type, who can't wait to leave this nasty world and get back to the sanitised environs of heaven. As I read the gospels now, I find a Jesus who was passionately involved, physically, mentally, and emotionally with people and with the natural world. Healing and helping and feeding and getting angry and weeping and eating and drinking and sweating and dying. His message to the world was uncompromising and impossibly demanding, but his way with hurt and sinful individuals was tailor-made and tender, unless the sin happened to be hypocrisy in church leaders, in which case he could be devastatingly angry. As far as I can tell, the invitation to continue his adventure and mission in this world is open to everybody, but it seems clear that nothing very startling happens in anybody's life until they start to do what Jesus laid down as a very clear condition of growth. Namely, to make the number one priority in your life, 'Seeking the Kingdom of God'. That's why I do what I do each day. I want to be in on the adventure. I don't want to huddle with other Christians twice a week for the rest of my life, indulging in religion as a hobby. I want God to take this grumpy, jealous, critical personality of mine, transfigure it somehow, and send me out to get my hands dirty in the real world, on his behalf. It's 'mission impossible' at the moment, but as Jesus himself said, 'What is impossible for men, is not impossible for God.'

My heart goes out to all those for whom 'being a Christian' has been like a marathon walk through ankle-deep mud. Some drop out, some keep going, all wonder what on earth it's all about. Why so many peaks and troughs? Why so little peace? Why do some Christians seem to have 'got it', whatever *it* is?

I've got no smart answers. I'm still trudging along myself most of the time, but I'm excited by three things. One is the person of Jesus, one is the fact that God likes me and wants me in his family, and the other is his assurance that nothing is wasted. To all my fellow-stragglers and Christian delinquents I say, with tears in my eyes as I write, God bless you in whatever way you need. Be wary about those once-for-all solutions, but hang on – he'll rescue you.

'That day – it is Yahweh who speaks – I will finally gather in the lame, and bring together those that have been led astray and those that have suffered at my hand. Out of the lame I will make a remnant, and out of the weary a mighty nation. Then will Yahweh reign over them on the mountains of Zion from now and for ever.'

Micah 4:6-7.

Saturday December 14th

Feel led to keep a diary. A sort of spiritual log for the benefit of others in the future. Each new divine insight and experience will shine like a beacon in the darkness!

Can't think of anything to put in today.

Still, tomorrow's Sunday. Must be something on a *Sunday*, surely?

Sunday December 15th

Another commercial Christmas! I shall send only ten cards this year. What is Christmas about, after all?

Our church is getting like an auction room. One blink and you get ministered to. Sit still and keep your eyes shining – that's my motto. This morning was Edwin Burlesford's fault. Forty-five minutes on 'sin'! A record nine-fruit-gum talk. Halfway through, I was checking supplies when Edwin suddenly shouted 'LUST!', and made me drop the packet under my chair. Put my head down between my knees to locate it, then couldn't get up because Doreen Cook pressed her hands down on the back of my head. She prayed that 'our despairing brother would move from darkness to light'. I was all for that – I couldn't see a thing. When she let me get up she had one of those roguish Christian smiles on her face. Came very close to really giving her something to forgive me for. Everyone thinks I've got a big lust problem now. At coffee time they all smiled reassuringly at me. Leonard Thynn hugged me. I signed Edwin's carol-singing list for next Saturday to show that I'm not all bad. Gerald's coming too.

Monday December 16th

My son Gerald says James Bond is on next Saturday evening. Pity it clashes. Still, carol-singing is the Lord's work.

Absent-mindedly bought a box of 50 Christmas cards. Never mind – that's enough for five years.

Tuesday December 17th

Dreamt last night that I *was* James Bond.

Wednesday December 18th

Is carol-singing scriptural? Rang Doreen Cook's husband, Richard, who thinks Christmas trees are wrong. No luck – apparently it's okay.

Bought another 50 cards.

Thursday December 19th

Could it be that God's trying to say I *should* watch James Bond? Opened my Bible at random and put my finger on the page. It said,

'The dogs licked up the blood'.

Went to bed. I don't understand God sometimes. . . .

Friday December 20th

Laid a 'fleece'. If a midget in a Japanese admiral's uniform came to the door at 9.04 precisely, I would know that God wanted me to sing carols.

9.05: A miracle! No-one came. That's that then. Leonard Thynn came at 10.30 selling charity cards. Bought 50.

Saturday December 21st

What an evening!

7.30: Film started. Surprised to find Gerald settling down to watch. 'What about carol-singing?' I said. 'Oh, no', he replied, 'I rang old Edwin on Monday and told him there was a good film on, so I wouldn't be going.'

Why don't I do things like that?

8.45: Edwin at the door, concerned as I hadn't gone carol-singing. Lost my nerve and told him I was still fretting over my lust problem.

11.00: Edwin left after counselling me for 2-1/4 hours. Missed the end of the film. As he left, Edwin said, 'I'm off home to watch that Bond film. The wife's videoed it'.

Gerald said it was the best ending to a film he'd ever seen. He grinned in a rather unchristian manner when he said this. He's a good lad though. Patted my head and said he thought God liked me despite everything.

Next year I am not sending *any* Christmas cards.

... Despite what???

Sunday December 22nd

Guest speaker at church today, dressed in a monk's habit. He said that God is nice and he likes us. Everyone looked at Edwin to see if we agreed. Difficult to tell as he was grinning like a happy little boy. Speaker kept quoting Mother Teresa of Calcutta, who is, of course, a *Roman Catholic!!*

Afterwards, Richard Cook whispered to us, 'Ah yes, but is she saved?'

Gerald whispered back, 'Ah yes, but how many filthy beggars have you washed this week, Richard?'

Anne said she thought the monk was wonderful, so he probably is.

Had some news today that would be really depressing if we weren't Christians. Anne's Uncle Ralph, who is the most vulgar man I have ever met, will have to spend Christmas with us. Wouldn't be so bad, only we've already got my Great Aunt Marjorie staying from tomorrow. *She* condemns wine-gums for their 'intoxicant potential'! Gerald rubbed his hands when he heard the news.

Oh, dear. . . .

Lay awake for a while thinking about what the monk said. 'God is nice and he likes me.' Felt oddly peaceful.

Monday December 23rd

Met Gerald in the hall when I got back from work. He said, 'The Titanic has docked.'

Found Aunt Marjorie looking through the TV magazines in the sitting room. After we had exchanged the customary kiss in which not even the tiniest part of my face touches the tiniest part of hers, she said, 'I am encircling with black ink, those programmes that are unsuitable and which we shall *not* be watching during the Christmas period!'

Gerald poked his head round the door, and said, 'There's a man at the door with a deliverance ministry.'

Turned out to be the postman doing a late round. A parcel and two cards. Counted the cards we've received so far after everybody had gone to bed tonight. Not as many as last year. Naturally, I forgive all those who've forgotten us, but you'd think they could make a bit more effort. After all, that's what Christmas is all about, isn't it?

Uncle Ralph arrives tomorrow.

What on earth will Marjorie make of him?

Gerald says he makes Bernard Manning look like the Archbishop of Canterbury.

Talking of Gerald I've decided I must *do* more with him. He's asked me to go along on Friday to hear the new Christian music group that he's formed with a few friends.

They call themselves 'Bad News For The Devil.'

I *shall* go.

I like music.

Tuesday December 24th

How is it possible for someone like Anne to have an uncle like Ralph? He arrived just after lunch, a short, very fat man, on a tiny motor scooter. Life is just one big whoopee cushion to Uncle Ralph.

Disastrous first encounter with Great Aunt Marjorie. Kissed her full on the lips, and said, 'No-one told me there was going to be some spare talent on the menu this Christmas. Stick around Marjy-girl. You could be right up little Ralphy's street!'

Aunt Marjorie turned puce, and has refused to look at him, let alone talk to him all evening, even when he flicked through the Radio Times and said, 'Heh! Good biz! Someone's gone through and marked off all the best progs!'

Anne and I arranged all the presents under the Christmas tree tonight. The ones from Uncle Ralph are all shaped like bottles.

Asked Anne what she thinks God loves about Uncle Ralph. She said, 'His niece.' Kissed.

Wednesday December 25th

Christmas Day!

Aunt Marjorie went off to a 'proper church' this morning.

Ralph not up by the time Gerald and Anne and I left for the Christmas service.

Enjoyed it all very much except for a point halfway through the prayer-time, when George Farmer, who was sitting behind me, stood up and began to swing his fist from side to side as he prayed fervently for good will among God's people.

Suddenly felt a heavy blow on the side of my head and slumped forward, momentarily stunned. Shook my head to clear it, and realised to my amazement that Farmer was still ranting on as if nothing had happened!

Didn't feel much good will.

I said to him afterwards, 'I forgive you for punching me in the head, George.'

He said, 'Did I really do that?'

Gerald said, 'Yes you did. It was on your twenty-fifth "just" – I was counting.'

Went home.

Spent the rest of the day rugby-tackling Uncle Ralph's jokes before they could cross the line. Became more and more difficult as he drank more and more whisky.

After tea, he went up to his room to get something 'really good' for a game he knew.

Came back with a rubber monkey attached to a long length of elastic, and told Great Aunt Marjorie she should stuff the monkey down her dress, pull it out at the bottom and pass it to him so that he could put it down his trousers, then pass it to Anne.

Thought for a moment she was going to faint.

She retired to bed early, leaving the bottle of gin that Ralph gave her this morning, unopened in the waste-paper basket near the foot of the stairs.

Gerald, who seems to have enjoyed the day enormously, asked Ralph if he knew any more 'good games'.

Ralph said the best game he knew was one where you sit in a circle and each person drinks a bottle of whisky, then one person goes out of the room, and the others have to guess who it was.

How can you run a Christian household with people like Uncle Ralph around?!

I could be a really good Christian if other people didn't mess it up all the time.

I've noticed this before.

Mentioned it to Anne in bed tonight.

She said, 'Well, I promise you, darling, that Gerald and I will try really hard not to stand in the way of your saintliness.'

Just a hint of satire there, I fancy.

Thursday December 26th

Richard Cook turned up this morning to invite us to the Fellowship New Year's Eve party.

Talked in the kitchen.

Dreaded Uncle Ralph appearing suddenly and saying something really awful.

Afraid I wasn't altogether honest.

I said 'Anne's Uncle Ralph is staying with us this Christmas, Richard. He's not a Christian, and he can be – well – let's say, difficult, but I honestly think part of our witness has to be showing a spirit of tolerance, and perhaps even giving the impression

200

sometimes that we enjoy or laugh at things that might be – well – not quite on.'

Said this because I hadn't been able to help laughing at one or two of Ralph's dirty jokes, and knowing him he was quite likely to say to Richard, 'Here's a good one! Adrian nearly wet himself when he heard this one!'

As for witness, it never crossed my mind in connection with Uncle Ralph. Not the Christian type, I suppose.

Amazed when we took our coffee into the sitting room to find that a miracle seemed to have happened. Ralph shook hands quietly and politely with Richard, and insisted on leading him to the most comfortable chair, saying, 'It's a real pleasure to meet one of Adrian's friends. Do sit down.'

As Richard put his weight on the chair, a most awful noise came from underneath him. Shot to his feet again, and Uncle Ralph lifted up the cushion to reveal a deflated rubber bladder with the words 'A REAL BRONX CHEER' printed on the side. Ralph was in hysterics of course.

Richard, obviously taking to heart what I'd said in the kitchen, started to cackle in his high-pitched artificial sort of way, and said, 'Oh, what a good joke against me! I don't disapprove of it. Oh, no! I think it's very funny. Ha, ha!'

Very ashamed.

Rang Richard later and confessed I'd not been very truthful.

Give old Richard his due, whether it's thick skin or love I'm not sure, but he doesn't bear grudges.

Told Anne and Gerald what had happened when they came in.

Anne, who'd been out on a disapproval tour of the area with Aunt Marjorie, was rather short with me.

Gerald made me tell him what had happened three times over. Could still hear him laughing hours later when we were all in bed.

Thank goodness Marjorie and Ralph are leaving tomorrow.

We've all had enough really.

Twinge of toothache tonight....

Friday December 27th

They've gone! Peace again.

Went to Unity Hall tonight to hear 'Bad News For The Devil' practising . When I got there, stood outside for a moment listening to a noise that sounded like a piano falling down a lift-shaft with someone trapped under the lid.

Turned out to be a number called 'Peace Will Come'.

Privately thought a better name for the group would be 'Rather Encouraging News For The Devil'.

Didn't say so though.

They're all very keen.

There's Gerald on the lead guitar, Vernon Rawlings on bass guitar, Elsie Burlesford on flute and William Farmer on drums (very loud), and vocals (unintelligible).

Turns out none of them are even *remotely* interested in fame or riches, only serving God through music.

Never seen Gerald so earnest about anything.

Edwin's invited them to play at the service in three weeks 'if they're ready'.

Hmmm. . . .

Saturday December 28th

Toothache slight but persistent.

Anne mustn't know!

Sunday December 29th

Got up.

Toothache.

Went to bed.

Monday December 30th

The lights are going out all over my head!

Tuesday December 31st

Awake at 5.00 a.m. with this blasted toothache. Gloom! Prayed hard in the lavatory. Maybe it'll just go away. Getting more and more irritable. Must be careful or Anne will guess.

To the Cooks' at 9.00 p.m. for the Church's New Year's Eve party. Earlier on I had said, 'We'll take quiche, shall we?'

Anne said, 'Cake would probably be better.'

Gently reminded Anne that scripture tells us the man is the head of the woman. We took quiche.

Everyone took quiche! No sandwiches, no cake, no puddings, just acres of – quiche.

Anne said, 'What now, oh Lord and Master?'

Gerald said the Lord's Prayer should change to 'Give us this day our daily quiche, because that's all Christians ever eat.'

Richard Cook was standing nearby and overheard. He said it was mocking the Word, and did Gerald really have assurance?

Gerald foolishly replied, 'Yes, I'm with the Woolwich.'

Richard stormed off towards the raspberryade. I wish Gerald wouldn't do it.

Left after an hour or two of loud embarrassing games organised by George Farmer.

In the garden on the way out, we found Leonard Thynn having a theological debate with a large garden gnome, and drinking something from a Tizer bottle. Took him home, Gerald insisting on staying to see him in and put him to bed. Typical Gerald. Not religious, but nice.

Wednesday January 1st

1.30 a.m. Anne's gone to sleep. I can't. My jaw's on fire!

Might as well write down my two New Year resolutions:

(1) *Every* morning – take Anne a cup of tea in bed. She deserves it.

(2) *Every* morning – have quiet time after making tea. Give God more of my time. He deserves it.

10.00 a.m. (at work) Disaster! So tired after sitting up late mulling over my resolutions, I forgot to set the alarm and we all overslept. Anne was very angry with me. Gerald grinned in that maddening way he has. Late for work. No quiet time.

Toothache's awful, but I feel the Lord is saying, 'I will heal you. Don't go to the dentist.' Prayer is what's needed. (Taking painkillers until prayer is answered.)

Thursday January 2nd

Toothache BAD!!! Wife ugly. Son ridiculous. God non-existent. Quiet time? Early tea? Huh! Why doesn't God heal my tooth if

he's so wonderful? Pockets awash with empty pain-killer pack-
ets. I think Anne suspects.

Friday January 3rd

PAIN! PAIN! PAIN!

Richard round tonight, apologising to Gerald for losing his
temper on Tuesday. Then Gerald apologised for making him lose
his temper, then Richard apologised for not coming round sooner,
then Gerald . . . etc, etc. So ridiculous! *They've* not got toothache!

Afterwards, Gerald said that an apology from Richard was like
GBH from anyone else. Felt a sudden, excruciating twinge and
called Gerald an 'arrogant little pagan'.

Anne looked hard at me, then nodded slowly. 'I knew it!' she
said. 'You've got toothache.'

She's getting me an emergency appointment for tomorrow!

TOMORROW, Lord! Please heal me before tomorrow! They
don't work on Saturdays anyway, do they? Surely?

Saturday January 4th

I've been to the dentist!!! He's fixed my tooth!! What a wonderful, glowing, beautiful world this is!

Floated home to my stunning wife, my charming son, chatting
happily as I walked, to God, who loves me so much!

Why on earth do people make such a fuss about going to the
dentist? What's needed is a little courage, that's all.

Sunday January 5th

Took Anne tea in bed without getting grumpy.

Long quiet time.

Invited Richard Cook, Leonard Thynn and Edwin Burlesford,
our elder, to Sunday tea. Gerald was on his best behaviour until
near the end. He leaned forward and said very seriously, 'Richard,
can I share a really amazing truth with you?'

Richard never learns.

'Yes?' he said – agog.

'Did you know,' said Gerald solemnly, 'that Gerald Coates can
be rearranged to make "God's ale crate"?'

Anne looked concerned.

I choked in my tea.

Edwin laughed.

Leonard cackled.

Richard said, 'Who's Gerald Coates?'

Monday January 6th

Went into the Christian bookshop on my way home from work tonight.

All those books!

Gerald says Christian paperbacks are like Chinese meals. Very satisfying at the time, but it's not long before you want another one.

Bought a really great book about faith this time, though. It's called 'Goodness gracious – in God's name, what on Earth are we doing for Heaven's sake?'

A very witty title I feel.

It's all about how Christians should be able to move mountains by faith, if they are really tuned into God.

Very inspiring.

Waited till there was no-one around, then practised with a paper-clip. Put it on my desk and stared at it, willing it to move. Nothing! Tried commanding it in a loud voice.

Gerald came in just then, and said, 'What's all the shouting about, Dad?'

Could hardly tell him I was shouting orders at a paper-clip.

Said I was practising voice-projection.

He said, 'What for?'

I said, 'I don't know.' Felt really stupid.

Anne tells me someone is moving into the empty house next to us in the near future. Be nice if they were Christians, or, at least, easily convertible.

Tuesday January 7th

Gerald has managed to get himself a Saturday job at one of the stores in town. He says it will help to pay for musical equipment for the band.

Anne said, 'Are you sure you won't be too tired after a week at college?'

Gerald laughed as though she'd said something really funny!

Had another go with the paper-clip tonight. I really took authority over it. Couldn't get it to budge.

Told God I'd give up anything he wanted, if he would just make it move half an inch.

Nothing!

All rather worrying really. If you only need faith the size of a mustard seed to move a mountain, what hope is there for me when I can't even get a paper-clip to do what it's told!

Wednesday January 8th

Richard and Edwin round for coffee this evening. We chatted for a while, then Gerald came in with an armful of leads and plugs and stuff.

Richard said, 'I hear you're going to be serving the Lord in Woolworth's on Saturday, Gerald.'

'That depends on whether he comes in or not,' said Gerald.

Funny thing – Richard, who eats, sleeps and breathes religion, looked awfully stern and disapproving when he heard this, but Edwin, who's an Elder and more or less in charge of our church, fell back in his chair with his feet in the air and laughed his head off. Odd!

Hoped Richard would leave before Edwin so that I could get some counselling re faith, but they left together.

Told Anne later that I'd heard about a man who tried to move a paper-clip by faith and couldn't do it. She yawned and said, 'Well, you always get your lunatic fringe, don't you?'

Thursday January 9th

Study-group tonight. We had a tape by Terry Virgo. Old Mrs Thynn said, 'Oh, yes, I've seen him on Pot Black. He takes off all them others, doesn't he?

Good prayer and worship time after that. Forgot about the paper-clip business for almost an hour, quite distracted by thinking about Jesus. Asked Gerald to get the numbers for drinks as the worship session ended.

He said, 'Right, you cuddly charismatics – hands down for coffee!'

I don't know how he gets away with it.

Rather odd couple here for the first time tonight. Mr and Mrs Flushpool. Said nothing all evening, just watched and listened. Edwin asked me quietly afterwards if I could ask them round for a meal one evening soon, as they'd just joined the church and didn't know anybody. Said I'd have to ask Anne about it. Edwin rushed off before I had a chance to put my faith problem to him.

Friday January 10th

Down to Unity Hall to see how the band's getting on. All that equipment! Sounded quite a bit better this time. Should think they've just about reached the stage where they could call themselves 'Not Particularly Good News For The Devil'.

They said that things like recording contracts were of no interest to them whatsoever, unless they were led in that direction, of course. William Farmer still seems somewhat over-vigorous to me. Someone's quite likely to stand up and exorcise him if he carries on like that in front of a few Christian audiences that I know.

Anne says the Flushpools can come on Thursday week. Didn't seem all that keen, though. Unusual for Anne. She's very hospitable usually.

Saturday January 11th

Got up early today to have a last go at that blasted paper-clip. Ended up hissing viciously at it, trying not to wake everybody up. When I gave up and opened the door, I found Anne and Gerald listening outside in their night-clothes, and looking quite anxious.

Anne said, 'Darling, why did you tell that paper-clip you'd straighten it out if it didn't soon get its damned act together?'

Explained with as much dignity as I could muster that I'd been conducting an experiment in faith, and had got a bit carried away when it didn't work.

Anne said, 'But, sweetheart, being a Christian isn't like joining the Magic Circle. Why would God want you to make a paper-clip move by faith?'

Gerald wiped his eyes and said, 'Dad, I think you're wonderful. I wouldn't swap you for anything.'

Rather liked him saying this. Anne did me a cooked breakfast. Felt quite happy really.

In Anne's bad books this evening. Had tea with Gerald when he came back from his first day at work, and asked him if there were any nice girls there. Developed into a discussion about women's looks.

Suddenly, Gerald said, 'When it comes down to it, I can't think of anyone who looks nicer than mum.'

Totally absorbed in the conversation, I said, 'Oh, *I* can!'

Anne put two more sausages on Gerald's plate, and took mine away before I'd quite finished.

Gerald can't have planned for that to happen . . . can he?

Sunday January 12th

Six-fruit-gum-talk on witnessing by Edwin this morning. Very good. Made you want to go straight out and witness to somebody. Drifted off into a pleasant daydream in which I began to preach in the street and ended up with a huge crowd of people, all repenting in tears, and being healed of their sickness just by the touch of my hand. Very near to tears myself during the chorus that followed, as I pictured myself addressing vast assemblies of needy people throughout the world.

Came to with a shock as I realised that Edwin was asking for people to volunteer to do some actual street evangelism next Friday.

Sat as low down in my seat as I could, trying to look like someone whose earnest desire to evangelise has been thwarted by a previous appointment.

Leonard Thynn, sitting next to me, started poking his elbow in my ribs and whispering, 'Go on, you'll be good at it! I will if you will'.

Honestly! It's nothing like this in the books. Thynn made it seem as if we were two girl-guides volunteering to share a tent.

Put my hand up, so did Leonard. In a special meeting afterwards, Edwin said we would go out in pairs. Leonard and I have got to talk to people going in and out of the fish and chip shop in the High Street.

Feel a bit depressed at the prospect. Supposing I meet someone I know! Very fond of Leonard, but he's not the most reliable person in the world.

Asked Anne and Gerald what they thought about it tonight. Anne very supportive and encouraging. Gerald said that in his view, haddock eaters would prove to be less open than other customers in the fish shop. Tried to stop myself asking why, but cracked after about two minutes.

I said, 'Why should haddock eaters be less open?'

'Because,' said Gerald, 'they don't believe in cod.'

He must lie awake thinking these things up!

Monday January 13th

Lay awake myself for a while last night worrying about Friday. I won't know what to say! Wish I was a frog-worshipper.

Found a note from Gerald on the breakfast table, suggesting that when I go out to change the world at the end of the week, I should bear in mind the important fact that Billy Graham is an anagram of 'Big rally ham'.

Richard phoned at lunchtime to ask if he could come round tomorrow evening with his son Charles to talk about a 'little problem'.

Rather puzzling. I thought Charles had already gone off for his second term at Bible School. All last term he wrote a letter a week back to the church, from which Edwin read occasional snippets. Gerald, who's seen the originals, says they make St Paul's epistles look like pagan telegrams.

Wonder what's gone wrong?

Tuesday January 14th

Went into the Christian bookshop again today, to see if they'd got anything good on street evangelism. Asked the man behind the counter eventually. There must be a special college somewhere, where they train Youth Hostel wardens, Lost Property officials and people who work in Christian bookshops.

I said, 'Have you got anything on street evangelism, please?'

'Street evangelism?' he said, with such annoyance and incredulity that I took an involuntary step backward, knocking over a life-size cardboard cut-out of Cliff Richard.

Panicked a bit. I said, 'Don't worry, it'll only take a second to resurrect him.' Picked Cliff up, then turned back towards the shop man who was breathing heavily through his nose.

'Yes,' I said, 'street evangelism – please.'

Came away eventually with what looks like a really great book, grudgingly excavated by the shopkeeper from the Christian Gardening section, where some frightened customer must have thrust it in his hurry to escape.

It's called 'Prayers, Principles, Practices and Probable Problems for Precinct Preachers' written by a man called A. P. Lunchington, who is, apparently, known affectionately in his part of the country as 'Lamp-post' Lunchington, owing to his untiring efforts to spread light on the pavements of his home town. I shall read it tomorrow when Richard's gone.

Richard arrived at 7.30 with Charles. Poor Charles looked a bit crazed, I thought. I said 'I thought your term started this week, Charles. Have you not been well?'

Charles said, 'The Lord has told me I'm not to go back to college. He would have me serve him elsewhere.'

Anne said, 'Where do you think he wants you to go, Charles?'

Charles said that he thought he should pack his bags and set out for the Near East as soon as possible, because God had made it clear that that was where he wanted him.

Anne said gently, 'How has he made it clear Charles?'

Charles leaned forward and spoke eagerly. 'It's amazing! Just about every time I open the Bible, there's something about Israel, or the Jews!'

Nearly laughed out loud, but Anne caught my eye. Richard looked unhappy.

Anne said, 'Charles, dear, what's going wrong at college?'

Had that feeling I sometimes have with Anne that I'd missed a whole chunk of conversation somewhere along the line. He hadn't mentioned a problem at college!

After a few tears from Charles and some more talk, it turned out that the poor old chap had felt lonely and useless and sinful all last term, and couldn't face going back for another three months of misery.

After a bit of prayer, lots of cake, and good advice from Anne, Charles said he thought he would go back after all.

Richard very pleased. Actually smiled! How did Anne know? Why didn't he talk to his own mother? I don't seem to understand anything!

Too late to start my new book tonight. Lay awake yet again, worrying about Friday. What shall I say, God? I don't know *any-thing*. What shall I say? What shall I say?

Wednesday January 15th

Sat down with Lunchington's book this evening, hoping to pick up a few good tips. What an amazing book! I don't know how the man finds time to eat or sleep. His life is literally one long succession of extraordinary miracles. Everyone he meets and everything he does could have come straight out of the New Testament. In fact the New Testament seems like an early and rather poor rehearsal for Lunchington's life.

The man doesn't know what it is to experience doubt or depression or failure or discouragement. Everyone he meets seems to get converted, and absolutely nothing gets him down. As for street evangelism – well! Lunchington has only to step out of his front door as far as I can see and instantly a hitherto deserted stretch of pavement will be thronged by a huge crowd, all jostling and shoving to get near enough to Lunchington to seek his help in making a commitment. Fell back in my chair exhausted at the end of the book.

Puzzled to find in the back of my mind a small but definite desire had arisen to kick Lunchington very hard, just between miracles. Dismissed this unworthy impulse as yet another ploy of the enemy, and dialled Leonard's number.

I said, 'Hello Leonard, I just wanted to tell you that I've been reading a really great book about witnessing, and I think we ought to do what this man does, and step out in faith on Friday night, dressed in our spiritual armour and know that the victory's won before we even begin!'

Thynn said, 'Oh, I agree, but can we pop into the George and have a jar or two on the way, just for a bit of Dutch courage, like?'

When I write *my* spiritual autobiography, Thynn will not be in it, except perhaps in a smartened-up form. Instead of suggesting 'a jar or two' he will say 'Amen, brother! Hallelujah!'

Thursday January 16th

Finished work early today. Took a walk out to the Mugley estate to visit Bill and Kitty Dove, our favourite old couple in the church. Found them eating crumpets and drinking tea by the fire. Bill and Kitty both smile as though a light's been switched on behind their faces.

Kitty said, 'Oooh, hurry up! Your crumpets'll get cold!'

Bill said, 'Here's a lovely cuppa. Get by the fire and tell us what that young Gerald's been up to.'

'Hee-hee-hee!' giggled Kitty. 'Young Gerald, hee-hee-hee!'

Told them about Christmas and Aunt Marjorie and Uncle Ralph and the band. They nodded and twinkled and nodded.

Bill said, 'What about you then? What've you been up to?'

Told them about the witnessing on Friday.

Kitty beamed at me. She said, 'Oh, you are a lovely man to want to tell folks about our dear Jesus. Oh, he will be pleased!'

Suddenly felt weepy and soft. I said, 'It's not quite like that. I'm not a lovely man at all . . .'

Bill said, 'Oh, yes you are! God loves you fit to bust. He's crackers about you, so you must be lovely! Have another crumpet and don't be so daft!'

Left the Doves', feeling well fed.

Good study-group tonight, except when Doreen Cook said, 'Just for prayer, and strictly in confidence, but have you heard about Raymond?', and Edwin told her off gently for gossiping.

That couple, the Flushpools, were here again tonight. Said nothing at all, except when Gerald offered Mrs Flushpool a cup of coffee, and she said, 'I used to in the natural, but not any more.'

Asked Anne later why she'd been so funny about inviting them round. She just shook her head slowly and said she didn't know. Strange. . . .

Wish I knew what Doreen was going to say about Raymond.

Friday January 17th

Silly, sweaty quiet-time. Started by asking God for a sign that it would go alright this evening. Then remembered that bit about, ' . . . it's a wicked generation that seeks a sign' and felt guilty. Then remembered John the Baptist losing his confidence in prison, and felt alright again, then remembered about Doubting Thomas and felt guilty again, then remembered Gideon's fleece and felt alright again.

Might have gone on like this forever, but Anne called out that it was time for work.

Gerald had left me a tiny silver cross to wear, and a note saying that witnessing is an anagram of 'sing in stew'.

Too nervous to eat before going out this evening. Spent a little while looking for a Bible that could have been 'The Guns of Navarone' for all anyone else knew. Found a smallish one eventually.

Leonard arrived at seven, clutching a huge brass-clasped family Bible under his arm. Said his mother wanted him to bring it because *her* grandfather had used it to preach in the street in 1906. Thynn was dressed in a peculiar, old-fashioned, black suit, that looked as if it had once been used by an undertaker. Said it was his *best* suit.

Took up our position outside the fish-and-chip shop. Leonard looked like a severely deranged religious maniac out for the evening with his keeper. Felt really miserable and hopeless. Every time I *did* say something to one of the people going in and out of the shop, Leonard just echoed everything I said.

ME: Evening!

CUSTOMER: Evening!

LEONARD: Evening!

ME: Still chilly, eh?

CUSTOMER: (Laughing) Cor, yes!

LEONARD: Still chilly, eh?

CUSTOMER: Pardon?

LEONARD: Still chilly, eh?

CUSTOMER: (Uneasily) Err ... yeh! (Departs hurriedly)

or

ME: Excuse me.

CUSTOMER: Yes, what . . . ?

LEONARD: (Paralysed with nerves) Excuse me.

CUSTOMER: Pardon?

LEONARD: Err . . . excuse both of us.

CUSTOMER: (Looking at Thynn's ridiculous suit and Bible) Yes, of course. You're excused. (Departs hurriedly)

Not the most dynamic religious exchanges of our time! In the end we both got hungry and went to buy some chips. Got talking without really trying, to a man called Ted who'd decided to eat his fish and chips in the warm before walking home. After we'd talked for a bit, Leonard, suddenly realising that this could be 'IT', started mouthing silently and intensely at me from behind Ted's shoulder, 'Go on, convert him!' Felt completely paralysed by this. Managed stumblingly to ask Ted if he'd ever thought that Christian values should be emphasised more strongly in society. Had quite a good discussion after that, ending, believe it or not, with Ted saying he wouldn't mind coming along to our church on Sunday morning!!

As we parted outside the shop, Ted said, 'Talking about values in society an' all that, that's why I come down 'ere for my supper on Fridays now. There's a gang of yobs makes an 'orrible noise with their so-called music every Friday night for about two hours in that Unity 'all next door to us. Now *there's* somethin' that needs stoppin'! Anyway, see you Sunday mornin'. Goodnight.'

Later, after Leonard had gone home, singing 'We got one, we got one . . .' to the tune of Loch Lomond, I made sure Gerald wasn't around, and told Anne what Ted had said about the 'orrible noise.

'What's going to happen on Sunday,' I said, 'when Ted finds out that the gang of yobs who drive him out every Friday night are playing at our church? And that one of the leading yobs is *my son!*'

Anne said, 'I don't know what'll happen, but I'm sure it'll be alright. Remember Lunchington. He wouldn't worry.'

Huh! Lunchington! I dare say he would've brought all the fried fish back to life and given them a tract each.

Just said one prayer tonight. 'God, please save Ted. Amen.'

Saturday January 18th

Spent almost half an hour in the bathroom this morning, flattening down two tufts of hair which kept sticking up whatever I did, and making me look like the devil. Finally subdued them, only to have my hair ruffled violently by Gerald from behind as I was about to crack my egg.

Talk about full of beans! He said, 'Tomorrow's the day, Dad! Edwin came to listen last night and he said it's all systems go for Sunday morning. Mum, Dad.' He was suddenly serious. 'You're going to be proud of me tomorrow.'

Anne said, 'I'm sure we are, dear.'

Opened my mouth, but my thoughts were strangling each other and no sound came out. Gerald didn't notice. He said, 'Must go, must go! Time for work! Fancy them being foolish enough to employ *me!*' Waltzed off through the door singing, 'That's the blunder of Woolworth's . . .'

Disappeared, then put his head round the door a few seconds later.

'By the way, Dad.'

'Yes.'

'This chap you met last night.'

'Yes?'

'Well, our music might be the thing that brings him to a point where he makes a real decision.'

'Yes, Gerald,' I said. 'You could well be right.'

Hmmm. . . .

Saw our future neighbour briefly through the hall window this afternoon, going in to do some measuring or something, I expect. He looks relaxed, contented, smokes a big comfortable-looking pipe, there's a sort of glow of happiness around him. Unlikely to be a Christian, I would think. We shall find out when he moves in.

Sunday January 19th

Gerald up and out early to help get the band set up in the church. Very excited of course.

Arrived at the church with Anne later, half hoping that Ted wouldn't turn up. Sat at the back as usual and watched the door. Suddenly saw Ted hovering rather nervously in the doorway. Felt a sudden surge of pride. That was my very own potential convert standing over there. Mine! Not anyone else's. Mine! Rose to my feet, intending to greet him with impressive, quiet modesty and warmth, when to my disgust, Thynn called out in a very loud voice, 'Ah, Ted, my old friend! When we asked you to come along to church the other evening, we weren't sure if you'd come or not. But here you are! Nothing to do with us of course. We all know that. Ha, ha!'

An outrageous exhibition to my way of thinking, and very frustrating. Could hardly stand up and say, 'Excuse me, everybody, but I was there as well. Actually, I did most of the talking.'

Leonard did at least bring him over to the empty chair that I'd saved next to me. Service began soon afterwards, led by Edwin himself, thank goodness. Edwin may stretch the old messages out a bit at times, but he doesn't mind if you sit or stand or wave your hands in the air, or dance, or don't dance, or mime the whole of Goldilocks and the Three Bears, or whatever you like as long as what you do makes you feel comfortable, and doesn't interfere with anyone else. Ted seemed to quite enjoy the singing and the prayers. Edwin's message (5 wholly consumed fruitgums and one unwrapped and halfway to the mouth) was a little disappointing. It was all about the Christian family and how we might get on better with each other, not the straight-down-the-line gospel message that I wanted Ted to hear. Kept looking sideways at him to see if there were tears in his eyes. Always a promising sign I feel. Not so much as a glisten as far as I could see, but he was certainly listening.

Then came the bit I dreaded. Edwin said, 'Now, everybody, I want you to listen to a brand new Christian band, made up entirely of young people from the church. They've been practising really hard for today. They're going to play one of their own compositions – 'Peace Will Come'. How about a nice encouraging round of applause for 'Bad News For The Devil!'

They *were* better, no doubt about that, but it was still pretty much a solid wall of noise, and young William Farmer drummed and sang like someone who'd got electric leads attached to some very vulnerable part of his body.

Noticed, rather nervously, that Ted was leaning forward in his chair with a puzzled expression on his face, listening intently to the music.

When it finished there was a stunned silence for a few moments, broken by old Mrs Thynn who said, 'What did 'e say they were called?'

Leonard said, 'Bad News For The Devil, mother.'

Hope for Gerald's sake, that the clapping which started just at that moment, obscured Mrs Thynn's reply of, 'Bad news for anyone, if you ask me.' Suddenly realised Ted was tapping me on the shoulder. ''Ere,' he whispered, 'this lot sounds just like the other lot down Unity 'all of a Friday.'

Cleared my throat, 'Actually, Ted, this lot *is* that lot, if you see what I mean. In fact, the one playing the lead guitar is my son – Gerald.'

'You mean,' said Ted, 'that when you asked me to come 'ere, an' afterwards I said about the yobs at . . . an' you still asked me?'

Suddenly realised Gerald had stepped forward to the microphone. All flushed and nervous, not like Gerald at all. Suddenly remembered him as a little boy.

'We're still pretty awful,' he said, 'but we're going to get better, and I just wanted to say that song we just did, is – well, it's dedicated to a new friend of dad's called Ted, who's sitting over there at the back, and we just want to tell Ted that we hope he – he – well, becomes one of the family soon.'

Couldn't swallow for some reason. Ted was frowning and shaking his head slowly. 'Ain't never 'ad a family,' he said fiercely.

When the service ended Ted said, 'I want a word with the bloke in charge.' I introduced him to Edwin. Couldn't help just hinting that I'd invited him. They went off together into one of the side rooms.

Floated home.

I AM A CHRISTIAN WHO WITNESSES AND BRINGS PEOPLE TO THE LORD!!!

If things go on like this, I could end up being asked to speak at Christian conferences!

Monday January 20th

Woke up this morning feeling older, sterner, more patriarchal, somehow. Hoped Anne and Gerald would respond with more respect than usual to the aura of calm holiness that I sensed was all around me. When I came downstairs, Anne said, 'The cat's been sick behind the settee. Will you clear it up? I've got important things to do.'

Gerald handed me a folded piece of paper before setting off for college. When I opened it up I found a note saying, 'Dear Dad, did you know that "Inflated ego" is an anagram of "Feel a tin god"?'

Went to work.

Tuesday January 21st

Stopped on the way home this afternoon to chat to a man working in his garden just down the road from us. Thought I'd try out my new gift of witnessing. When I said I was a Christian, he said, 'Well, in that case, why don't you cut your – ing hedge back a bit, so that we pagans don't have to step into the gutter every time we walk past your house?'

Walked on with flaming cheeks. What a horrible man! Needn't think he can tell *me* what to do and when to do it! Coincidentally, I *did* decide to have a go at the hedge today, but NOT because of what he said. Borrowed an electric trimmer from Mr Brain, our elderly neighbour, who comes to church sometimes, and did it in no time.

Didn't mention to Anne what the man said. She has gone on a bit about the hedge – since last summer in fact.

Gerald tells me he *will* be in when the Flushpools come tomorrow. Says he's curious.

Wednesday January 22nd

Phone call from Kitty Dove at work today. Says that Ted came to tea at their house yesterday, and said he wanted very much to follow Jesus, but Edwin had told him to think very carefully about it for a couple of weeks, and in the meantime, spend some time with the Doves.

'He speaks so highly of you, dear' said Kitty, 'and I think he's quite right!'

Why is it that when the Doves say nice things to me, I *really* want them to know I'm not as good as they think?

'He's asked if he can come and see us for the next two Friday evenings,' went on Kitty. 'Very particular about that, he was. Said Friday would be the best night for him if we didn't mind. Isn't that lovely?'

Smiled to myself. 'Yes,' I said, 'it is lovely.'

Gerald answered the phone at six o'clock this evening. Came back looking mystified.

He said, 'That was Mrs Flushpool. They can't come, she says her husband's laid up with an old disease that still affects him in the natural, and they'd like to come next Thursday, God willing, if that's alright. Can you 'phone back if it isn't?'

Isn't it WONDERFUL when something that *was* going to happen even though you didn't really *want* it to happen but you thought it *ought* to happen because it was right, doesn't happen after all, and it's *not* your fault?

Spent a very cosy evening with Anne and a bottle of wine. Gerald ate his own, Mr Flushpool's and Mrs Flushpool's share of the food, then went out for the evening. All very satisfactory.

I'd *love* to know what Doreen was going to say about Raymond last week. For prayer I mean....

Thursday January 23rd

I keep thinking about the man down the road. I wish I hadn't cut the hedge now. Bet he smiles smugly every time he walks past our house. He thinks I've cut the hedge because of what he said.

Huh! That's all he knows. If I wasn't feeling Christian forgiveness and goodwill towards him, I'd like to kneel on his chest and make him eat the hedge clippings.

No wonder St Paul says we mustn't be yoked with unbelievers. He was obviously thinking of people like this man, who doesn't understand things like love and peace and Christian charity.

Not that it bothers me. Why should it? I feel that the Lord is saying I mustn't make contact with him again, so I won't. So that's that! I won't give it another thought. Not another thought.

Study group at someone else's house tonight. Didn't go. Felt rather ill and down. Anne and Gerald came back very happy and nauseatingly healthy. Perked up a little later on when Gerald told me that Mrs Thynn described tonight how her grandmother had not been able to afford to pay for her father's funeral, but the Lord had 'wonderfully undertaken'.

Friday January 24th

Had an awful nightmare last night. Really bad! It all happened in church. I was standing up at the front behind a barber's chair and somehow I knew that I'd just finished shaving all the members of the congregation, men, women *and* children. I was the only unshaven person there. In fact, my beard, which was bright green for some reason, came down way below my knees.

Suddenly (in my dream) the doors at the back crashed open and the man down the road stormed in, pointed an accusing finger at me, and shouted, 'He shaved others! Himself he could not shave!'

Woke up sweating and trembling. Had to reach out and touch Anne's shoulder to make sure everything was alright.

Stupid, meaningless dream!

Still feeling grotty. Anne wouldn't let me go to work today. Just a mild spot of 'flu I expect. Prayed for healing but wasn't. Why don't people like Lunchington put that sort of thing in their books?

When Anne came up to bring me a hot drink and my favourite creamed mushrooms on toast, I waited 'til she'd tidied the bed and stopped fussing round me, then I said, 'Anne, just tell me one solitary thing that shows God cares about me being ill.'

She said, 'He's provided you with a full-time nurse who doesn't ask to be paid, and loves you very much. Will that do for a start?'

Thinking to brighten up Anne's day with a little joke, I replied, 'Great! When does she arrive?'

Had to have a slight relapse later to make Anne sympathetic again.

Saturday January 25th

Felt a little better this morning. Two visitors while Anne was out. Richard came round to say that he'd had a 'picture'. Why don't I ever have pictures? He wondered if his picture might be connected with my illness.

He said, 'I saw, as it were, a dartboard, and, impaled upon the dartboard by means of a dagger, was a small jellyfish, and, as I watched, it was revealed to me that the creature's name was Stewart.'

I shall never understand why Richard says these things in front of Gerald. Gerald nodded gravely, and said, 'Well, there you are dad. That's it. It's "The Revenge of the Jellyfish", like in the horror films. Obviously at some time in your life you must have stepped on one called Stewart while you were paddling, and now they've found a way to get their own back by giving you the 'flu.'

Richard said, 'That doesn't explain the dartboard.'

I said, 'Isn't it time for you to go to work, Gerald?'

Thanked Richard for sharing his picture with me. Said I couldn't see an obvious connection, but I'd bear it in mind.

Next visitor was Edwin with some mint imperials, which I love, and the offer of a chat. Started to tell him about Richard's picture, but he stopped me and said, 'Don't tell me the details. Dear old Richard means well, but he does get a bit carried away sometimes. The thing about these "pictures" is that every now and then you get one that really is from God. You just have to think them through, pray about them, and decide calmly for yourself.'

Did all that later. Didn't take long. Jellyfish! Really!

Just before dozing off this afternoon, I said to Anne, 'You know that man down the road who looks like a jellyfish?'

'No,' said Anne.

'Well, he's fattish and – well, fattish.'

'No.'

'Roses in the front.'

'Oh, yes, – fattish, yes.'

'You don't know his name, do you?'

'No.'

'You don't know if he's called Stewart?'

'No.'

'Oh.'

'Why?'

'Nothing . . . it doesn't matter.'

Sunday January 26th

Much better, but decided to stay in today so as to be fit for work tomorrow. Gerald left me some of the band's song lyrics to read while he and Anne were at church. Had a look at the one they did on Sunday last. 'Peace Will Come'. I am copying the words into my diary. There are two verses.

Verse I   Peace will come,
Peace will come,
Peace will come,
Peace will come,
Peace will come,
Peace will come,
Peace will come,
Peace will come,
Peace will come,
Peace will come,
Peace will come,
Peace will come,
What will come?
Peace will come.

Verse II   Peace has come,
             Peace has come,
             Peace has come,
             Peace has come,
             Peace has come,
             Peace has come,
             Peace has come,
             Peace has come,
             Peace has come,
             Peace has come,
             Peace has come,
             Peace has come,
             What has come?
             Peace has come.

(Repeat verses I and II three times)

Gerald said they spent hours polishing up the lyrics on this one!
Seems a bit of a waste of time to me. By the time *any* words have
fought their way out between William Farmer's tonsils they could
sound like anything at all. Still, Gerald's keen. Mustn't be discouraging.

Monday January 27th

Quite well again. Went to work. Have decided to walk *up* the
road and through the cemetery every morning from now on. It's
a bit longer, but the exercise will do me good.

Just as I left Anne said, 'Oh, by the way, what about him?'

Pretended not to know what she was talking about.

She said, 'You know, you were rambling on about him in bed
on Saturday afternoon. Something about jellyfish, and was he
called Stewart? The man down the road – with the roses. What
about him?'

Panicked. I said, 'Oh, yes, I remember now. I – I saw him in
his garden one day, and thought I'd like to – to write a poem
about him. It's not finished yet.'

Anne said, 'You're writing a poem about the man down the road?'

'Yes.'

'The man you think looks like a jellyfish, and might be called Stewart?'

'Err . . . yes. There's err . . . a dartboard in it too. Anyway, I must go, Anne. I'll be late for work.'

Left Anne silently mouthing 'dartboard' to herself. I'd only got a few yards up the road when she called me from an upstairs window.

'Darling, that's not the way to work! I know you haven't been for three days, but you can't have forgotten already.'

Tried to call back casually. 'Oh, it's okay. I know it's a bit longer, but it'll do me good.'

Anne said, 'Darling, it's nearly a *mile* longer, and you're late already. What *are* you talking about?'

Felt like screaming! I said firmly, 'Anne, I feel led to go this way, and go this way I shall!'

Late for work. Felt guilty and confused all day. Worn out by walking the long way home this evening. Feel like killing somebody! The man down the road for instance.

Anne kept looking at me as if I was a loony.

Just after switching the light off tonight, she said, 'Have you finished your poem yet, darling?'

Foolishly replied, 'Yes.'

Anne said, 'Oh, good. You must read it to me in the morning.'

Waited till she was asleep, then crawled out of bed to write the damned thing! What am I going to do if Gerald's there when I read it? He knows all about Richard's 'picture'. What a stupid mess! Hope Armageddon's scheduled for tonight.

Tuesday January 28th

Woke with a headache.

At breakfast Anne said, 'Can I hear your poem now, darling?'

Gerald said, 'Poem? Has *dad* written a poem?'

Said it as though he'd just heard about a pig who'd been taught to dance Swan Lake. *He* can talk. 'Peace will come'. Huh!

I said, 'Yes, Gerald, I've written a poem.'

Anne said, 'Your father is very struck by a man down the road, Gerald. That's what the poem is about. Go on, darling. Read it to us.'

Anne turned away for a moment just then, so I was able to look pleadingly at Gerald and put my finger to my lips. He looked intrigued but co-operative. Read the poem out.

> Oh, man down the road,
> You with the roses,
> And a face like a dartboard,
> Were you fathered by a jellyfish?
> Or what?
> You, whose name may not be Stewart,
> How I'd love to watch Eric Bristow,
> Practise on you.
> Or anybody really.

Looked at my wife and son as I finished, and realised that once again, they are, quite reasonably, convinced that I am going round the bend.

Came home tonight (the long way) to find that Ted had phoned earlier. Could I phone back? Rather pleased really. Reflected, as I dialled the number, that Ted probably sees me as a sort of spiritual giant, silly, but quite understandable.

When I got through he said, 'Oh, good stuff! Thing is, there's this bloke at work 'oo might be interested in – well, you know, God an' that. Kitty Dove said why not bring 'im round to see you, 'specially as 'e lives in the same road as you. Watcha think?'

I said, 'What's his name?'

'Simmonds,' said Ted.

'No, no, I mean his first name. Is he called Stewart?'

Ted sounded puzzled. 'No 'e's called Norman. But listen. Can I bring 'im round tomorrow evenin' at about seven o'clock?'

'Yes Ted,' I replied. 'Yes. Please do bring him round. See you tomorrow. 'Bye.'

His name may be Norman, but something tells me that, without any doubt at all, the chap coming to my house with Ted tomorrow night, is the chap who told me to get my--ing hedge cut.

Wednesday January 29th

8.00 a.m.

Woke up in deep gloom. A near-fatal road accident would just about hit the spot as far as I'm concerned today. Don't want to actually die, just be severely – and painlessly – injured, enough to distract everybody from this lunatic fever-dream of hedge-cutting and dartboards and walking the long way to work and the man down the road being interested in God.

Wish the J.W.s had got to him first. No I don't. Yes I do. No I don't. Oh-BISCUITS!

This may be the last entry in my diary. I'm setting off for work now, and I'm a troubled, dangerous man. I may *never* come back!

6.00 p.m.

Back at the usual time. Slightly cheered by a phone-call at work from Bill Dove.

He said, 'Hello, mate! Got time for a chat with an old sinner?'

'Yes, Bill,' I said gloomily, 'if you've got time for a chat with a middle-aged idiot.'

Bill chuckled. 'I know, I know,' he said. 'You've got yourself in a real pickle, haven't you?'

'*How* do you know, Bill?'

Another chuckle. 'Just know, don't I? Now listen! It's all planned out – got that? It's *all* planned out.'

'Planned out?'

'Certainly. Now, I want you to call me tonight, late, and say either "Bill, you're a silly old fool, and I'm never going to listen to you again," or – "Hello Bill, God's in charge." Got that? Good! See yer.'

Midnight: Ted and the Simmonds man arrived at seven o'clock precisely. We all sat stiffly around the sitting room waiting for someone to say something. Everyone seemed to be staring at *me*.

I could feel a sort of mad laugh bubbling up in me, when the doorbell rang suddenly and broke the tension. Anne answered it, and came back a second or two later with our new pipe-smoking neighbour, who smiled round at everybody without any self-consciousness, and introduced himself as Frank Braddock.

'Moved in today,' he announced easily. 'Thought I'd stroll over and say hello to my new neighbours. Anyone mind if I smoke?'

Looked intently at me suddenly.

'Now, your name is . . . ?'

'Adrian,' I said rather feebly. 'That's my name.'

'Ah! Adrian is it? Right!'

He pointed his pipe-stem at me.

'You know . . .' he smiled richly, 'you're the only man I've ever seen cutting his hedge in near-darkness in the middle of winter as if his life depended on it. And I said to myself that day – I said "When I move in I'm going to *ask* that man *why* he was doing that. So – why were you?"'

Braddock plumped down into an easy chair and began filling his pipe with calm enjoyment.

Never felt so embarrassed in my life.

Looked down at the carpet to hide my burning face. Thought how much Simmonds must be enjoying this moment. Suddenly thought – what the heck? I'll tell 'em all what happened, they can all have a jolly good laugh, then they can do what they like. Looked up, and was about to speak, when I noticed to my surprise that Simmonds, who only has hair on the sides of his head, was also one big blush.

'Actually,' he stumbled, 'I was hoping that wouldn't get brought up tonight . . .'

'What on earth do you mean?' said Anne.

'Well . . .' Simmonds cleared his throat, 'You see, I'd had the mother-and-father of a row with the wife that day, and when you came along . . .' – he pointed at me – ' . . . and started talking about being a Christian, well – I just blew my top and gave you all the aggro that I'd piled up ready for the wife. The first thing I thought of was your hedge, 'cause I walk past it to work every day, and it *did* stick out a bit, but not much. But then . . . !'

He leaned forward, very animated.

'Instead of giving me a mouthful back, like I deserved, you went off and started cutting the hedge! And I thought that was – well, I thought you must be quite – well – I dunno – quite unusual.'

His blush deepened.

'Anyway, I lost my nerve after that. You won't believe this, but I even started walking the other way to work so I didn't have to go past your house and run the risk of seeing you.' He laughed ruefully. 'That's the kind of idiot I am, I'm afraid.'

Caught Anne's eye and looked away hastily.

'And then,' Norman resumed, 'old Ted here told me he'd got interested in what was going on up at the church, and I thought I'd like to find out what it was all about, so he suggested coming along here tonight. Well ... when I saw which house it was when we got here just now, I nearly did a bunk! But then I remembered the way you went off and did that hedge and I thought, Oh, well, in for a penny, in for a pound, so here I am.'

He leaned back, obviously glad to have got it off his chest. I looked round. Ted was staring at me as if I was a modern-day St Francis. Anne looked like someone who's just finished a difficult jigsaw puzzle. Gerald's face was in his hands, but his shoulders were gently shaking. As for Frank Braddock, he was leaning forward, elbows on his knees, pipe clenched between his teeth, gazing fixedly at me with a funny little expectant smile lighting up his eyes.

I said, 'Norman, you're all wrong about me. I cut the hedge because I was embarrassed, and I wanted to make you eat the clippings to get back at you for making me feel stupid. And ... (A difficult one this) ... I walked a different way to work as well, and I told Anne that – that it was because I felt led to go that way, and – and, oh, Lord ...!'

All got sorted out after that. A lot of laughter and chat. Braddock didn't stay much longer. Saw him to the door. Just before closing the door, I said, 'Frank – can I ask you, are *you* a Christian?'

He raised a bushy eyebrow. 'Guess!'

Didn't know what to say. What an embarrassing question! Still don't know the answer. When I didn't say anything, he just clapped me on the shoulder and strode off down the path, shouting 'Goodnight mate!' as he went. Strange man!

After they'd all gone, Anne hugged me and made a cup of tea. 'Darling,' she said, 'why let things get so complicated?'

Gerald said, 'Come off it, mum! Dad wouldn't be dad if he didn't complicate things.'

Just about to follow Anne up to bed, when I remembered Bill Dove. Phoned him straightaway. I said, 'Bill, you're a silly old fool, and I'm never going to listen to you again.'

He chuckled, 'It went alright then?'

'Yes Bill,' I said, 'God's in charge.'

Thursday January 30th

Walked to work the *short* way this morning.

Suddenly felt oppressed by the prospect of the Flushpools' visit this evening. Would have been nice to just enjoy the uncomplicated atmosphere for once. Still, as a Christian, you're lumbered aren't you?

Came home to find Anne tired and tense after cleaning and baking and preparing the meal all day. Gerald breezed into the kitchen as we were enjoying a cup of tea, peered at a rather sad looking sponge on the side, and said, 'I see you've made a Bishop of Durham Cake, Mum.'

'What do you mean, Gerald?' said Anne, quietly but icily.

'All the right ingredients, but nothing's risen,' replied Gerald cheerily. Dodged the wet dish-cloth with ease. Slipped hastily out of the door before she could find more ammunition.

I said, 'You've got to laugh.'

Anne said, 'Have you?'

Flushpools arrived at about seven-thirty. We all sat down straightaway in the dining room. Mrs Flushpool, who looks like a collection of black plastic bags half-filled with water, glanced around and said, 'Dear Anne, such a problem keeping a room of this size *really* clean. How we need the presence of the mighty one, even in our most intimate wifely duties.'

Mr Flushpool, who bears a remarkable resemblance to those old photographs of Crippen, said, in a deep tomb-like voice, 'Amen to that!'

From that point onwards, Anne said hardly anything. Mrs Flushpool described at great length how she had been converted from fleshly works and appetites since being washed in the blood, and how, in consequence, she was now able to turn her back on those things that she used to do in what she called 'the natural'. Everything she said seemed to have a sort of dampness about it. She and her husband refused wine, saying that Christians should be ashamed to have it in the house, as it led to carnal excess. At this point Mr Flushpool let out another sonorous 'Amen to that!' Coffee was also frowned on as something that was wont to stimulate inappropriately in the natural.

Gerald, with a perfectly straight face, asked Mrs Flushpool if she used to go swimming in the natural. She replied fervently that her bodily flesh would never again rouse any man to a fever of sensual lust.

Mr Flushpool opened his mouth very wide to say, 'Amen to that!' but thought twice and shut it.

Mrs Flushpool went on to talk, with gleaming eyes, about the dangers of the occult, becoming so vehement, that she started to froth slightly at the mouth, and had to use a red paper napkin.

Quite glad when they got up to go at about 10 o'clock. As she left, Mrs Flushpool said, 'Thank you so much for supper, *dear* Anne. You must come round to us soon, and have a *proper* meal.'

Through the closed door we heard a final 'Amen to that' as Mr Flushpool marched to his nightly fate.

I said to Anne, 'Well, what did you think?'

Rarely seen Anne look so grim. She said, 'They have a certain emetic quality. I'm going to bed – in the natural. Are you coming?'

'Yes,' I replied. 'Amen to that!'

Friday January 31st

Strolled down to Unity Hall again tonight to hear B.N.F.T.D. Gerald tells me that Elsie (flute) and William (vocal hysteria) are deeply in love with each other. Doesn't seem to have slowed him down at all. When he sings, the words still come out of him like rats from a burning building. He told me afterwards that if the

Lord leads him into being an international rock star, he's prepared to be obedient, even if it means travelling all over the world and staying in expensive hotels, and earning huge amounts of money. The only drawback at the moment, he said, is that his father wants him to work in the family fruit shop in the High Street.

Said that if he's going to spend the rest of his life selling bananas and turnips to fat old ladies he might as well die right now.

Young Elsie, who was listening, flushed with sympathetic indignation, and said she would stand by William to the 'absolute death', and anyway, they both felt led to carry on and make Bad News For The Devil into one of the greatest Christian rock bands of all time.

Felt rather flattered being taken into their confidence until, on the way home, Gerald said, 'Sorry you had to listen to all that, Dad. They say the same thing to anyone who's stupid enough to stand and listen. They're just loopy about each other.'

Got my own back later on when, after much thought, I was able to announce that 'Gerald Plass' was an anagram of 'All pa's dregs'. Gerald gave me another of those 'pig dancing Swan Lake' looks. Think he was quite impressed really, though.

Anne says we ought to visit another of her Great aunts tomorrow, Aunt Felicity, who used to be married to a sailor. Suppose I'll have to go. Somehow I always end up feeling depressed after an encounter with this particular old lady. Oh, well, it probably won't be too bad. They say she's got very senile lately.

Saturday February 1st

Off in the car this morning to visit Aunt Felicity at the Eight Bells Home for Maritime Relics. Anne went into the room first to explain quietly that we'd come to visit while I waited outside the open door.

Anne said, 'Hello, Auntie, it's Anne, your niece. I've come to see you. Adrian's here too – he's just outside the door.'

''E can't be,' replied Aunt Felicity in a shrill squawk, ''e's dead, thank gawd!'

'Now Auntie,' said Anne, 'you know you don't mean that really. Look, here he is now, come to visit you.'

Aunt Felicity sat up a little, inspected me closely with her beady little black eyes as I walked into the room, and then relaxed back onto her pillow, and squawked triumphantly, 'There you are! Told yer! I said 'e was dead!'

Felt a bit non-plussed. Leaned right over her and said in a loud voice, 'Auntie, it's me! Adrian! I'm alive!'

She stared up at me for a moment, then said dispassionately, 'You want to get 'im cremated, Anne love, 'fore 'e starts to smell.'

Gave up and said nothing for the rest of the visit. There's something deeply discouraging about being in the same room as someone who's convinced that you're a corpse.

Sunday February 2nd

Lay awake for some time last night, thinking about getting old like Auntie Felicity, and dying all alone in some nursing home. Wanted to wake Anne and Gerald up and do something like playing Monopoly – all cosy together. In the middle of the night I'd have gladly given up my glorious resurrection if we could just stay as we are. I don't want to die!'

If I'd known George Farmer was leading the service this morning I wouldn't have gone. He started by shouting things at the congregation in a loud, thirty-six-visions-before-breakfast sort of voice.

G.F.: Good morning!

CONGR: (feebly) Morning . . .

G.F.: (Not satisfied) I said GOOD MORNING!!

CONGR: (forcing slightly more volume out between tired tonsils) Good morning!

G.F.: Are we joyful?

CONGR: (in a strangled bleat, like a herd of dyspeptic sheep) Ye-e-e-s

G.F.: Well we don't *sound* very joyful! I'll ask you again! ARE WE JOYFUL?

CONGR: (Panicked into believing that lack of volume is a sin) Y-E-E-E-s!

G.F.: That's more like it! And are we glad to be in the House of God this morning?

CONGR: (Playing the game well now) Y-E-E-E-S!!

G.F.: (Cupping his hand playfully round his ear) And where do we all hope to go one day?

CONGR: H-E-A-V-E-N!!

minus one

THYNN: T-E-N-E-R-I-F-E!! (Pause – all look at Thynn)

THYNN: Sorry – H-E-A-V-E-N!!

As a token of appreciation I passed Leonard my penultimate fruit-gum. Greater love hath no man . . .

Just before Anne went up to bed tonight, I said, 'You know all the business about death and going to heaven, and all that?'

'Yes,' said Anne, yawning loudly.

'Well – I'm completely confused about it.'

Anne smiled a very weary smile. 'Well there's one thing, darling. At least you're consistent.'

Was that a compliment? I've been sitting here for half an hour since Anne went up, and I'm still not sure.

It's good to be consistent – isn't it? Surely?

Monday February 3rd

I don't want to die.

Gerald invited Vernon Rawlings and William Farmer round this evening. They're all young. They don't even think about dying. All William Farmer thinks about is the band, and how badly he's getting on with his dad. It appears that George left him in charge of the shop for half an hour on Saturday, with clear instructions to write a big sign to go over the fruit and veg., out on the pavement. Unfortunately, William was so distracted by the sight of Elsie unpacking the water-melons that he left out a vital word, and when George came back he found a little crowd of people outside the shop all picking up fruit and squashing it in their hands. When George asked them what on earth they were doing, a fat little girl holding a plum in one fist and a peach in the other, nodded towards the sign that William had propped up against the shop window and said, "S'alright – look!'

The sign said 'PLEASE DO SQUEEZE THE FRUIT'

William said that when his father stormed, wild eyed, into the back room, where he and Elsie were counting each other's fillings, and shouted, 'There's no not in it! With no not it means do! Why the hell didn't you put a not in it!', he thought his dad had gone completely mad. It didn't help that Elsie, who is a very spirited, if rather foolhardy girl, put her hands on her hips, looked George straight in the eye, and said, 'Now's your chance to *prove* you're a Christian, Mr Farmer!'

Poor old George. I don't think I would have felt very Christian if someone had just crushed my fruit. Still, he was alright by Sunday morning. *He* seems to be looking forward to dying and going to heaven. Rang Richard Cook tonight and asked him what *he* was most looking forward to about going to heaven. He cleared his throat into religious gear and said, 'I am looking forward to being able to worship and adore the Lord for all eternity. What greater joy can there be than this?'

Well, of course I go along with that. I mean – yes, absolutely …

Tuesday February 4th

Still feeling gloomy about death. Keep looking round at all the old familiar people and things, then trying to imagine swapping them for something like one of our Sunday meetings only going on for ever, instead of an hour and a half. Gerald tried to cheer me up by pointing out that Ishmael is an anagram of 'I lash 'em!'

Nearly smiled.

Wednesday February 5th

Am I a Christian? Don't want to die.

Don't want to go to heaven. Certainly don't want to go to hell. Asked Anne tonight if she thought I'd enjoy heaven. She said, 'Only if they give you your own special little corner to moan in.'

Charming! When have I ever moaned?

Thursday February 6th

Frank Braddock round tonight after study-group. Just appeared at the door, strode through to the sitting room, and collapsed in an armchair. Still don't know if he's a Christian, even after what happened next. The doorbell rang and Anne came in after a few seconds with Mrs Flushpool who said she'd discovered the loss of an intimate personal item after arriving home from the study-group, and as she wasn't sure how long it would be before Anne tidied up again, and she didn't want to put temptation in anyone's way, she thought she'd just pop back to see if it had slipped down behind a cushion. No sign of whatever unspeakable object she was looking for, so she turned her attention to Frank Braddock, sitting happily in a little cloud of sweet-smelling tobacco smoke. I introduced him.

'Well, Mr Braddock,' she said, lips pursed in diapproval 'and are you one of the elect?'

Braddock stared at her for a moment, rose slowly to his feet, and spoke with deep gravity and immense dignity.

'Madam,' he said, 'I am a member of the M.C.C..'

'And what, pray, is the M.C.C.?'

Braddock replied with deep reverence. 'The Marylebone Cricket Club, Madam.'

Momentarily taken aback, Mrs Flushpool rallied her forces, gave the black plastic bags a little shake, and returned to the attack.

'And may I ask, Mr Braddock, how membership of this *club* will be of assistance to you when you stand before the judgement seat, and things of the natural are of no account?'

Braddock's gaze was unwavering.

'My M.C.C. membership card, madam, guarantees me, at any time, and at all times, admission to the Lords Enclosure.'

Mrs Flushpool tried hard to think of a reply to this, but it was clear that she was defeated, and she hadn't even *started* on the pipe! After murmuring something perfunctory, she was gone, leaving Anne hugging herself with satisfaction, and Frank puffing away calmly in the armchair.

As Frank left later, I said, 'You still haven't told me, you know. *Are* you a Christian?'

'Guess!' he said, just like last time.

Later I asked Anne if *she* thought he was a Christian. She laughed helplessly. 'You are a funny man,' she said. 'Of course he is!'

Friday February 7th

I don't want to die, despite the ludicrous evening I've just been through.

Elsie Burlesford rang me when I got home tonight. She said I'd been so understanding last week she thought I might agree to talk to William's father about his cruel treatment of his only son. Reminded Elsie that William has two brothers. 'Well, one of his only sons then,' she said.

Rather pleased to be asked really. Said I'd do what I could. She said thanks, and could I not tell William she'd phoned, as he was very independent and brave, and wouldn't want help from anyone else.

Five minutes later William phoned to ask if I'd mind having a word with his dad about the band meeting tonight. Apparently George told him on Saturday that part of his punishment would be not going to B.N.F.T.D. practice for two weeks. Could I possibly change his mind, and would I mind not telling Elsie he'd phoned as she was very sensitive and mustn't be upset? Said I'd have a go. Felt a bit like Henry Kissinger.

Ten minutes later Gerald came crashing in to ask if I'd try to get William's dad to let him come to band practice this evening. Didn't wait for an answer. Just said 'Thanks, dad,' and rushed off again, then rushed back to ask if I could please not tell William or Elsie that he'd asked, because he knew they'd hate to think anyone was interfering. Rushed off again, shouting, 'Ta, dad! You're a real pal. See you later!'

The moment the door slammed the phone rang. It was Anne. She'd stopped off on her way to late shopping to ring me. She'd run into Elsie Burlesford a little earlier and heard about how upset William was. 'The poor little girl's in a terrible state about it all,' said Anne. 'George likes you. Can't you give him a ring and suggest a chat. Oh, and don't tell Elsie I told you. It was all strictly confidential. You know what Elsie's like! See you later, darling. Bye – love you!'

Felt a bit dazed as I put the phone down. Felt even more dazed when it rang *again*. It was Edwin, Elsie's father. Said that Elsie had just been expressing the view that George Farmer needed to be delivered from a spirit of intolerance and anger, and was Edwin, as her father, and the Elder of her church, prepared to 'see to it'.

'The thing is,' sighed Edwin, 'you know what old George is like. It's nothing to do with a spirit of anything. He's just a very passionate type, and, sometimes he goes over the top. After all young William was a *bit* careless. Anyway, what I was going to

239

say was that George thinks a lot of you, so why don't you talk to him – cool him down a bit? Elsie's going to burst if something doesn't happen soon. She'll be up at the Farmer's with a wooden stake and a sprig of garlic before long. Oh, and, if you don't mind, keep this call to yourself, Elsie didn't want anyone but me to know how she felt. Is that okay?'

'Yes, but . . .'

'Super! See you on Sunday. Cheers!'

My only consolation as I put the phone down yet again, was that there was no-one else left to ring. Made the fatal mistake of getting into the bath. I'd just said, 'Aaaah!' as I sank back into the hot water, when the damned thing rang *again*. Went back down in a towel, determined to give short shrift to whichever member of the Elsie Burlesford fan club was on my back now. Sensitive indeed! From what I'd seen of Elsie she was about as sensitive as an avalanche. Picked up the phone.

'Ah! Hello, Adrian – hope I'm not interrupting anything.'

'Ah, George,' I said, 'I was going to ring you about . . .'

'Listen, brother!', boomed George. 'I need a favour from you. Y'see . . . well, fact is I got a bit snappy with young William the other day – little blighter forgot to put a not in it . . . anyway, in the heat of the moment I said he had to miss band practice for a couple of weeks, and – well, I guess I got a bit carried away really. Thing is, I want to let him off, but I don't want him to think I've gone soft. So . . .'

'Yes George?'

'So would you mind if I told him that you'd talked me into changing my mind. Would that be alright, brother? Would it?'

'Yes George, that's fine. You go ahead. Goodbye, George.'

Went back to my not quite hot enough bath and said to God, 'You *do* work in mysterious ways, don't you?'

Later, at Unity Hall, after William's usual impression of a man who's stubbed toes on both his feet, Elsie came up and gazed at me with wide admiring eyes.

'D'you know who you remind me of, Mr Plass, even to look at, a bit?'

Here we go, I thought, the old Henry Kissinger bit. Ah, well, a spot of hero-worship never did anyone any harm.

'Who's that then?' I asked.

'Claire Raynor,' said Elsie.

Saturday February 8th

Thought there might be something in the Christian bookshop about confusion. When I asked the shopkeeper, he said, 'Confusion?!' as though I'd asked for a bag of coal. Finally unearthed a tape cassette at the back of the Christian Plumbing shelf entitled 'Collected Correctional Courses for Confused Christians', by Doctor William Worplesdon, or 'Windolene Worplesdon' as he is commonly known. Settled down this evening to listen. Really looking forward to some clear teaching about death and heaven and all the things I've been worrying about. This is how the tape began:

'My name is Worplesdon. Greetings to you, confused brother, or confused sister. My message divides into three sections, the first of which consists of two parts, Part "A" being approached from four perspectives, the most immediate of which can be sub-divided into two areas, the initial one breaking down into four main categories, beginning with a multi-faceted topic, the primary facet being contained under six main headings, and I would like to look at number one from two points of view, the first consisting of five components, the commencing item of which falls naturally into seven sections, starting with a three point introduction to part one of the opening item in the first stage of the primary point of a six-step argument on the subject of confusion in the church ...'

Must have been the click of the cassette player switching itself off that woke me up. I dread to think what Worplesdon's like when he's speaking to people who *aren't* confused.

Dragged myself miserably upstairs to bed. Anne's asleep so I can't talk to her. Gerald's left a note on my pillow to say that Alvin Stardust is an anagram of 'I trust vandals', and now *he's* fast asleep.

There's just me – me and God.

Help me, God! I'm confused....

Sunday February 9th

That monk who came at Christmas was in church again today. Edwin had asked him to do a question and answer session. Put my fruit-gums away unopened. Father John looked pale and tired, but I honestly thought they'd rigged a spotlight up at the back because there seemed to be a sort of shininess round his face as he sat quietly on a stool at the front.

Mrs Flushpool asked the first question.

She said, 'I find it strange, reverend – I cannot call you Father as I have scriptural reservations – that on your previous visit you barely mentioned the judgement of God on sin committed in the natural. Perhaps you do not feel sinful?'

Father John blinked. 'Oh, I'm a ratbag,' he declared, with enthusiasm, 'but I do feel so *very* forgiven. You see, God's crazy about me, just as he's crazy about you. Salvation was his idea you know – not ours.' He pointed at Mrs Flushpool. 'If you were to commit a foul sin with every person in your street, and then you said to God "I really am honestly and sincerely most awfully sorry," he would say, "Great! Let's start all over again." Marvellous, isn't it?'

Mrs Flushpool, presumably wrestling inwardly with the image of herself committing foul sins with every person in her street, splashed back down into her seat, looking rather breathless.

Leonard Thynn leaned across and whispered in my ear, 'He knows a different God to the one I do. His God's *nice!*'

Suddenly found myself on my feet. Felt about six years old as I spoke.

'I don't want to die ...'

'No,' said Father John, 'neither do I. Life can be very good. I'm sure Jesus didn't want to die either. His friends and family, the natural world, laughter, tears, work – he loved it all I'm sure.'

'But heaven – the idea of heaven seems so ... I don't know ...'

'What is your name?' asked the monk.

'Adrian ...'

'Adrian, what are you interested in – *really* interested in, I mean?'

'Cricket.' Didn't mean to tell the truth. It just slipped out.

242

'So,' said Father John, 'for you, Adrian, God has to make sure that heaven is at least as exciting and stimulating and satisfying as scoring a century against Australia at Lords. Is that your wife sitting next to you?'

Anne smiled and nodded.

'If Adrian keels over suddenly, my dear, and he's on the point of death, you'll know what to do now?'

'Yes,' laughed Anne, 'I'll buckle a pair of pads on him – quick.'

Felt as if someone had opened a window and let air into a stuffy room. Went home for a very enjoyable lunch. I invited Leonard who brought *three* bottles of wine! Anne and I, knowing poor old Leonard's problems in this area, drank as much of it as we could before he could get his hands on it. Leonard stayed sober, Anne seemed unaffected, but I ended up in the same position as the football team that Gerald supports – struggling at the foot of the table....

Monday February 10th

I HAVE BEEN HAPPY ALL DAY!!!

Still don't want to die, but I have a feeling it's all in hand.

Insisted we all went to the cinema tonight. When we got there we found it was a choice between 'Confessions of a Brain-damaged Tomato', and 'Lucky the Lonely Raccoon'.

Didn't want to just go home again, so we watched the raccoon film. Anne and I quite enjoyed it, but Gerald said he used the time to work out that Sheila Walsh is an anagram of 'Lah, she wails!'

Thank goodness none of these people will ever see my diary!

Tuesday February 11th

On the way home today, met Mr Lamberton-Pincney, who runs a little group called 'Spot it and Stop it' in the church. They look for things to ban. Mr Lamberton-Pincney, who insists on his full name at all times, said that the group's annual outing was due this week, but as yet the nature of the event was undecided.

Told him about the cinema. I said, 'There's "Confessions of a Brain-damaged Tomato" on Studio One.' Mr Lamberton-Pincney winced in horror. 'Or there's a sort of nature film on at Studio Two.'

'Hmmm . . .,' he said, 'that *might* be appropriate. You are sure it is not – unsuitable?'

'Oh, yes,' I said, 'Anne and Gerald and I saw it last night. It's just a film about wild creatures doing – well, wild things. Real family entertainment.'

Mr Lamberton-Pincney said that he would probably take his group to the film on Friday evening. 'You are *sure*,' he said as we parted, 'that it is a *suitable* film?'

'Oh, yes,' I replied airily, 'quite harmless.'

Wednesday February 12th

Edwin rang this morning to say that there's going to be a special healing meeting on Wednesday week, led by a visiting speaker from the north. Places would be limited, so did I want to reserve some seats? Said I'd ring back in five minutes. Lay on my back on the hall floor with the soles of my shoes against the front door, and after wriggling about a bit, discovered that my legs were exactly the same length as each other. Wish I'd realised that Anne and Gerald were watching from the kitchen. I'd like to have ten pounds for every time I've seen that mixture of compassion and anxiety on their faces when they look at me.

Gerald strolled into the hall with a sort of therapeutic casualness, and said, 'Don't worry, Dad. We won't let anyone in that you don't want to see.'

Silly boy! He must have *known* there was a rational explanation. Told him about Edwin's call.

'The thing is,' I explained, 'that most of these healing meetings nowadays seem to end up with a lot of sick people finding that the root of their problems is one leg being longer than the other, so I was just checking mine before ringing Edwin back.'

'And . . . ?' said Anne, who'd joined us.

'Well . . . I think they're the same, so I'll call him back and say I'd like to go.'

'And if one *had* been shorter than the other?' asked Gerald, looking even more puzzled.

'Well, then I wouldn't have gone, of course,' I replied, trying not to sound too impatient.

'In case you got healed?' queried Anne.

'Exactly! What could be more embarrassing?'

Rang Edwin and asked him to reserve three seats, then left for work, conscious that Anne and Gerald were still standing in the hall staring blankly at me as I went out of the door.

Not the first time I've noticed this dullness of intellect, especially in Gerald. Quite recently, for instance, he tried to persuade me that I should buy my petrol at a different garage a little further away, because they charge a few pence per gallon less than my usual one. I pointed out to him that as I always buy five pounds worth of petrol, the difference in price per gallon wouldn't affect me. Talk about stubborn! He ended up kneeling on the floor punching cushions. Just couldn't accept being wrong. Still – he's young.

Thursday February 13th

Gloria Marsh came to the study-group tonight. Doesn't often come.

A very attractive widow lady.

Not that I'm in the slightest attracted to her of course, though I do think *she* has a bit of thing about *me*. When she came in Gerald leaned over and whispered, 'Pull your stomach in, Dad, Gloria's here.'

Ridiculous!

When old Mrs Thynn said, in the course of discussion, that she had been a believer from childhood to adultery, everyone smiled, but Gloria *winked* at me! Tried to look shocked and disapproving in a desirable sort of way. Not easy. Really embarrassed later on when someone asked Gloria to describe what Christian forgiveness really meant. She said it meant that when someone smacks you on the bottom you have to turn the other cheek. Although she wasn't looking at me when she said this, I could feel my face reddening for some reason. Hope no-one noticed.

At coffee time Gloria made a beeline for me, and was soon confiding in me her problems about a large telephone bill which is beyond her means. Suddenly occurred to me that I could help. Popped upstairs and wrote a cheque, then handed it to Gloria just as she left. Went through to the kitchen and told Anne.

'You should've seen her face,' I said, 'surprised isn't the word.'

'I'm quite *sure* it isn't, dear,' said Anne, rather tartly, I thought.

Gloria rang a little later, reversing the charges, to thank me again for the money. Called me a honey-pot. Said to Anne jokingly, "Why don't you ever call me a honey-pot, Anne?"

She said, 'Because you're not one, darling.'

Friday February 14th

Woke at 6.00 a.m., and remembered with a shock that today is Valentine's day. Dragged my clothes on as quietly as I could, crept out of the house, and staggered up to the corner shop.

Found a little clutch of haggard-looking husbands sorting through the remaining Valentine cards. Ended up with a card that had a picture on the front of a cow's backside, with the cow looking round and saying 'I LOVE YOU'. Then, when you opened the card, it said, 'FROM THE HEART OF MY BOTTOM'.

When Anne opened it at breakfast-time she said, 'Oh, darling, you're an incurable romantic. You must have spent hours choosing this.'

She laughed though. Gave me a beautiful card and a long lingering kiss over the marmalade, interrupted by Gerald coming in and saying, 'Your tie's coming to a sticky end, Dad.'

Intrigued to see that Gerald received one of those huge padded cards, with an enormous velvet heart on the front, and hundreds of kisses done in biro on the inside. No name, though.

I said, 'Who's the secret admirer then, Gerald?'

'It's probably a joint offering from all the local girls,' he answered coolly, but you could tell he was pleased. Gerald's never had a real girlfriend – not that I'm worried about that.

Why should I be? I'm not. Never have been.

Rather surprised tonight to see that Elsie walked home from band practice with Gerald, to 'help carry his guitar'. Hope the girl who sent that Valentine didn't see them together. It might give her the wrong idea and put her off. Stupid of Elsie, when she's so devoted to William.

Saturday February 15th

Woke up with one of those rare, everything's-alright feelings. Strolled down to the shop for a loaf of bread after breakfast. Walking back, couldn't help reflecting that, although I might make the odd small mistake from time to time, generally speaking I get things right.

Felt quite a warm glow inside despite the cold.

Disconcerted to discover, when I got back to my front gate and glanced through the living-room window, that Mr Lamberton-Pincney was there, sitting on our most uncomfortable chair, and looking *very* grim.

Hid in the garage for a while reading the sports news in a ten-year-old newspaper and hoping he'd go away. Driven in by the cold in the end. Last bit of warm glow evaporated as Anne met me at the door and hissed, 'You're an idiot! You're an absolute pea-brained dumbo! Why didn't you check they'd be showing the same film Friday that they showed on Monday? I don't understand how you can be so stupid!'

Gathered something had gone pretty wrong.

Mr Lamberton-Pincney addressed me in Vincent Price tones.

'Following your guidance, Mr Plass,' he said ominously, 'myself and my little group attended the Studio Two cinema presentation yesterday. Being a little late, we purchased our tickets hurriedly, and entered without pausing to peruse the customary publicity material. After all ... '

He fixed me with an accusing frown.

'We had the word of a brother Christian that the entertainment was not ... unsuitable.'

Cleared my throat nervously. 'What err ... was the err ... actual film that you actually err ... ?'

Mr Lamberton-Pincney braced himself. 'The film, Mr Plass, was entitled "Hot Thighs in Wet Grass".'

Tried to explain and apologise. Mr Lamberton-Pincney accepted my apology heavily, then left, glancing suspiciously to left and right when he reached the road, as though he was frightened of being run over by something obscene.

'There's one thing, Dad,' said Gerald, who'd been listening outside the door, 'you did tell Mr Thingummy-Whatsit the film was about wild creatures doing wild things . . . '

'And . . . ?'

'Well, from what I've heard about "Hot Thighs in Wet Grass", that'll be exactly what he saw!'

Anne called out from the kitchen, 'Where's my loaf?'

Thought for a moment. 'In the garage,' I called back.

Anne came through and stood staring at me.

Gerald said gently, 'You'll never get the car in the bread bin you know, Dad.'

Anne went off muttering, 'It won't be the *bread* bin he ends up in . . . '

Sunday February 16th

Wish there was an easy way of knowing when thoughts are just thoughts, and not messages from God. Had a thought just after quiet-time today. Just came into my head suddenly.

'Buy a tree-frog and call it Kaiser Bill.'

Sounds utterly absurd, but why should a thought like that just pop up from nowhere? Was going to tell Anne and Gerald but decided (especially after yesterday) I would just be inviting ridicule, like Richard and his impaled jellyfish. I've written the words down on a piece of paper, and put it in the inside pocket of my second best suit. After all, you never know!

Off to church.

Found that old Ephraim Trench, one of the local farmers was preaching.

Only preaches twice a year or so. Dear old fellow, but makes a real meal out of saying hardly anything at all.

Stood up today after the worship, took out a huge silver pocket-watch on a chain, checked it against the wall-clock, checked it again against Edwin's wristwatch, checked it once more to be sure against young Vernon Rawling's amazing digital chronometer, which Gerald says would probably cook a three course meal for you if you pressed the buttons in the right order, then laid the watch solemnly down on the table in front of him, and drew from his trouser pocket an enormous white handkerchief.

Treated us to a virtuoso display of nose-blowing such as has never before been seen or heard in our church. Seemed to go on for hours. Featured very fair impressions of most known wind instruments, varying from long high trumpeting blasts, to deep, sonorous, tuba-like effects. At last the old man tucked the sheet-size piece of material back into his pocket, and was just about to pick up his Bible, when the clock struck the hour and Ephraim, after counting the strokes carefully, picked his pocket-watch up again and made further minute adjustments before replacing it on the table. One or two people who'd had nothing to say Hallelu-jah about for ten minutes, were getting a bit restless, especially as, for one awful moment, it looked as if the old chap was going for the handkerchief pocket again, but it was a false alarm. With maddening slowness, he drew his spectacles out of the other trouser pocket, cleaned them meticulously with a soft cloth, and finally put them on. Picked up his well-thumbed old Authorised Version, and peered sternly round the room like an old-fashioned Sunday School teacher.

'Roight!' he said, ' 'ere we go! 'Smornin' we're gonna look at a psalm ain't we? We're gonna look at psalm twenny-three! An' oi'm 'appy to say, the Lorrrd 'as revealed to me a way of foindin' it quick-like in moi bible, an' oi'm gonna pass it on to all of you 'ere 'smorning'! It goes loike – as follers.'

Ephraim spoke in prophetic tones.

'Psalm twenny-three can easily be found moi brothers an' sis-ters, 'cause the Lorrrd in 'is wisdom 'as placed it immediate after psalm twenny-two an' just previous to psalm twenny-four! Allylooyer!'

Gerald and Anne and I said, 'Hallelujah!' very loudly to support Ephraim. He's a good old chap.

Elsie round this afternoon to ask Gerald's advice about a song she's writing. Must be taking her music very seriously to give up an afternoon when she could have been with William. Gerald showed me a copy of her song later. It begins like this:

> I'm in love with someone special,
> He means so much to me,
> He's a very lovely person,
> And his name begins with 'G'.

Said to Anne tonight how great I thought it was that a girl of Elsie's age could write such a positive song about God. She looked at me rather oddly. Don't know why.

Monday February 17th

Something interesting this evening. Heard next door's front gate click open and clang shut, and when I looked out of the hall window (to see what the weather was doing) I saw that monk, Father John, waiting at Frank Braddock's front door. Rushed through to the kitchen and found some empty milk bottles to put out on the step. Got out there just in time to see Braddock throw open his door, and shout, 'Bungles! Well, stap me vitals! Come on in, mate.'

The monk, chuckling, and saying something that sounded like, 'Avast there, Smelly', disappeared into the house and shut the door behind him.

Interesting!!

Felt a twinge of my old back trouble this evening. Hope it doesn't get any worse. I'd hate to miss that healing meeting on Wednesday week. I want to actually *see* someone being healed.

Tuesday February 18th

Spent a pleasant hour with the Doves after work today. Kitty rather poorly, but still twinkling and smiling. Told them about my problems over dying and going to heaven and messing up Mr

Thingummybob-Pincney's outing and – well, everything really. Bill said I was a very unusual person, and Kitty said God must be using all these mistakes and problems to train me up for a special job that only I could do. Never thought of it like that. Felt quite bright when I left.

Bill walked down to the front gate with me, and told me quietly that Kitty's going into hospital soon for tests, but she doesn't want a fuss made.

Told Anne and Gerald about Kitty when I got home. I said a little prayer, and we all said 'Amen!', louder than usual.

Leonard round to play Scrabble with Gerald and I tonight. I got told off for taking too long as usual and Leonard kept putting down words like 'vquex', which, according to Thynn, is defined in the full length Oxford Dictionary as 'a cross between a ferret and a giraffe'. Gerald objected on the grounds that the mating act would be geometrically impossible between two such animals, and the rest of the conversation became rather more ribaldly vulgar than I care to record in what is after all a Christian diary.

Back still a little painful. Laughed immoderately on the stairs when Gerald said that Gavin Reid is an anagram of 'vain dirge', and gave it a bit of a twist.

Wednesday February 19th

Can't help worrying that Gerald's getting obsessional about these anagrams. Came downstairs at one o'clock this morning after hearing a noise, and found Gerald still up in the sitting room clutching a pencil and surrounded by pieces of paper with letters scribbled all over them. Looked at me with wild triumphant eyes, and said "Vile creed!'

Backed off a bit nervously.

'Eric Delve!' he said, waving one of the sheets of paper. 'Eric Delve is an anagram of Vile creed!'

Went back to bed. Honestly! Stupid boy!

Felt led during quiet-time this morning, to give poor, quaint old Mr Brain, our ex-actor neighbor, a little financial gift. Remembered that verse in the bible about giving secretly. Didn't even tell Anne what I was doing. Popped it through his letterbox in a plain envelope when I got home from work. Hung about for a bit, hoping he'd spot me through the window.

Edwin popped in tonight. Says he's invited a special guest speaker, Dwight Hackenbacker, who's a Californian, to talk about the 'Gifts', on Sunday.

Thursday February 20th

Couldn't help feeling a sort of glow inside all day at work, thinking of Mr Brain's pleasure. What a joy and a privilege it is to give!!

Had a discussion at study-group tonight about unity in the church, and whether it was a good thing or not. Richard Cook said he didn't mind as long as we didn't have to change the way we worship, or mix with people from other churches who were not 'truly in The Way'.

Old Mrs Thynn said that she didn't mind getting together with other Christians, but she didn't want to have to go into the sort of churches where you walked through the door and 'all you could smell was incest'.

252

We all laughed, but Edwin said we should take this important subject seriously, and reflect on the fact that we are all parts of the Body of the church, and therefore need each other.

Good discussion after that, ending with each of us saying what part of the body we thought we were. Anne started, by saying that she thought she was probably a bit of dried skin on the elbow, but Edwin, bless him, said that he thought she was much nearer the *heart* than that.

Haven't seen Anne blush like that for ages!

Rather fortunately, I thought, Gerald got up to answer the telephone in the hall at this point. As he squeezed past Richard, he said, 'Excuse me Richard, but you are truly in the way.'

We all agreed that Edwin is an ear, because he's good at listening, and George Farmer said he knew he was a mouth. Thynn said he was a left shoulder blade for some obscure reason, and Norma Twill said she thought she might be a dimple. Couldn't think what *I* was, and dismissed Thynn's assessment of me as a small, unimportant vein in the right foot. All good fun really!

Gerald reappeared just as we were winding up, and said he'd thought of a good name for the church if all the denominations formed a united group.

'It's simple,' he said, 'we'll call ourselves the Maptocostal Angloholics!'

Asked Gerald later who he'd been on the phone to all that time.

'Oh,' he said, 'that was Elsie ringing up to say she'd finished her song, and just ... chatting.'

Quite pleased really. Must be good for a girl like Elsie to have a close platonic friendship with a member of the opposite sex. Said this to Anne at bedtime. She laughed and said something quite inexplicable.

'Darling, if you ever decide to have a secret affair, you'd better let me organise it.'

Friday February 21st

Came home from work tonight to find a note on the mat addressed to me.

Dear Mr Plass,

In the remote past you took possession of my excellent mechanical hedge trimmer. You described the transaction as a 'loan'. Possibly the terms 'loan' and 'theft' are synonymous in your vocabulary. If not, perhaps you would return my property. Otherwise I must invite you to explain your verbal idiosyncrasies to my solicitors, from whom you will shortly hear.

From your frail elderly victim,
Percival X Brain.

Showed it to Anne. She said, 'What a scream! He's a real character, isn't he?'

I said, 'Yes, Anne. He's a real character.'

Took the blasted trimmer round to the silly old fool. When he came to the door I said, 'Anything good happened this week, Mr Brain?'

Brain said, 'The Lord has provided, young man, through some soul whose nature it is to give rather than take. A lesson there for *you*, Plass! A lesson!'

Wagged his finger at me. I nearly trimmed it. Went home and sulked for an hour. In the end Anne tickled me from behind and said, 'Aaah … Diddums got the sulkie-wulkies 'cos nasty Mr Brainy-Wainy finks diddums is a big nasty man. …'

Couldn't help smiling. Sulk ruined.

Gerald in late tonight from B.N.F.T.D. practice, looking very thoughtful. Asked him what was up. He said, 'Nothing for you to worry your pretty little head about, Dad. Just band stuff – you know.'

Saturday February 22nd

Secret giving's hard!!!

At the moment I feel like strangling Brain, and telling him about the money just before he dies. Fine Christian I am! Asked God to make me a better person.

No noticeable improvement by this evening.

So there can't be a God after all, can there?

1.30 a.m. Didn't mean that last bit. Just being flippant. Course there is.

Sunday February 23rd

To church.

Dwight Hackenbacker, the Californian, spoke powerfully about Word of Knowledge. He said it was a gift for today's church, and that we could all practise it 'RIGHT NOW!' if we really wanted to.

There was a short silence, then young Vernon Rawlings stood up, pointed dramatically at Ephraim Trench's youngest girl, Bessie, and said, 'You've got a pain in your lower abdomen!'

Bessie went pink and said she hadn't.

Vernon said she had.

Bessie said she hadn't.

Vernon said she had.

Then Bessie said she hadn't, and she should know because it was *her* lower abdomen.

Vernon said that he *knew* she had a pain in her lower abdomen, and perhaps she didn't have the faith to feel it. Edwin stepped in then, thank goodness. I think if I'd heard the words 'lower abdomen' once more I'd have gone mad.

At coffee time some people seemed a bit confused. Deaf old Mrs Thynn asked Dwight if Word of Knowledge was made by the same people as Cluedo and Monopoly, because she'd like to give it to her grandson for his birthday.

Left early, feeling flat. Brain on my mind.

Monday February 24th

Edwin popped in just after tea. 'Just to tell you,' he said, 'how pleased the Lord is about your generosity to Mr Brain.'

I just stared. 'How on earth did ... ?'

Edwin smiled. 'You were at church on Sunday, weren't you? See you later!'

Went round to Mr Brain's house later. Said I'd come to see if there was anything I could do for him. He said the most useful thing I could do was drink a pint of his home-made bitter, and listen to some stories about his experiences as a 'thespian'.

Awful beer, but I drank every drop. Excellent stories – enjoyed every word. As I left he said, 'I would be obliged, young man, if in the future, you would address me as "Percy", a more informal, and significantly less cranial term than "Brain". By the way, I feel it incumbent upon me to offer you something in the way of an apology for the style and content of my recent communication to you. The fact is . . .'

The old man suddenly looked very vulnerable.

'The fact is that I am, as it were, devoid of familial comforts, and I had entertained hopes that the loan of my trimming machine might have signalled the commencement of a . . . might have marked the genesis of . . . of a relationship. I fear that disappointment was the main motivator for my somewhat aggressive missal. Perhaps we might now consider ourselves to have embarked on a . . . on a . . .'

'Friendship?', I suggested.

'Precisely!' said Percy, beaming happily. 'A friendship. Precisely! Ale and conversation! We shall be friends and brothers!'

Isn't God nice sometimes!

(I mean *all* the time, of course. Sorry God.)

Tuesday February 25th

Got up early this morning to check the length of my legs again, ready for the healing meeting tomorrow night. As far as I can reasonably tell, they are absolutely identical, so that's that.

Confessed everything I could possibly think of in my quiet-time, so that no-one in the meeting can minister to some secret sin in my life, and did a few exercises to check my back's alright. No pain at all, so it's all systems go for tomorrow. I'd just like to see one person really healed. That would be really amazing! Not an internal organ or something that you can't see. I want to see someone get out of a wheelchair, or throw away their crutches – that sort of thing.

Not that I don't believe God can do it, of course. I know he can. He *does* do it! I've read about it. I just . . . want to see it.

Gerald has suggested we have a party soon. Anne thinks it's a good idea too, so we've decided to have it on Friday week, as long as the rest of Gerald's band don't mind missing a practice.

Gerald said, 'Is it going to be a Christian party or a real party?'

Didn't know what he meant.

'What do you mean by a Christian party?'

'*You* know,' he said, 'all flans and fruit juice. Let's have some french bread, and different cheeses and a few bottles of plonk, then we can ask all sorts of people.'

I know what Gerald means, but there are some of my non-Christian friends who I'd be a bit nervous about putting in the same room as a lot of wine and some of my *Christian* friends. I'll have to give it some thought.

Wednesday February 26th

Went through yesterday morning's routine again today. All well. Roll on tonight!

Set off to walk down to Unity Hall with Gerald and Anne at about 7.15. Felt quite excited really. Our seats were around the middle, not too far forward. The evening started with choruses, led by one of those people who Gerald says have 'A' levels in Ecstasy. All very enjoyable until someone went up to the front and whispered something into the ecstatic fellow's ear. When she'd finished, he spoke to us in one of those close-to-the-microphone voices.

'That sister has shared with me her feeling that the Lord is saying there are folk here who are not released in physical expression of their joy. He would have them know the joy of true freedom in worship.'

Adopted my expression of prayerful calm concern.

Took years to develop – absolutely essential in this sort of situation. With a slight swaying motion that could possibly be construed as dancing, and a subdued but dignified handclap, I can get through most of these awful periods without too much trouble.

Gerald is much cruder. Just ignores it all. He leaned over and whispered in my ear.

'We'll find that "sister" afterwards, and duff her up, shall we?'

Disappointed to note, as the speaker rose to his feet at last, that there were no wheelchairs or crutches in evidence. Still, you can't have everything.

Jolly good, simple talk by the speaker. Very down to earth – northern accent. At the end of his main talk, he said, 'Right, now it's not much use coming down here and talking about how God can heal, if at the end of it all, nobody is. So let's have a look at you!'

Sat back happily, confident in the knowledge that my legs were the same length and my back didn't hurt.

He said, 'Right, first of all there's a young lady here who has injured her arm in the kitchen this morning. The Lord's going to sort it out, so step up quick, we've got a lot to get through.'

A girl stood up looking dazed and incredulous, and went up to the front. She had a bandage on her arm. After he'd prayed over the arm, the speaker said, 'Well, come on, take the bandage off! Hold your arm up and let 'em all see what God's done for you!'

She held her bare arm up and said, 'It's . . . it's better!'

'Course it's better,' he said, 'sit down yer daft thing!'

Suddenly felt scared. Hadn't banked on there really being a God who really told people real things about real people. Wanted to hide. But where?

' . . . and now I think there's a couple of folk with back problems. One of them's a bruise at the base of the spine . . .'

Relief! Mine had been much higher up near the shoulder-blades. Phew!

' . . . and the other is much higher up near the shoulder-blades . . .'

Oh, no! But I wasn't actually in pain . . .

' . . . and it's not painful just now, but every now and then it gives you some real stick.'

The bruised base of the spine surfaced and was dealt with pretty quickly, then told to go for a run round the car park to make sure it was really healed.

A silence fell. Nearly jumped out of my skin when Gerald leaned across and tapped me on the knee.

'Go on, Dad,' he said quietly, 'It's you – you know it is!'

No escape! Trailed reluctantly up to the front, and whispered urgently to the speaker.

'My legs are exactly the same length you know!'

'Well that's useful – for things like walking,' he whispered back, with a broad grin.

'And my back's not hurting at all at the moment,' I added.

'Great!' he said, 'and it's not going to hurt you in the future either.'

Put his hands on my back and prayed. Felt a sort of heat go through me, but nothing else. As I turned to go back to my seat, he whispered, 'God likes you, lad, he really does!'

No really dramatic healings after that.

When we got home I rang Bill Dove and told him what had happened.

'The thing is, Bill,' I said, 'I was scared when it looked as if God was really there and really did exist. So does that mean I never really believed in him before?'

Heard Bill chuckle at the other end of the phone.

'Doesn't mean any such thing,' he said. 'It just means that up to now you've had faith bunged away in your heart, but tonight you had it shoved into your head. Always a bit of a shock. You'll handle it – don't worry.'

I said, 'How's Kitty, Bill?'

'Booked for home, I'd say,' said Bill quietly. 'I reckon she's booked for home.'

Thursday February 27th

I wish dirty jokes weren't so funny sometimes. Heard one this morning from Everett Glander who works at the next desk to me. Really side-splitting!

All about General Custer, a mackerel, and lots of Indians. My usual polite-smile-followed-by-a-tut-of-distaste almost didn't work. Glander does it on purpose because he knows I'm a Christian. He's enjoyed baiting me ever since the time when I had a bit too much at the office party two years ago, and he came up and said, 'How about us talking about *my* beliefs for once?'

After a year of crinkling my eyes into a Christian smile every time he asked his incessant questions about 'Who made God?', and 'What about suffering?', I'd run out of patience, and with four unwise pints of best bitter inside me, I looked at Glander, hated him, and said, 'Stuff your beliefs!'

Apologised later, but he's cashed in ever since.

All the same – pity there's no-one I *can* tell the General Custer joke to. It's *so* funny! Toyed with the idea of telling it to the study-group as an example of the sort of joke we shouldn't tell as Christians. Decided it wouldn't go down too well, really.

(Memo – Everett Glander is precisely the sort of person I *don't* want at this party of ours. The thought of him telling his awful jokes, and letting all my Christian friends know that I once got drunk and told him to stuff his beliefs, makes me go all hot and cold.)

Good tape at study-group tonight, by a man who does Christian meditation. Apparently he gets up very early every Saturday morning, and meditates on something like 'eternity', or 'love', or 'creation' for anything up to two hours. He says the rest of the weekend is filled with a special kind of peace for him and his family as a result. Think I'll try it this Saturday.

Do wish Leonard would make his mother turn her hearing aid up when she comes to meetings. When the tape finished, and Edwin asked for comments, she said, 'Well, I feel sorry for 'im. I should think 'e can 'ardly move with all that lot sloshin' around inside 'im. Wouldn't make me feel peaceful!'

After a long blank silence, it turned out that she thought the man on the tape had said he took *medication* for two hours every morning. Anne had to explain in the corner for ages. I dunno!

No sign of Gloria Marsh again this evening. Not that it matters to me personally, of course. Mentioned to Anne that Gloria hasn't been for two weeks.

She said, 'Perhaps she finds you so irresistible, darling, that she decided to do the sensible thing and keep away.'

How ludicrous! That's almost certainly *not* the reason!

Friday February 28th

Nearly told Gerald the Custer/mackerel/Indian joke at breakfast this morning. Felt guilty at the last moment and didn't.

Spent part of my lunch hour today thinking about the party next Friday. Pity they don't sell anti-invitation cards.

> Dear Everett Glander,
>   We are holding a party on
>   Friday next, and would be
>   very pleased if you would
>   not attend, as your presence
>   would be embarrassing and
>   unwelcome.
>   Yours, very sincerely, etc.

Couldn't help chuckling at the thought. Glander heard me and said, 'Still thinking about the old Custer joke? Good'n', eh? Told it to the wife yet?'

'I wouldn't consider passing a joke of that type on to anyone,' I said, with the sorrowful smile I use for Everett. 'I don't really find jokes of that kind very funny I'm afraid, Everett.'

'What *were* you laughing at then?' said Everett in the persistent way he has sometimes. 'Some nice clean Christian joke?'

Suddenly went cold and guilty inside. I'd been laughing about the idea of sending a cruel, nasty letter to the man I worked next to every day. The Custer joke didn't seem all that bad in comparison. Cleared my throat.

'Actually, Everett, I was thinking about a party we're having next Friday. Anne and I would . . . would be pleased if you could come and . . . well come.'

Never seen him so taken aback.

'You're asking me to a party at *your* house next Friday?'

'Yes – and your wife, of course. About eight o'clock if that's okay.'

'Well, yes,' said Everett, eyes still screwed up in puzzlement. 'Yes, I'm sure we'd love to come. Bring a stock of funnies and a couple of bottles of holy water, eh?'

Felt quite good about this at the time, but it wore off. Haven't dared tell Anne Everett's coming.

'Funnies and Holy water.'

WHAT HAVE I DONE??!!

12.30 a.m.

Had intended to go to bed early so as to be wide awake at 5.00 a.m. for meditation, but got seduced by the snooker on television. Decided that if I was a famous snooker player I'd like to be known as 'Pinkball Plass'.

To bed! I've set the alarm for 5.30, and I shall meditate until half past seven.

Saturday March 1st

Alarm clock exploded dead on 5.30 a.m.

Wondered for a moment what lunatic had set it for such a ridiculous hour, then remembered it was me. Anne half woke and said sleepily, 'Darling, *what* are you doing?'

I whispered, 'Go back to sleep, Anne. I'm just going to go and think about eternity for a couple of hours.'

As I tiptoed out of the room I distinctly heard Anne say, 'To think I had a proposal of marriage from someone normal once ...'

Crawled downstairs and knelt, bleary eyed, in the sitting room. Put my watch on the floor in front of me so as not to carry on past seven thirty.

Started contemplating eternity at exactly 5.34 a.m. Kept my eyes shut and tried to concentrate on things going on for ever and ever. Not easy. Found my thoughts drifting off to holidays, and why you don't see those wicker waste-paper baskets any more, and what a cross between a ferret and a giraffe could possibly look like. Was just imagining a creature with a ferret's body, and a neck so long that it could put its head right down a rabbit hole without moving its legs, when I remembered what I was *supposed* to be thinking about. Clenched my mind and really tried hard.

After about an hour, opened my eyes to check the time. It was 5.44 a.m.

Thought about eternity for another couple of minutes, but my head began to ache. Tried going back to bed but I couldn't sleep. Got up again. Anne came down at a quarter to eight.

She said, 'Of course, you've been meditating, haven't you, darling? How much of your two hours did you do?'

'Twelve minutes,' I said.

Told her I'd been too tired and my head hurt.

'But you came to bed so late,' she said, 'no wonder you were too tired.'

Afraid I've been bad tempered and sulky all day since then. Obviously twelve minutes isn't long enough to produce that 'special kind of peace' for oneself and one's family. Spent quite a long time out the back this afternoon, talking to Brenda, our rabbit. She might think I'm irritable and annoying, but she can't say so.

Sunday March 2nd

Forgot to get fruit-gums at the corner shop on the way to church today. Felt occupationally naked during Edwin's talk on the authority of the Bible. Slightly enlivened at the end when Edwin said that some books were apocryphal, and old Mrs Thynn said in a very loud voice, 'A pocket full of what?'

Spent the afternoon and evening with Anne writing out our invitations to the party. We seem to have invited an awful lot of people, Christians *and* non-Christians.

Hope it'll be alright! Still haven't told Anne about Glander. Still, there's one comfort – Uncle Ralph's not invited, and he's too far away to hear about it in any other way. That would be *too* much!

Asked Anne this evening whether she believed every word of the Bible was true. She said she'd always had to wrestle with profound doubts about one particular semi-colon half way through Zephaniah. Said I thought this was nit-picking, but she just burst into laughter and asked how we were going to keep Thynn away from the booze on Friday. Good point. How?

Asked Gerald the same question about the Bible later on.

'Well,' he said, 'I tend to go along with the views of St. Boglash of Flinge, who wrote a fascinating 53 volume work on the use of the apostrophe in Bible literature. He died in 1371 when a set of his own volumes fell on him as he knelt at prayer and ...'

'Okay, okay!' I interrupted. 'No need to go on. I'm not that stupid. I know perfectly well there's no such place as Flinge.'

Had him there! He really looked taken aback. I only *pretend* to be naive from time to time.

Prayed for Kitty again tonight. Surely God doesn't want someone like her to die ...

Monday March 3rd

At breakfast Anne said, 'I've got a little confession to make, darling.'

Don't have many opportunities to be magnanimously forgiving towards Anne. Felt rather pleased in a way. Leaned over the table and took her hand.

'Whatever it is, I forgive you in advance,' I said. Smiled encouragingly.

Anne said, 'I've invited Uncle Ralph to the party.'

Quite flabbergasted! 'Anne, how could you?' I shouted. 'Are you mad?! Ralph doesn't just *lower* the tone of a party, he buries it! Why on earth did you do such a stupid thing? You must be off your head! you stupid, stupid ...'

SUDDENLY REMEMBERED I'D INVITED EVERETT GLANDER!!

Could see Anne's lower lip trembling.

'I'm awfully sorry, darling,' she said with a little sob. 'It's j-just that he's all alone and no-one really l-likes him and it suddenly seemed so m-mean not to ... I *know* it was silly, but ... you did say you'd forgive me in advance ...'

Knew I'd be lucky to leave the room alive.

'Oh, I just over-reacted,' I said airily. 'After all, we all do silly things from time to time.' Stood up and edged towards the door. 'Take me, for instance. You may have invited Uncle Ralph, but I've ... I've invited ... I have actually invited ...'

'Oh, no . . .' said Anne, 'Not him – surely not him! Tell me you haven't invited that awful Glander man to our party!'

Both started to laugh suddenly – thank goodness!

'Uncle Ralph and Everett Glander,' I said. 'God help us!'

'I'm banking on that,' said Anne.

Noticed Anne and Gerald whispering together at teatime. Asked what was going on. Anne said, 'How's your back, darling?'

'Fine,' I said, 'Why?'

They just smiled at each other.

Another odd incident later on. Elsie came round at about half-past seven to tell Gerald that William had managed to book Unity Hall for a practice tomorrow night instead of Friday, then stayed chatting for a while. I said, 'Has Gerald told you about the big Valentine's card he got this year, Elsie? Some cow-eyed girl's really got it bad for this young man! Go and get it Gerald – show it to Elsie, it's hilarious! The poor girl must be a bit simple. She spent hours doing hundreds of tiny kisses in biro. Gerald and I were in fits, weren't we Gerald? I bet you wouldn't go to all that trouble for your William. Did *you* send *him* a card this year?'

Suddenly realised, as I finished speaking, that these perfectly harmless comments were producing rather odd responses.

Elsie was bright red, opening and shutting her mouth like a goldfish, and Gerald had screwed his eyes shut like you do just before a crash. Felt, in some inexplicable way, that I'd lost my Claire Raynor image. Anne called me into the kitchen just then, so I didn't get a chance to ask what was wrong. These young people!

(*Another* odd thing. When I got to the kitchen Anne had forgotten why she called me, but was annoyed with *me* instead of herself! I can't help thinking now and then, that I'm surrounded by some very funny people!)

Tuesday March 4th

Hadn't planned to go down to the band practice tonight, but Anne said the way things were with Gerald and Elsie, perhaps we ought to be there. Couldn't think what she was on about, but she's usually right, so off we went.

Terrible atmosphere when we got there. William Farmer sitting in a corner on one of those miniscule play-group chairs, looking very black indeed, Vernon Rawlings draped over a radiator picking his ear with a plectrum, and Gerald leaning against the wall, gazing at the ceiling and whistling tunelessly to himself. No sign of Elsie. It all looked like very *good* news for the devil, whatever *it* was.

Was just going to say something, when Elsie came out of the Ladies, red-eyes and sniffing. Homes in on me like an exocet missile.

'Mr Plass!' she said dramatically. 'You tried to push William and I together a month ago when you must have realised we were never really suited . . .'

'But you asked me to . . .'

' . . . and I want to tell you – I feel *led* to tell you that however much you may try to keep us apart, Gerald and I are *meant* for each other!'

Glanced at Anne in bewilderment, but she looked as if she already knew what was going on!

She said, 'Elsie, my love, if you and Gerald want to go out together, that's fine with us, absolutely fine – honestly it is.'

'Fine . . .', I echoed feebly.

Elsie revved furiously in neutral for a moment, then, obviously feeling we were sufficiently cowed, turned to Gerald and said, 'It's going to be alright, Gerald darling!'

'Oh, err . . . good, good,' said Gerald. 'That's err . . . good, Elsie.'

The dark figure in the corner grunted sardonically.

Anne moved over to speak quietly to William.

Felt a bit troubled really. Didn't like the idea of our Gerald trailing submissively behind a sort of female Rambo. Needn't have worried. Gerald put his hands on Elsie's shoulders, looked deep into her eyes, and said, 'Elsie, there's something I want to tell you – something I want you always to remember. Promise you'll never forget what I'm about to tell you.'

Elsie's eyes shone.

'Of course, Gerald! I promise I'll never forget!'

'Well then ...' He paused. Vernon suspended his ear picking.

'Yes Gerald?' Elsie's eyes couldn't have opened wider.

'I want you to know,' continued Gerald in a deep throbbing voice, 'that Mother-in-law is an anagram of Woman Hitler. Never forget that!'

By the time we left, the band – including William, who seemed almost miraculously restored to good spirits – had launched itself frenziedly into one of its orchestrated epileptic fits, and everything seemed more or less normal again.

Asked Anne on the way home what she said to William to perk him up so quickly.

'Oh,' she said, 'I just told him that if he put all the raw passion he feels about Elsie into his music, he'll be the nearest thing to a Christian Meatloaf that anyone's ever heard ...'

'What's a Christian Meatloaf, for heavens sake?'

' ... and I told him that if I was a teenager, I'd be at the front of the queue now, and glad to see the back of Elsie, especially as she never did *really* understand him. That's what I told him.'

'What's a Christian Meatloaf?'

'Ask Gerald later, darling. He knows more about it than I do.'

Asked Gerald later, 'What's a Christian Meatloaf?'

He said, 'Mum means he could become something big in heavy metal. I don't personally think he's quite in the "Bat out of hell" class, though, do you?'

Something big in heavy metal?

Not in the 'Bat out of hell' class?

Are we all going mad???

Never mind, Gerald's got a girlfriend, so he's certainly not gay. (Not that I ever thought he *was*.)

Wednesday March 5th

(Not that I'm prejudiced against gay people.)

Rang Leonard up and arranged to meet him for lunch (not in a pub!). Before getting round to the subject of the party, I asked him what he'd ended up thinking after Edwin's talk on Sunday.

He looked pleased. Doesn't usually get asked for an opinion. Overdid it of course. Leaned back in his chair, put his fingertips together and tried to look wise.

'Well, I did sit right up at the front on Sunday.'

'Yes.'

'So I was very close to Edwin as he talked.'

'Yes . . .'

'And I did end up doing something I'd never quite managed before.'

'Yes – and that was . . . ?'

'I counted Edwin's teeth. He's got thirty-six.'

Thynn amazes me. Seems an awful shame to waste all that space in his head. Gave up and asked him what he was going to do about drinking at the party. Leonard loves parties.

'Well,' he said, 'I've just been trying a new lager-free alcohol that mother found. I'll bring some of that. We teetotallers don't want to embarrass you drinkers.'

Wasn't till I got home this evening that I realised what Leonard had said. Lager-free alcohol? He *did* mean the other way round. Didn't he? Please!!!

(Not that I think it's right.)

Thursday March 6th

(Being gay I mean.)

8.30 a.m.

Won't have much time for diary entries today. We've only got till the study-group starts, to do all the shopping for the party. Don't want to leave it till tomorrow. Norma Twill just phoned to say she's got a job interview at the marshmallow factory this afternoon and would I pray for her. Said I would, but it'll have to wait till I get to work now.

10.00 p.m.

I blush to record what happened at the study-group tonight. Most charitable thing I can think is that Uncle Ralph *didn't* know there was a group of people praying in the sitting room when he arrived this evening. The group had just got onto Doreen Cook's knee (praying about it I mean, not sitting on it), when a hand appeared round the door that opens from the hall, holding a pair of pink-sugar lady's legs, and a voice said in a sort of music-hall French accent, 'Voulez-vouz jig-a-jig?'

Anne leaped to her feet, pushed the hand back into the hall and followed it, closing the door behind her. There was a brief, hissed, verbal scuffle, then silence. Pretty sure everyone had seen the legs. *Absolutely* sure everyone had heard the voice.

Long embarrassed silence. Could have fried an egg on my face.

Bit difficult to concentrate on poor old Doreen's knee after that. Anne came back after a while and apologised for Uncle Ralph. Said she'd sent him to bed without any supper. Everyone except the Flushpools laughed and said it was alright, but you could see that they were all a bit shocked.

What's he going to do at the party, for goodness sake?

As they left, Norma Twill drew me aside and whispered excitedly, 'I got the job, Adrian.'

'Job?' I said, 'What job?'

Norma's face dropped.

'You know, the job! You've been praying about it for me today. I've got it! They're putting me on the pink and whites. I just wanted to thank you for praying this morning.'

'Oh, you mean *that* job!' I gabbled. 'Oh yes, of *course* I know what you mean, and congratulations! Well done!'

'Well, thank you anyway,' smiled Norma. 'I'm sure your prayers helped.'

Would have to be a very different sort of man to have admitted to Norma that I'd forgotten to pray.

'Oh, no,' I protested modestly, 'it was nothing – really nothing.'

Very troubled later. Explained to Anne.

'Perhaps you shouldn't be so quick to promise,' she said, 'but don't worry too much. *You* may not have prayed – but *I* did. You owe me half an hour of prayer!'

Good old Anne.

Rotten old Ralph.

Muddled old me.

Wish we'd never thought of having a party.

Wonder how Kitty is? Don't want to ask, really.

Friday March 7th

9.00 a.m.

Had a totally unrecordable dream last night, provoked, I'm quite sure by Norma Twill's news that she is going to be working with those pink and white marshmallows. So vivid, I decided to tell Anne. Changed my mind and didn't.

1.00 p.m.

Sat down with Ralph this morning to lay down the law as far as the party's concerned.

'Right!' I said, 'There are a few little things I want to talk to you about, Ralph. Things like getting drunk, and making suggestive comments to ladies, and dirty stories, and vulgar practical jokes, and games involving drink, or sex, or both!'

'Fine!' said Uncle Ralph, rubbing his hands, 'You mean you want us to plan the party.'

'No,' I said, 'that's *not* what I mean, Uncle Ralph. What I *mean* is that I don't want any of those things to happen. A lot of the guests will be young Christians.'

'What am *I* then?' demanded Uncle Ralph, 'An old pagan?'

Yes, I thought, that's just what you are. 'Look, all I'm saying is that the people at the party are Christians, and they don't much like all those things I mentioned just now, so could you just chat pleasantly, have a couple of drinks, and be just – well – pleasant?'

'Just chat?'

'Yes.'

'A couple of drinks?'

'Yes.'

'No dirty stories?'

'No.'

'No practical jokes?'

'None!'

'Be pleasant?'

'Yes please.'

Uncle Ralph sighed, his little fat face a picture of gloom.

'Doesn't sound much of a party to me,' he said, 'still, I'll try.'

1.00 a.m.

Too tired to write about the party tonight. Do it tomorrow. Gerald has a strange brain. Leaned on the doorframe just now, yawned, and said, 'Did you know that Robert Runcie is an anagram of 'C.E., but in error?'

At 1.00 a.m.!!!

Saturday March 8th

11.00 a.m.

All cleared up! Mostly Anne and Gerald actually. Said they didn't wake me early because they preferred doing *all* the cleaning themselves, to being helped a *bit*, by me in a bad temper. I'm *not* like that! Got quite angry with them when they said I'm always irritable early in the morning.

Anyway . . .

Party! What a strange evening. Far as I can recall, events were as follows. Worth putting down in detail, I reckon.

7.45

No-one had arrived. Worried that nobody would come. Popped next door to borrow a few extra glasses from Percy Brain. Asked him if he was coming. Said he'd come when it had 'warmed up'. No-one ever wants to *do* the warming up!

8.00

Came back to the house to hear laughter and glass-clinking coming from the sitting-room. Uncle Ralph suddenly emerged, the old beam back on his face, and a large glass of scotch in his hand.

'Here, I say, old man, I don't half like these Christian friends of yours. The first one's just come and he's brought a bottle of whisky – this is some of it he poured for me – and he's just told me a great story about General Custer and a mackerel and some Indians. You see this bloke decided . . .'

'I've heard it!'

Just my luck! Everett Glander and Uncle Ralph getting together right at the beginning of the party. Felt like disaster, especially as the very next guest was Leonard Thynn, clutching four cans of (thankfully) alcohol-free lager, but with an excited gleam in his eye.

Next hour was like a nightmare. Anne and I spent our time welcoming guests then rushing back to the living room to prevent Leonard from drinking and Uncle Ralph and Everett from turning the whole thing into a sort of Bernard Manning show. Slipped upstairs eventually and hid in my bedroom for a few minutes to escape the noise and commotion. Suddenly realised the row had died down. Anne opened the door and said, 'Come and look!'

Went back down and listened outside the sitting room. Only one voice to be heard. Opened the door as quietly as possible and tip-toed into the corner. Frank Braddock was sitting in an armchair at the far end of the crowded room, a pint glass in one hand and his pipe in the other, talking easily to the rest of the guests, who seemed to be listening with close attention to what he was saying.

'He was a nuisance *then*,' said Braddock, 'and he's a nuisance now. He won't let you work out cosy little systems and call 'em "churches", and he won't let you get away with having four meetings a week to discuss what you're going to do in next week's meetings. If *that's* what you want, you'll find Jesus a real pain in the neck. He says awkward, difficult things, like "Love your enemies", and "Invite the people who really need it to dinner", and "Love God before anything else". He's terrible like that. They couldn't pin him down then, and you can't pin him down now, but I'll tell you something . . .'

Braddock leaned forward in his chair and stabbed the air with his pipe stem. His eyes were filled with excitement. Amazed to see Everett Glander and Uncle Ralph listening like small children.

' . . . if you want to pay the cost, there's no-one else worth following, and nothing else worth doing!'

Braddock took a long satisfying pull at his pint, and leaned back in his chair.

Mrs Flushpool, sitting on a hard chair at the side of the room was clearly impressed despite herself, but not entirely won over.

'Mr Braddock,' she said, 'would your message not be more convincing if you were to abstain from strong drink and noxious substances, such as tobacco? Stenneth and I neither drink nor smoke. Scripture issues grave warnings on these matters!'

(Stenneth?!)

Braddock blew a long stream of smoke towards the ceiling.

'Ah, scripture!' he said. 'Scripture certainly does warn that those whose strong faith allows them freedom in these things, must be careful not to harm those of a weaker faith who have abstained altogether.'

He held up his glass and his pipe.

'My dear Mrs Flushpool, if my drinking or my smoking is tempting you unbearably, I shall never drink or smoke in front of you again. Say the word!'

'Stenneth and I are *not* tempted to drink or smoke, or indulge in any other vice,' said Mrs F. firmly.

'Amen to that!' responded Mr Flushpool, with just a hint of sadness in his voice.

Braddock went on speaking to the assembled guests until about 11.30. No-one got drunk, Uncle Ralph seemed quite happy, Everett Glander looked very thoughtful as he left, and the rest of the guests said how much they'd enjoyed the evening. Edwin asked Frank Braddock if he would come and speak in our church one day. Frank said he would if Edwin would come and play snooker at his club one evening. Edwin laughed and agreed.

As Frank left, I said, 'Which church do *you* go to Frank?'

'Just an ordinary local one,' he said, 'but, . . .' He smiled, ' . . . I like to use the word 'church' as a verb, as well as a noun. See you! Thanks for the party. Night!'

Didn't really understand.

(No-one's called Stenneth, are they? Surely?)

Bill and Kitty Dove both got invitations to the party, though we knew they wouldn't come, of course. Rang Bill tonight, hoping he'd say Kitty was better. No change. No better, no worse. Just have to wait.

Sunday March 9th

Wouldn't ever say this to anyone, but it strikes me that to go through life with a name like Stenneth Flushpool, and then to marry Mrs Flushpool, is a most extraordinary run of bad luck!

Uncle Ralph left early after shaking my hand and giving me an electric shock with some infernal machine hidden in the palm of his hand.

Watched him disappear, a little round shape, wearing a little round crash helmet, perched on a little round scooter, and wondered if God loved him.

Hope so.

Only saw Gerald at church today. Out with Elsie somewhere or other the rest of the time. When he came in tonight, he waited till Anne went out of the room, then he said, 'Dad, I've got this great joke to tell you. Uncle Ralph told it me before he went this morning. It's about General Custer. You see, there was this man . . .'

'I've heard it!'

That joke's like a mosquito. I have to keep swatting it.

Monday March 10th

Wish Gerald and Anne wouldn't have these little private jokes together. This morning Gerald said 'How's your back, dad?'

'Fine,' I replied, 'never better. Must be the change in temperature. Why?'

Sniggers! Then Gerald said, 'Did you know that Ian Andrews is an anagram of 'Weird 'nanas'?'

'No,' I said. 'What's that got to do with it?'

Sniggers!

Edwin phoned this evening to ask if we could accommodate his little niece, Andromeda, for a few days, while her mum's in hospital. He added for some reason, that Andromeda's mum, Mrs Veal, is an ardent Christian feminist. Don't see what that's got to do with anything. Agreed to have the little girl, naturally. We love children, and, though I say it myself, I'm really rather good with them. Quite looking forward to it really.

Tuesday March 11th

Richard Cook round this evening. Brought young Charles with him, back for a couple of days from his second term at Deep Joy Bible School. What a difference from the miserable young man who came round that evening half way through January! Bit *too* much of a difference I thought. Kept looking at Anne and I with that I-can-see-right-through-you-because-I'm-ablaze-for-the-Lord expression you see on people's faces sometimes. Rather hoped Gerald wouldn't come in. He's in love and more flippant than ever. Charles was just in the middle of explaining to us how the holy spirit *really* operates, when Gerald came bouncing in.

'Hi, Charlie-boy,' he said, 'how are things down at the old Muppet factory?'

Anne and I glared, knowing how upset Richard gets sometimes, but Charles just looked very, very patient, and invited Gerald to a local meeting tomorrow night.

'I have a feeling,' said Charles meaningfully, 'that your needs will be mightily met there, Gerald.'

'Oh,' said Gerald, 'you mean they're having a bar?'

More patience from Charles, and a stern look from Richard. Gerald put his hands in the air and said, 'Alright, I give in, I give in! I'll come to the meeting!'

Hope it'll be alright. . . .

Wednesday March 12th

Andromeda Veal – age seven – has arrived!

Small but powerful. Conversation consists mainly of the phrase, 'I'm afraid I don't think that's very funny'. Clothes covered in obscure badges. Didn't like to ask what they all meant.

At bed-time I asked her if she'd brought any little dolly-friends along to go bye-byes with her. She called me a tool of the male sexist regime, and a false gender labeller. Thought this sounded a bit unsavoury, but was a little unsure of my ground, so didn't argue the point. What a cheek, though! Fumed inwardly as Anne wrestled her off to bed.

Wonder how Gerald's getting on at this meeting? He's a bit vulnerable at the moment, what with Elsie and . . . Elsie. Hope he's alright.

Thursday March 13th

Gerald very gloomy at breakfast. Says last night's speaker, someone called Bernard Brundle, has a special ministry to people who've somehow escaped feeling miserable and guilty. Now he feels *both!*

Andromeda spent most of the morning pointing out to Anne those aspects of our life-style that fall short of the socialist ideal. Anne reckons that when Jesus said we should all become like little children, he couldn't have met the Jewish equivalent of Andromeda Veal. Luckily, Andromeda adores Gerald's stereo headphone set. She's a bit confused though. Keeps referring to it as 'Gerald's personal problem'. Never mind. It keeps her occupied. Had to be almost nailed into bed again tonight. A tiring child!

Study-group led by 'my' convert, Ted, tonight.

Amazing! He's further on than I am. But then *he* hasn't got a family, has he?

Prayed for Kitty during the meeting. Apparently she's worse.

Friday March 14th

Gerald offered to settle Andromeda tonight before going to band practice. Said he'd got a plan. Absolute silence from upstairs after only a few minutes. Waited till Gerald came back down, then asked him what he'd done.

'Oh,' he said, 'I just told her that if she didn't go to sleep the bogey-person would get her. She's not frightened, just baffled.'

Still worried about Gerald. Very low since that meeting on Wednesday. Not like him at all.

Anne and I prayed for him and Kitty for quite a long time tonight.

Saturday March 15th

Really worried about Gerald now! Never seen him so miserable. When I got back from town today, he told me that Charles came round earlier to check he hadn't backslidden into happiness. He doesn't want to see Elsie this evening in case his gloom is infectious.

Met Andromeda on the stairs this afternoon. She asked me when I planned to release Anne from bondage, then stood outside the lavatory waiting for me to come out and give her an answer. I cannot *stand* people tutting and scuffing and sighing outside the lavatory when I'm *inside!!*

Terminated my stay somewhat prematurely, found Gerald's personal stereo, and stuck the headphones on Andromeda in midrhetoric.

Peace at last!

Bit of a surprise this evening. Edwin phoned, and happened to mention that tomorrow's guest speaker is Bernard Brundle, the man whose talk upset Gerald so much, earlier in the week! Didn't say anything to Edwin, but I'm a bit concerned. How's Gerald going to react to a second dose?

Sunday March 16th

To church with Anne, Gerald and Andromeda.

Told Gerald about Brundle, but he said he'd rather come to church and be made to feel guilty, rather than stay at home and feel even more guilty about not coming to church to feel guilty. *Think* I know what he meant.

Andromeda very watchful, and ominously quiet, during the first part of the service. Like sitting next to a small, slowly boiling, pig-tailed kettle.

I see what Gerald means about Brundle. Towards the end of his talk, he got an empty chair, set it in the middle in front of everybody, and looked round at us all in a here's-something-you-haven't-thought-of-before sort of way.

'Imagine if Jesus was sitting here in this chair right now,' he said. 'Wouldn't you feel bad? And wouldn't you just want to hide your face and creep away when you thought about all the things in your life that are not as they should be?'

Really did try to feel all those things, but I couldn't. Just felt excited about the idea of meeting Jesus. Shows I've got an awful long way to go, I suppose.

At chorus time the little kettle boiled.

Andromeda stood up on her chair, stuck her chin out, and sang, 'SHE-E-E-E IS LO-O-ORD . . .', at the top of her voice. Raymond Pond, our organist, who's been very stable for a long time now, lost his head and launched into 'Home, home on the range'. Wouldn't have mattered so much, but a few people started to sing the words with raised arms and passionately sincere expressions on their faces. Vernon Rawlings, completely carried away, shouted out, 'We want to be those Antelopes for *you*, Lord!'

Everything ground to a halt eventually. Andromeda triumphant. Gerald almost crying with laughter, Anne and I highly embarrassed.

Edwin came round this evening to collect Andromeda. Said not to worry – he knows his niece of old.

Relieved to see Gerald's spirits are quite restored. When we were all drinking cocoa tonight, he said, 'That chair *winked* at me this morning.'

Monday March 17th

Mrs Veal rang at *dawn*. Sounds like Andromeda cubed. She wanted to know why Andromeda was demanding a personal problem just like Gerald's.

Explained and laughed.

She said, 'I'm afraid I don't find that very funny,' and put the phone down.

Anne and I were very relieved to find a note on my pillow tonight from Gerald.

> Dear Dad,
>   Did you know that Selwyn
>   Hughes is an anagram of
>   Shye welsh gnu?
>   Love, Gerald.

Back to normal. Thank you, God.

Tuesday March 18th

Spent yesterday evening enjoying the Veal-less atmosphere and reading a marvellous book called 'Two Thousand Things You Need To Know About Living The Victorious Christian Life'.

Written by Carlton S. Calhoun the third, who is, I believe, an American. Struck particularly by the section on giving. I see it all now! My motives for giving Mr Brain that money were all wrong. Paragraph 1,416 of the book says we must give cheerfully, without thought of reward or our own inconvenience. Explained this to Anne and Gerald at breakfast.

Gerald said, 'Can I have your bacon then?'

Anne said, 'There's a funny noise in the washing machine. Will you mend it for me?'

Why don't people take me seriously?

Wednesday March 19th

Edwin rang to ask if a small group could use our house on Saturday night to plan the Easter service. Agreed cheerfully and without etc etc. It works!

Anne mentioned the washing machine again. I said, 'Is it actually working, Anne?'

She said, 'Yes, but ...'

Honestly! Women!

Thursday March 20th

Mildly interested to note that Gloria Marsh made another of her rare appearances at the study-group tonight. She mentioned casually at coffee-time that her car was going for repairs, so she would have transport problems for the next two days. I thought how incredible it was that on the one night when she comes, she should have a problem that I could help with. What a great opportunity to give without etc etc. Told her on the spot that she could have ours. Talk about surprised! Still protesting after I handed her the keys. Kissed me on the cheek. I think the poor helpless soul sees me as a sort of father figure.

Suddenly saw Anne glaring at me through the hatch. Must show her that book. She doesn't seem to understand giving.

Friday March 21st

Cold atmosphere at breakfast. Asked Anne why she wasn't speaking.

She said, 'I'm saving my energy for when I *walk* into town later.'

Told her what Mr Calhoun says about giving without etc etc.

She said, 'Yes, but you're giving without thought of *my* inconvenience, not yours! She only came last night because of the car, and now she's got it!'

Appalled by this uncharitable assessment of Gloria. I intend to remain cheerful about it, whatever happens.

Saturday March 22nd

Things still very cool. Suddenly remembered I'd forgotten to tell Anne about the meeting here tonight. Tried to get Gerald to tell her, but he wouldn't. Eventually told her through the hatch.

She said, 'Actually, it doesn't matter, because we can't go out anywhere much without the car today, so I'll just stay in here all day, and make food for this evening.'

Heard Gerald singing 'Fight the Good Fight' somewhere upstairs. Very funny – I don't think!

Meeting started at 7.30 p.m. There was Edwin, Leonard Thynn, Richard Cook and George Farmer. Gerald asked if he could stay for a minute because he had an idea. Someone was silly enough to say he could.

Gerald said, 'Right! Here's my idea for the Easter service. What we do is, we run a wire from one end of the church to the other, and just before the service ends, we slide an enormous artificial chicken along over people's heads, then when it gets to the middle it lays a great big egg into the centre aisle, and when it lands it cracks open, and – this is the *really* good bit – Richard's inside, dressed in a fluffy yellow chick costume and he stands up and

281

shouts 'New Life!' Then we release twenty or thirty live chickens into the congregation just to make it a real *experience* for everybody. What do you think?'

Smiles all round except for Richard, frozen in a listening position, sausage roll poised uneaten in front of his open mouth. Thought Gerald might've gone too far this time. Richard slowly grounded his sausage roll, then looked up very gravely at Gerald. He said, 'Where would we get the chickens from?'

Stupid Thynn showered us all with puff-pastry at this point. Had to be patted on the back and given sips of water.

I'll kill Gerald one of these days!

Good meeting after that. *I'm* to do a testimony in the Easter Sunday service.

Car still not back. Anne tight-lipped. Never mind. Surely Gloria will bring it back in the morning. I'm still cheerful!

Sunday March 23rd

Felt uncomfortable at church today. Don't know why. Couldn't even smile when George Farmer said he wanted to hear a spontaneous burst of applause after the next chorus.

On the way home our car passed us, full of Gloria and several men, all singing and laughing. Some of them seemed to be holding bottles.

Anne said, 'Look, the poor helpless soul has organised some sort of charity outing.'

Car still not back tonight. Read Mr Calhoun's advice again and took courage. Who am I to judge?

Anne said 'Washing machine' in her sleep.

Monday March 24th

Car not back.

Tuesday March 25th

Car not back. Civil war imminent. Anne says go round and ask her what she thinks she's doing. Can't. I'm chicken. Prayed instead.

Wednesday March 26th

I WANT MY CAR BACK!!!

If that idiot Calhoun was here, I'd send him round to Gloria's to get it, then I'd give him a right hook cheerfully and without thought of reward or inconvenience to myself.

Thursday March 27th

10.00 a.m.

I'm supposed to be giving a Christian testimony in three days time, and I hate everybody I meet!

WHERE'S MY BLOODY CAR?!?!

6.00 p.m.

Gloria at the door. She'd brought the car back. Said her car had taken a teensy-weensy bit longer to repair than she'd expected, and she hoped I didn't mind. Also she'd had the itsy-bitsiest little bump you ever saw with another horrid car, and there was a titchy little mark on one of the wings. But she was *so* grateful, especially as, on Sunday, she had been able to take out a couple of dear friends who weren't able to get about much these days and it was all because I'd been such a dream-lover about the car.

Cleared my throat loudly to cover Anne's snort from the kitchen.

Went and looked at the car when she'd gone.

It was crouching miserably by the kerb, looking exhausted and reproachful. The titchy mark was a huge dent. Anne and Gerald came out too.

Anne said, 'She's bent it.'

Gerald said, 'Dolly Parton's suckered you, Dad.'

Too fed up to even tell him off.

After study-group, spent two hours staring at a blank sheet of paper. Testimony? Me? Huh!!!

Friday March 28th

Good Friday.

Anne's being very nice but I just feel stupid and useless. Praying's like shouting into a concrete bucket. I'll never be ready for Easter. Terrified about this testimony. I'll have to make it up.

No-one ever felt like I do tonight.

(N.B. Must have a look at that washing machine.)

Saturday March 29th

9.00 a.m.

Rang Edwin. Said couldn't he ask someone on a spiritual high to give a testimony instead of me. He said, gently but firmly, 'You do it. Just talk about where you are. Be honest.'

I'm dreading it.

(Nearly looked at washing machine. Couldn't face it in the end.)

10.30 a.m.

Who should ring but Gloria Marsh! Could she speak to Anne? When she came back through, Anne said, 'Gloria's got to go into hospital unexpectedly in the next hour. She's terrified. She asked if I would go with her and look after her.'

I said, 'I bet you gave her a short answer to that!'

'I did,' said Anne. 'I said "Yes". I'm off straightaway. Back after tea sometime.'

Couldn't believe my ears.

'But what about the pictures with Brenda Rawlings this afternoon,' I said. 'You've been looking forward to it for weeks. And what about all that business with the car? You said that . . .'

Anne smiled at me in a funny way she does sometimes. Came over and kissed me. She said, 'Darling, go and read paragraph 1,416 again.'

I did.

Got some flowers to send to Gloria.

Wrote my testimony.

Played Scrabble with Gerald. He won by using naughty words.

Sunday March 30th

Easter Day!!

Thanked God quietly at church for Jesus and Anne. Did more or less the same in my testimony. Felt odd telling the truth in church. Good though! So happy I nearly danced. (Only nearly!)

Monday March 31st

First really happy breakfast for some time. Gerald announced that my name is an anagram of 'Sprain salad'. We all laughed.

Good quiet-time. I shall never get low again!

Tuesday April 1st

8.30 a.m.

Gerald must think I'm stupid!

Knowing he has a friend living in Northern Italy, I calmly laid aside a letter from Rome, inviting me to take up the post of Deputy Pope, and promising a salary of one million lire per week, with as much fish as I could eat. I shall walk to work now, comfortable in the knowledge that I have emerged unscathed from my son's annual attempt to make an idiot of me.

9.15 a.m.

Three people came up from behind me on my way to work, looked into my face, laughed, and shook my hand. Looked in the mirror when I got to work and found a big notice stuck to my back. It said,

'IF THIS MAN'S FACE REMINDS YOU OF A DISAPPOINTED CAMEL, PLEASE SHAKE HIS HAND.'

Sometimes I think Gerald's sense of humour needs pruning!

Wednesday April 2nd

Enjoyed quiet-time again this morning. Life felt perfect. Couldn't imagine anything going wrong.

8.30 p.m.

Everything's gone wrong!

The Flushpools appeared at the door this evening. Sat in a row of two on our sofa. Said they'd felt led to come round after hearing my testimony.

I said, 'What about my testimony?'

Mrs Flushpool said, 'You shared with us that your marriage had moved into Satan's camp for a season.'

I said, 'I don't remember saying that.'

Anne said, 'She means that you said we'd had a few rows lately.'

Mrs Flushpool didn't seem to hear. She said, 'The Lord would have us ask you if there are physical problems in your union. We have a special ministry to those with ... physical problems in their union.'

Completely mystified. Told them I don't belong to a union.

He said, 'We speak carnally, brother.'

To my surprise Anne suddenly got up and said, 'I'm awfully sorry, Mr and Mrs Flushpool, I don't think we can help you. There must be people around with problems like that, though. I'm sure you'll find somebody. Good evening. Why don't you see them to the door, darling?'

Sometimes I honestly wonder if I'm a bit slow on the uptake. Found myself at the door saying goodbye to the Flushpools, without really knowing what had been going on. Mrs F. seemed almost angry for some reason. But she smiled sweetly at me as she went out, then stopped on the doorstep and said, 'Can I say something to you in love, dear brother Adrian?'

Thought – oh, no! Said 'Yes. Please do.'

She said, 'Of course, your testimony wasn't really a testimony, was it? Descriptions of the way in which you have failed The Lord can hardly be said to glorify God, can they? I do hope things are soon better between you and *dear* Anne. Goodnight, dear, and God bless you.'

Felt very uneasy after they'd gone. Maybe she was right. Was I *too* honest? I think I probably was ...

Thursday April 3rd

She *was* right! I let God down on Sunday.

Friday April 4th

No-one's ever felt as bad as I feel tonight.

Anne and Gerald haven't noticed! Why not?

Saturday April 5th

Easter seems so far away now. Feeling really low. What use is a twit like me to God?

Wasted an entire evening looking miserable but bravely cheerful. At last Anne said, 'Are you alright, darling?'

'Oh, yes,' I lied heroically, 'I'm fine; you don't have to worry about me.'

'Thank goodness for that!' she said. 'I'm off to bed.'

Fancy believing me!!!

Sunday April 6th

Gerald arrived bleary-eyed but quietly content at the breakfast table. Announced that Graham Kendrick is an anagram of 'Grandmah Kicker'. Anne laughed like a drain. I produced a rather good shuddering sigh.

They didn't even notice!!

Good job I'm not the self-pitying type.

To church.

Why is George Farmer allowed to lead services? Told us to look around as we sang choruses, expressing Christian love to any brother or sister who caught our eye.

Groaned inwardly.

Stared fixedly at the overhead-projector screen, screwing my eyes up to look as if I didn't know the words well enough to look away. Glancing aside in an unguarded moment, I was impaled by a sisterly beam from pretty Norma Twill. Tried to smile back in a brotherly, going-on-well-with-the-Lord sort of way, but a muscle in my face just refused to work. The side of my mouth dropped open in a horrible leer, and one eye began winking uncontrollably. Norma turned pale, then looked compassionate. Went all hot as I realised she was remembering my so-called 'lust problem', back in December!

Afterwards, at coffee-time, I said, 'Sorry, Norma, a muscle in my face got stuck.'

She fell about laughing.

Later, at home, I told Anne, Gerald, and Leonard Thynn (who'd come to borrow the cat for some insane reason) about Norma. I sometimes think I'm just a one-man comedy show. They were all in hysterics!

Monday April 7th

Still low.

Quiet-time *too* quiet.

Prayed for an encouraging sign. Suddenly the door-bell rang. Rushed downstairs quite excited. It was Leonard Thynn returning the stupid cat.

Tuesday April 8th

God's on holiday. . . .

(Why borrow a *cat*?)

Wednesday April 9th

Edwin phoned to confirm that the study-group could meet here tomorrow night. I suppose that's all I'm good for – providing a house for others to be spiritual in!

(A cat???)

Thursday April 10th

Study-group began as usual about eight o'clock. Deliberately sat on the floor near the door, so that I could escape easily if I had to.

Started with a discussion on euthanasia. Deaf old Mrs Thynn shocked everyone by saying that she thought it was absolutely lovely, and she'd like her grandchildren to have a chance to sit and watch it from beginning to end!

Stunned silence until Anne suddenly giggled, and said, 'She thinks it's a Walt Disney film.' General atmosphere of relief, except from Richard Cook, who'd obviously been about to fire several rounds of scripture from the hip.

Discussion droned on.

Kept my eyes open during the prayer time. Everyone else locked in the 'shampoo position', as Gerald calls it. Wondered how many were sincere. Decided not many.

Edwin stayed on afterwards. Said he wanted a 'chat'. Felt a little nervous. Edwin *knows* things sometimes.

'Cheer up!' said Edwin, 'I've got a little job to offer you.'

Panic!!! 'What err . . . job's that then, Edwin?'

'Well, I think – I'm not absolutely sure, mind – but I *think* the Lord wants you to be a study-group leader.'

Started babbling about being bad and useless and not clever enough. Edwin interrupted me.

'It was during your testimony at Easter that the idea first came into my head. I was very impressed with how honest you were. Helped a lot of people, you know.'

Started to say something, but he held up his hand to stop me.

'Don't give me an answer now. Think about it. Let me know tomorrow. Ask *Him*.

11.45

Prayed in bed with Anne just now.

She said, 'I think Edwin's right.'

I like Anne being sure. 'Yes,' I said, 'so do I.'

Sat for a while, thinking/worrying/feeling pleased. Suddenly remembered what I'd meant to ask Anne.

'Anne, why did Leonard want to borrow the . . . ?'

She was fast asleep.

1.30 a.m.

Still awake. Hope my group don't go all quiet. Hope George Farmer's one of my group. He'll keep 'em on their toes. . . .

Friday April 11th

Rang Edwin first thing this morning to tell him my decision. Sounded very pleased. Told Gerald at breakfast. He *didn't* make a joke!

> *I* am a study-group leader!
> I *am* a study-group leader!!
> I am *a* study-group leader!!!
> I am a *study-group* leader!!!!
> I am a study-group *leader*!!!!!

Thanked God in my quiet-time that I am not a proud man. Can't help feeling a new sense of importance, though. *Me!* A study-group leader! Well, well!

Saturday April 12th

Ridiculous incident this morning, just as I was enjoying my new sensation of deep, spiritual dignity. Busy washing up and thinking about my first study-group as a leader, this Thursday, when I put my hand into the washing-up bowl and cut my thumb quite badly on the bread knife. Started to bleed quite heavily.

Gerald, who was drying up said, 'How did you do that, dad?'

'Like this,' I said, and put my other hand in the washing-up bowl. Cut my other thumb. Ended up with an absurd, white bulbous bandage on *both* thumbs.

Anne and Gerald both very sympathetic, but had to take turns going out of the room to laugh. How embarrassing!

Bet Billy Graham never had to face his public with two bulging bandaged thumbs. Bit of an early set-back really. Can't help feeling nervous about church tomorrow. I know what'll happen – Leonard Thynn will just cackle, Doreen Cook will want to lay hands on my thumbs, and everyone else will be very compassionate and secretly want to ask me how on earth I could've injured *both* thumbs!

Sunday April 13th

What a relief. Edwin rang early to say that there's no church this morning. Gave me a list of names (*my* study-group!) to phone and pass on the news to. Asked him why church was off. He said, 'Oh there was a mix-up in the bookings for Unity Hall. Nobody's fault really, but the local cage-bird society have got it for the morning.'

When I told Gerald about this, he said, 'Oh, it'll be business as usual up at the old hall this morning, then.'

Now that I have a position of responsibility in the church, I don't intend to allow this kind of foolish comment from Gerald. Gave him a look that was supposed to combine fundamental acceptance with loving but firm chastisement.

Gerald said, 'Thumbs giving you stick, eh, Dad?'

Went off to meet Elsie before I could put him straight.

Decided this afternoon that, as a study-group leader, a dramatic improvement is needed in my prayer-life. Intend to pray for two solid hours *every* night after Anne's gone to bed. Two hours should be enough – don't want to overdo it.

1.30 a.m.

So far so good. Prayed from 11.15 until 1.15. Feel tired but mystical. Must keep it up.

Monday April 14th

Rather a shame Anne and Gerald can't make the same efforts over consideration for others as I'm making over prayer. The row they made getting up this morning when I was trying to get a bit of extra sleep!

Forgave them.

Seven separate people at work asked how I 'did my thumbs'. Everett Glander made what can only be described as an unsavoury suggestion about the cause of my injuries. If I wasn't a Christian and a study-group leader I'd push Glander's head through the shredder.

Hope these bandages are off by Thursday!!

About to start my new extra prayer-time this evening, but got distracted by the quarter-finals of the North-East Bedfordshire indoor bowls championship on TV. Suddenly it's 1.00 a.m.! Too tired to pray. Why have I watched bowls instead of praying? I don't *play* bowls! I'm not *interested* in bowls!

Never mind – tomorrow, I'll get it *right*.

Tuesday April 15th

6.00 p.m.

Overheard Gerald on the phone when I got home just now.

' . . . and then, Elsie – *then*, he put the *other* hand in, and – oh! Hello Dad . . .'

If the Bible's right about long life depending on respect for parents, Gerald will be lucky to make it to Saturday, let alone three score years and ten.

2.00 a.m.

Really, truly, honestly, *did* intend to pray tonight. Got caught up in a long Albanian film with sub-titles, set in a kitchen. Kept thinking something was going to happen, but it never did, and suddenly the film finished.

Have crawled to bed. . . .

Wednesday April 16th

Felt exhausted and morose at breakfast.

Anne said, 'How's the late prayer going, darling?'

Couldn't meet her eye. 'Alright,' I mumbled.

Gerald said, 'Were you speaking in tongues most of the time, dad? I could have sworn I heard you speaking in Albanian for ages.'

Very funny! Deliberately didn't smile later on when he asked if I knew that David Owen was an anagram of 'An odd view'.

Fell asleep at work today.

Leonard Thynn came round this evening while I was asleep in my chair after supper. He drew little faces on my thumb bandages with felt-pen and wrote 'Thynn was here' underneath, on both of them. Anne and Gerald just let him! They were all sitting with foolish grins on their faces when I woke up. Thynn can be very silly sometimes. Suggested *all* the members of our study-group should wear bandages on their thumbs, like a secret society. Gerald suggested our theme tune should be 'Thumb enchanted evening'. Thynn cackled at this, then said he knew a way to cope with problems such as my thumbs. Asked wearily what it was. He told me to go and stand behind the television. Decided to humour him. Stood behind the TV and said, 'Alright, Leonard, how does this help?'

'Well,' said Leonard, 'it teaches you how to face set-backs!'

They all roared.

Forgave them.

Thursday April 17th

Was absolutely determined to get the prayer thing right last night. Knelt down at 11.00 p.m. and closed my eyes. Woken and man-handled to bed at 4.00 a.m. by Anne. Didn't seem over-sympathetic really.

Fell asleep at work again. Glander poured ice-cold water on me, then claimed to have raised me from the dead when I sat up at my desk and shrieked.

So tired!!

Got home to find Anne with one of those okay-this-is-going-to-get-sorted-out-right-now expressions on her face.

She said, 'Darling, tell me why you can't go to bed early and then get up early to pray.'

'Oh,' I said, 'I don't like getting up …'

'Quite!' said Anne. 'And I don't like being joined every morning by a guilty, exhausted, disillusioned mystic. Besides …'

She smiled shyly.

'I … well, I miss you at night. Couldn't you just *try* the other way? Just for a while?'

Promised I'd try.

10.00 p.m.

My first meeting as a study-group leader is over.

Not a particularly good start to the evening. Apart from feeling exhausted and still wearing my ridiculous bandages, the members of the group seemed to have undergone a mysterious change since last week. Last time we met most of them were pleasant, easy-going people who co-operated with group aims. This week they were awkward, late, (some of them) difficult to quieten down when it was time to start, and generally unresponsive.

Really wanted to throttle Thynn, who does tend to wear a joke out. He went up to each person as they came in, and sang 'Thumbwhere, over the rainbow …' and pointed at me with a stupid smirk on his face.

Wondered why I'd not noticed before what a rebellious crowd of people these are. When we got going at last, I noted that Norma Twill was insufficiently joyful during the choruses, Vernon Rawlings yawned in the middle of the scripture reading, and Percy Brain had his eyes open during the prayers.

Profound silence for an hour and a half as I delivered a study on 'The function of fruit in the Old Testament'. Asked if there were any questions at the end. Long, rather disappointing silence, until young Bessie Trench raised her hand.

'Yes, Bessie?' I said, 'What's your question?'

Really pleased someone had been listening.

Bessie twisted her fingers together and cleared her throat.

She said, 'How did you do your thumbs?'

10.15 p.m.

Going to bed now. Seems ridiculously early, still …

Friday April 18th

9.00 a.m.

Up at 6.00 a.m.! Good prayer-time. Glad I decided to switch to the morning. Asked Anne at breakfast why she thought people were deliberately making things difficult for me now that I'm a study-group leader.

She laughed!

'It's not *them* that have changed, darling. It's you! You're a leader now. It's just that all their funny little ways didn't bother you before. Now you notice everything, and you think it's something to do with how they feel about you. They're not there to make *you* feel better, you know; you're supposed to be serving *them*, not the other way round.'

Yes ... well ... perhaps ...

Bandages off my thumbs before going to work this morning, thank goodness. No more silly comments. Great!

6.00 p.m.

Small boy stopped me on the way home from work just now ...

'Oi, mister! ow come yer fumbs is all white 'n' crinkly, an' the rest of yer 'ands ain't?'

(Don't dare ring Bill Dove to ask about Kitty at the moment.)

Saturday April 19th

Anne and Gerald off early in the car to visit Mick and Samantha Rind-Smythe who used to live in Frank Braddock's house. I can't go because of work. Just before going, Anne said, 'Whatever you do, don't forget to feed the rabbit, and if you could just take a look at the washing machine – it really is getting worse. The rabbit's the main thing though. You *won't* forget it will you?'

Really – you'd think I was a complete idiot! I may not have had much to do with Brenda, our rabbit (Anne usually feeds her), but I'm not likely to forget to feed her.

Leonard Thynn's looking after the cat. Anne says he's borrowed it again. Must remember to ask her why....

Sunday April 20th

Forgot to feed the rabbit yesterday. Old Miss Seed, whose garden backs on to the end of ours, came to the door early this morning, carrying Brenda, who'd escaped from the hutch and spent the night eating Miss Seed's 'treasured' plants. Miss Seed rather annoyed but quite nice about it really. Promised to reinforce the hutch. Patched it up a bit.

To church.

Very challenging talk from Edwin today. Short (two fruit-gums) but good. Said we should all be aware of chances to witness to our immediate neighbours. Percy Brain and Frank Braddock are already Christians, so that just left Miss Seed, who we've hardly ever spoken to. Thought how amazing it was that this 'rabbit' connection had happened earlier. Decided to contact Miss Seed after lunch.

Got home from church. Saw Brenda from an upstairs window, sitting in Miss Seed's flower bed, stuffing herself with more plants. Crept along under the hedge at the end of our garden, rattling food in a bowl and whispering, 'Come back, Brenda! I have dominion over you!'

Brenda can't have read that scripture.

Hid indoors, but had to answer the door after repeated knocking. Miss Seed with a scratch down one arm and Brenda under the other. Rather cool this time. I babbled apologies foolishly. 'Won't happen again ... etc etc.' Not the moment for evangelism really. ...

Can't do any more with the hutch until the shops open tomorrow. Have put Brenda in the house for the time being. It'll be alright as long as I keep the front and back doors shut!

Monday April 21st

10.00 a.m. At work.

Went out the back after prayer-time this morning to check what I needed for the hutch. There'll be no mistake about it *this* time! Closed the front door very carefully behind me as I left for work. I'll get wire-netting and staples on the way home, and that'll be the end of the problem.

10.00 p.m.

Got home from work to find that I'd left the *back* door open. Rushed round the house, hoping against hope that Brenda was still there somewhere. Lots of little round black pellets, but no rabbit. Spotted her eventually through the hedge, chewing smugly at me, with bits of Miss Seed's plants sticking out of the sides of her mouth, and her stupid great ears sticking up like two black exclamation marks.

Nearly fainted at the prospect of facing Miss Seed again. Prayed for the Second Coming. No luck. Phone went. It was Miss Seed. Said she realised it might be a little upsetting for me, but she didn't intend to spend the rest of her life cultivating food for my rabbit. Would I collect it – at once! Got Brenda back after a long undignified chase punctuated by a series of unsuccessful flying leaps. Shoved her hutch right up against the brick wall in the yard, and stapled two layers of thick wire-netting over the rest of it. Brenda sat inside chewing over ideas like a little one-rabbit escape committee. She won't get out this time, though! Secure at last! Life was beginning to seem only about great big black rabbits.

Tuesday April 22nd

10.00 a.m. At work.

Woke feeling peaceful for once. Off to work in a relaxed frame of mind. I can give a bit more thought to my study-group now that I don't have to worry about the rabbit. Also, I've forgotten that originally, I was planning to witness to Miss Seed, and I haven't. As soon as I get home, I'll ring her.

7.30 p.m.

Rang Miss Seed shortly after getting home. I said, 'Miss Seed, there's something I want to share with you.'

'Other than your rabbit, you mean?' she said icily.

Went all hot and cold.

'You mean ... you don't mean ... ?'

'Yes, Mr Plass! I *do* mean.'

Realised to my horror, that Brenda, wearing whatever Super-rabbit costume she dons when nobody's looking, must have squeezed between the hutch and the wall, and sprinted tri-umphantly down to eat Miss Seed's succulent vegetation again.

'I'll nail the hutch to the wall,' I promised wildly.

'Why don't you nail the rabbit to the wall?' suggested Miss Seed acidly.

Took over an hour catching Brenda. When I arrived in Miss Seed's garden, she hopped through the hedge into our's. Rushed back round to our's just in time to see her disappear through the hedge into Miss Seed's. Rushed round ... etc etc. I swear that animal grinned at me with her two big white front teeth, as I lurched wearily after her each time. Got home exhausted, and deeply anti-rabbit.

Nailed her hutch to the wall.

Wednesday April 23rd

Bad dreams all night about being chased by a huge rabbit which changed into Richard Cook just as it caught me, and said, 'Feed me! Feed me!'

Woke at 5.00 a.m. Checked Brenda every fifteen minutes from 5.15 onwards. No work today. By the time Anne and Gerald came back I was a nervous wreck. Told Anne all about the rabbit, then slumped down in an easy chair while she went out to put the kettle on. Everything seems much calmer and safer when Anne's here.

Bit later, Gerald came in and said, 'Cor, Dad! You've really boxed the old rabbit in, haven't you?'

Nodded wearily.

'I've let her out for a little hop-about,' said Gerald, 'just to ...'

Launched myself at his throat with a wild strangled cry. 'You what ...?!!!'

'Only joking, Dad! Only joking ... Mum told me all about it ...'

Didn't kill him.

Rang Miss Seed after talking to Anne. Anne said to make friends first, *then* think about witnessing.

'Don't judge me on my rabbit retention record, Miss Seed,' I pleaded on the phone.

'As long as you don't judge *me* on my rabbit rejection record,' she responded.

We laughed and arranged coffee tomorrow.

Later, Gerald said, 'You remember when you went out with Leonard, dad, the night you met Ted?'

'Yes,' I said, 'what about it?'

'Well, you remember I said that witnessing as an anagram of 'sing in stew'?'

'Yes, so . . . ?'

'Well, I forgot to mention something at the time.'

'What?'

'It's *rabbit* stew.'

Thursday April 24th

Spent part of my prayer-time this morning thinking about what Anne said on Friday. She's absolutely right! My job is to serve the study-group, not tell them what to do and judge them. After all, look at me and the rabbit. 'Let he who is without rabbits . . . etc'

No . . . from now on I'm going to put myself entirely at the disposal of the members of my study-group, ready and willing to pour myself out for them in every way that's necessary. Hallelujah! Oddly enough, when I expressed all this to Anne, she looked a bit worried. Perhaps when one takes a spiritual step forward (albeit very humbly), as I feel I've done, it's bound to threaten others a little.

Have decided to give a duplicated letter to each of the people in my group tonight offering my services as a Christian friend and counsellor at any time of the day or night. Spent the time between getting home from work and study-group, getting the letter ready and planning the meeting. Afraid I had to speak a little sharply to Anne once or twice. She's still fretting about the washing machine and odd bits of rabbit dung that got trodden in the other day. I feel that the Lord would not have me troubled with these things at this time.

10.00 p.m.

What an amazing meeting! We were all mightily blessed! (Thynn says he wasn't, but I told him he was in ways that he knows not of.)

My letter received with great enthusiasm. Amazed to find one or two people approached me *this evening* with problems that will need dealing with in the next few days!

There is a world of need! I hear the call! I am ready!

Friday April 25th

Out. New washer: Norma Twill.

Saturday April 26th

Out again. Percy Brain: Doubt.

Sunday April 27th

Church.

Out: Norman Simmonds – Furniture moving

„ : Norma Twill – check washer

„ : Deaf old Mrs Thynn – Explained that old Mr Verge next-door (who she hit with one of Leonard's Doc Martin ten-holers) said he wanted to '*speak* with her', not '*sleep* with her'.

Monday April 28th

Out. Vernon Rawlings: Lust and allied problems.

Tuesday April 29th

Out. Study-group leaders' meeting: (I'm one)

Wednesday April 30th

Out. Stenneth Flushpool: Dominoes while Mrs F. was out. Very excited. (Him I mean)

Thursday May 1st

Out before study-group. Ephraim Trench: Pregnant cow. (Rang me by mistake instead of the vet)

Great study-group. Planning/talking about the Lord's work. Reminded everybody that I'm always available.

Friday May 2nd

Out. George Farmer: Prayer re fruit.

Have had to cut morning prayer right down to save energy for church work in evenings.

Saturday May 3rd

Out. Norma Twill: Double check washer.

Sunday May 4th

Church.
Out.

Monday May 5th

Out.

Tuesday May 6th

Out.

Wednesday May 7th

Out.

Thursday May 8th

Out – study-group – out.

Friday May 9th

Out.

Saturday May 10th

First time I've had the chance to write much in my diary for a while. Life is good! Being a study-group leader is a real privilege. Never felt so humble. Constantly busy with pastoral work. Hallelujah!

Sorry to say Anne and Gerald are not totally supportive. Anne seems obsessed by this fault in the washing machine. Can anything be of more importance than the Lord's work?

As for Gerald – if he says 'Keep your hair on, Moses' one more time, there'll be trouble.

Sunday May 11th

To church. Can't understand people who don't join in at church. I really question their commitment. Makes life so difficult for us leaders. Gerald didn't come today. Said he was suffering from a pain in the neck, and wanted a rest from it. Odd way of putting it!

Anne asked about the washing machine again this evening. Suddenly remembered Percy Brain's ear ache. Felt led to pop round and pray with him. Stayed late, listening to Percy's theatrical stories. Hilarious! Left, feeling I'd really brought joy into the old boy's lonely life. Home at midnight to find Anne hand washing clothes in the sink.

I said, 'Anne, love, scripture teaches the body is the temple of the holy spirit. Shouldn't this have been done earlier?'

No reply, but something about her back showed she was really listening. Straight to bed. Asleep in seconds.

Monday May 12th

Decorated the Thynn's hall tonight with Leonard. Stayed for Scrabble afterwards. Felt right, as it's a very relationship-building activity.

Back late to find a note from Gerald saying that Roger Forster is an anagram of 'Frog restorer'. Tore it up. I will not tolerate disrespect in this house!

Tuesday May 13th

About to tackle washing machine when the phone rang. It was young Vernon Rawlings asking what passage we would be studying on Thursday. Dropped everything and said I'd be round immediately to explain.

Anne looked furious. Funny – I thought she liked young Vernon.

Wednesday May 14th

Really annoyed! Gerald's tinkered with the washing machine and made it worse. Reminded him that scripture says we must be good stewards and not go round causing extra expense by meddling.

A little later, as I was leaving to help the Cooks with young Charles' problem about free will and predestination, I distinctly heard Anne and Gerald arguing in the log shed about who should use the axe first. Curious!

Thursday May 15th

Are Anne and Gerald undergoing a spiritual crisis? I have discerned that their general attitude is cold and unresponsive. Neither of them said anything at the study-group tonight.

Later, while she was washing-up the coffee cups, I said to Anne, 'Anne, I think I've got a word for you.'

She said, 'And I've got one for you if that machine's not soon fixed!'

Prayed for her.

Friday May 16th

6.15

Home at six to find everyone out and a note on the side from Anne, alerting me to the fact that an abandoned family has turned up in Humph's cafe, just round the corner from us. Could I deal with it? Great! Spiritual adventure! I feel like the Red Adaire of the Christian world. I shall go out now, armed with the Spirit and the Word, to face and do battle with whatever forces of darkness await me!

8.30 p.m.

Got round to Humph's cafe about 6.30, but apart from Humph, the only people in there were Anne and Gerald! They were sitting by a table right at the back, drinking tea. Couldn't think what was going on. Sat down at the table with them. I said 'Where's the abandoned family?'

Gerald said, 'We're it.'

'But it was just ... I was just ... just doing the Lord's work ...'

Anne said, 'We thought perhaps *we* might be the Lord's work as well – just now and then, if that's alright?'

Gerald bought chips all round. I promised to mend the washing machine. I said sorry. We all laughed. We reckoned God laughed too.

Saturday May 17th

Mended the washing machine this morning. Took seven minutes. Went for a walk with Anne afterwards. She tells me the 'abandoned family' was Frank Braddock's idea. Also said Frank told her he was at school with Father John, hence the Bungles/Smelly business. Both converted on the same day apparently. Ended up different but the same – funny really.

Feel as if I've woken up after a long feverish dream today. Rang Leonard after lunch and asked him what he'd give me out of ten for my performance as a study-group leader so far.

He said, 'Absolutely *no* doubt about that. Ten out of ten! Easily!'

I said, 'How many if you tell the truth?'

'Minus three,' said Thynn.

Thanked him for telling the truth and said things would be changing now. Just about to put the phone down when I remembered something.

'Leonard, why did you borrow the . . .'

He'd put the 'phone down.

Sunday May 18th

About to set off for church this morning, when the phone went. Almost left it, but decided it might be important. It was Bill Dove.

'Just wanted to tell yer,' he said quietly, 'that Kitty's gone. Six o'clock this mornin'. She smiled that little smile of 'ers and said, "Time's up, love, see yer later", and that was it.'

Couldn't speak.

'She gave me a message for you last night,' went on Bill. 'Made me promise to pass it on soon as she'd gone.'

Could barely manage a whisper. 'What did she say?'

'She said, "Tell 'im, Bill, that Kitty said God loves 'im more than she does, so everythin's gotter be alright."'

'Thanks Bill . . . thanks . . . Is there anything I can . . . ?'

'Nothin' just now,' said Bill. 'See yer, mate.'

Told Anne and Gerald. We put our arms round each other for a little while, then went to church.

She always made me feel good.

Monday May 19th

Reminded by Anne this morning that it's only six days until we set off for our annual trip to 'Let God Spring into Royal Acts of Harvest Growth', the big Christian festival down at Wetbridge in the Westcountry. A whole group of us are going from the church. Rather looking forward to it this year. Other years we've rented caravans. This year we've bought a tent! Can't wait! Bacon sizzling deliciously on the primus every morning – the healthy feel of open-air living – soft talk under the stars each evening – good fellowship with other campers and caravanners – marvellous! Roll on Saturday!

I've insisted that we leave *very* early, probably about 4.00 a.m. Gerald groaned and Anne sighed when I said this, but it's the *only* way to do it. Up with the lark!

This evening Gerald said, 'Are you sure your back will be okay for camping, dad? Might be a bit cold down at Wetbridge.'

I said, 'Should be alright – I haven't felt so much as a twinge since . . . ooh, must be February or March – touch wood.'

Why does my back make Anne and Gerald laugh?

Tuesday May 20th

Rather embarrassed this evening. Edwin, Richard, Percy Brain and Leonard came round for the evening. After a bit Leonard said, 'What's the silliest thing each of us has ever done?'

Quite amusing after that, until it got to Gerald's turn. Instead of talking about the silliest thing *he'd* ever done, he reeled off a long list of the silliest things *I've* ever done. Edwin and Percy were in fits! When Gerald described how he and Anne had found me lying in the hall with my feet up against the door, I thought Edwin was going to do himself an injury, and when he got onto me shouting at a paper-clip, Thynn *did* do himself an injury. He was lying on the floor, on his front, weeping with laughter, and banging the carpet with his fist, when he accidentally punched himself on the nose. I was pleased. Gerald was just about to get on to the 'Hot thighs in wet grass' saga, when Anne came in carrying a suit on a hanger in one hand, and a piece of paper in the other. Felt very glad she'd interrupted.

'We're just talking about one or two of Dad's sillier moments, Mum,' said Gerald.

'Vastly entertaining!' chuckled Percy.

Thynn still prostrate, heaving weakly from time to time. Edwin smiling and shaking his head.

Saw Anne glance at the paper in her hand.

She said, 'Oh, well, I won't interrupt. It's just that your suit's back from the cleaners and there's a note ... I'll come back later.'

Didn't want to get back to 'Hot thighs in wet grass'! I said, 'It's perfectly alright, Anne, carry on – there's a note, you said? A note about what?'

'I don't think ...'

I said, 'Look, Anne, we weren't talking about anything important, just some silly incidents that have perfectly rational explanations. Please go on, Anne.'

'I don't ...'

'Please, Anne!'

'It's just that the cleaners found a note in your pocket before they cleaned the suit, and I wondered ... I'll come back later.'

'Anne, please read the note! What's the matter with you?'

'I don't ...'

'Anne!!'

'Well, alright ... if you say so. The ... the note's in your handwriting, and it says ... I'll come back later ...'

'Anne!!!'

'It says "Buy a tree-frog and call it Kaiser Bill".'

Unable to provide the perfectly rational explanation for my memo-to-self, because no-one would listen. All helpless and collapsing with laughter – even Richard, braying like a donkey.

Reminded Anne and Gerald tonight that we're leaving at *four* on Saturday. I know them. They think I'll forget.

Wednesday May 21st

Prayer time's settled down to an hour each morning now. Just right. Having to fend off some of the visiting requests from my study-group. All my own fault of course, but really! Raymond Pond wanted me to come round and feed his gerbil this evening. When I asked why, he said he was nicely settled by the fire next to the telephone, and he didn't feel like getting up. Honestly!

Said to Anne and Gerald this evening, '*What* time are we leaving on Saturday?'

'Seven, wasn't it?' said Gerald.

'Eight o'clock?' said Anne.

'Four!' I said 'F-O-U-R, FOUR!'

Thursday May 22nd

Strange moment at work today. Glander came across to me and said sneeringly, 'You know that loony mate of yours who was at the party – Thynn, his name is?'

'Yes?' I said, surprised.

'Well,' said Glander, 'a friend of mine told me that, not so very long ago, he saw Mr 'Christian' Thynn, very much the worse for wear, being peeled off the pavement outside the Plough and Bottle, by a couple of the lads in Blue. I thought as he's such a good friend of yours and supposed to be one of Jesus' little sunbeams, perhaps you ought to know about it.'

For one, awful, dark moment, was about to say that Leonard wasn't all that close a friend, and the rest of us in the church weren't like that, but suddenly thought of Anne and Gerald and Kitty and Leonard and Jesus, all waiting to hear what I'd say.

I said, 'I did know about that, Everett. Leonard's one of my best friends, so I hear about most of what happens to him. He's got a problem with drink. I've got a problem with getting things twisted up and making mistakes. All of us in the church have got problems. We're not very good people, but God keeps on forgiving us. Does anyone forgive you for what *you* do, Everett?'

308

Can't believe *I* said all that! Expected Glander to laugh his head off, but he just frowned and grunted and went back to his desk. Came up to me at the end of the day and *almost* apologised! Who knows – one day ... ?

No study-group tonight, everybody's getting ready for Saturday. Gerald had a surprise letter today from Andromeda Veal, who stayed with us back in March.

Dear Gerald,

How are you? How is your persunnul problem? I asked muther for one, but she said I must be out of my tiny mined. She is not a soshulist with her own cash. I corled her a thacherite laccy, so she sent me to bed without any mewsli and said I'm afraid I don't think that's very funny. Cum the reverlooshun she'll get hers eh Gerald. When I'm grown up I'm going to live in Rusher. The soshulist ideel is propperly upheld there by Mr Gorgeouschops. I am willing to marry you one day Gerald as long as I can be a mizz and you are soshulist with your cash.

Love
Andromeda

P.S. If you wear your persunnul problem out can I have it?
P.P.S. How's that fashist you live with?

Fashist – I mean, Fascist? Me? Asked Anne where she would place me in the political spectrum. She said she thought I was slightly left of gauche ...

Friday May 23rd

Came through the front door after work today to overhear Elsie's voice coming from the sitting-room.

'I'm sorry, Gerald, it doesn't matter what you say. It's over, and that's that! Poor William has suffered greatly. I feel led to go back to him and that's what I'm going to do!'

Heard Gerald say, 'But Elsie ...', then Elsie came flying out of the room, swooned carefully round the obstacles in the hall, and

309

slammed dramatically out of the front door without speaking to me. Found Gerald sitting in an armchair with his head in his hands. Went over and put my hand on his shoulder.

I said, 'I know it's hard, Gerald . . .'

Gerald looked up and grinned. 'Telling me it's hard, dad! It's taken nearly a fortnight to persuade Elsie that us breaking up is her idea!'

I dunno!

9.30 p.m.

Early to bed tonight so as to be up and ready to go at 4.00 a.m. I've set the clock for 3.30 a.m., and that's when we're *all* getting up. Gerald smiled that infuriating smile at me just now as he went off to bed. He thinks I'm going to mess it up – set the clock wrong or something. Anne looks pretty sceptical as well. We shall see. Roll on tomorrow morning. This is the one thing that *won't* go wrong!

10.30 p.m.

Having a little trouble getting to sleep because of worrying about waking up.

11.30 p.m.

Still can't get to sleep. Bit worried now. If I don't go off soon I shall sleep right through the alarm. Must try not to try to relax.

12.15 a.m.

Still awake! Only three and a half hours until the alarm goes off!

12.19 a.m.

Dozed off for one and a half minutes. Dreamt I was awake, and woke up worried about not being asleep.

1.00 a.m.

Too late to think about sleeping now, I must stay awake until 3.30. I must!! Going down to the kitchen to drink coffee.

2.00 a.m.

Still awake! Eyes heavy and blurred – all I want to do is sleep. Hour and a half to go. Mustn't lie down – that would be fatal!

2.45 a.m.

I think I'm going to make it. Feel like death but I'm still asleep – I mean awake.

3.00 a.m.

Good as made it, can't stop yawning but swill atake wade awike ...

3.29 a.m.

Made it! That'll show 'em. Just sitting in the armchair for a moment till the alarm goes off dun it! What a trium. . . .

Saturday May 24th

11.00 a.m.

There are times when my family is insufferable!

Anne and Gerald woke me at ten o'clock, and pretended to be very upset because we hadn't made an early start. Gerald said I might at least have gone to bed and *tried* to sleep instead of sitting up all night and dozing off in the armchair. Anne said it was no use my having a quiet-time because God had set off for Wetbridge hours ago. Very funny I don't think. Felt like a dead slug when I tried to get out of my armchair. Feel a lot better now I've had a wash and something to eat. Wetbridge here we come! We're meeting the others down there. Must make sure I take my diary along. I'll be able to sit quietly outside the tent each evening and record the events and revelations of the day. Can't wait!

10.00 p.m.

Arrived at 'Let God Spring into Royal Acts of Harvest Growth' around mid-afternoon. Anne and Gerald and I erected our new 'Tornado-Tough' frame tent in no time, despite high winds and sheeting rain. After checking out the toilets, we walked up to the shop. Passed our magnificent new tent, standing tall and proud in the face of the gale. A little further on, our magnificent new tent passed us, flying through the air like a huge, loony, red and blue sail. Caught it eventually, just outside Richard and Doreen Cook's 'Super-Safari-complete-Comfort-Vacation-Van. Could see Richard inside, drinking tea and reading a bible in the warm. He nodded and smiled and mouthed the words 'Praise the Lord' at me, as I wrestled with my horrible pile of soggy canvas.

Mouthed something back.

Everything soaked! Down to Wetbridge launderette to dry it all. Too late to pitch the tent again when we got back. Went to the 'Let God Spring into Royal Acts of Harvest Growth' office, where a wild-eyed person (who kept saying this was the last year she'd do it) gave us the key to a tiny refrigerated cowshed, where we're about to stay the night in strange contorted positions.

Sunday May 25th

Down to Wetbridge launderette with clothes soaked by rain coming in through holes in the refrigerated cowshed. Surprising number of people down there at 7.30 in the morning. One couple who'd spent the night in six inches of water, were anxious to get back in time for the marriage fulfilment seminar. Seemed a bit desperate really.

Got back and pitched the tent again. Drove pegs through anything that flapped.

Off to the first Celebration this evening with our church group. Relieved Leonard Thynn of a three-pint can of bitter and two bottles of Valpolicella on the way. Explained to him what this kind of Celebration means.

Pleased to see Gerald concentrating hard during the talk. Turned out all his mental energies had gone into working out that

Lyndon Bowring was an anagram of 'Born lying down'. Got a bit annoyed with him.

Monday May 26th

Forgot to put clothes away properly last night. All soaked. Down to Wetbridge launderette again. They should have a seminar *there*.

Pete Meadows spoke tonight. Gerald said afterwards, 'Now that was a really good talk, Dad.'

Guiltily confessed that I'd spent most of the time working out that Pete Meadows is an anagram of 'Sweated poem'.

Tuesday May 27th

Back from the Wetbridge launderette this morning to find deaf old Mrs Thynn waiting to tell me how disappointed she was that they hadn't had the chance to save anyone from drowning in her seminar yet.

Stared blankly at her.

'But aren't you in the house to house visitation seminar?' I asked. 'That's right,' she said, mouth to mouth resuscitation.'

Honestly! You'd think Leonard would have explained, wouldn't you?

Some problems over *my* seminar this morning. Was to be in Marquee 9, but had been changed to Marquee 6, only Marquee 6 had blown down, so Marquee 9's seminar was moved to Marquee 14, and the new Marquee 6's seminar was moved back to Marquee 9, only, by now, Marquee 9 had also blown down. Our group ended up wandering disconsolately round the site, looking for an empty marquee, and discussing stability in the church as we went.

Overheard two fellow campers in a local shop later on, while I was waiting to buy fruit-gums for the evening talk. One said the bad weather and the tents blowing down was God's way of saying that these huge gatherings were wrong. The other said it was God's way of testing our perseverance in something that was unquestionably *right*. The old local chap behind the counter interrupted them to say that it always 'bloody rained' down here at this time of the year, and he couldn't understand why they 'kept on 'aving it!'

Wednesday May 28th

Same good old crowd down at Wetbridge launderette this morning. Asked everybody if they'd come to 'Let God Spring into Royal Acts of Harvest Growth' again. They all said they would, because the church thrives under persecution.

Back to the site. Went down for a wash. Funny washing in front of strangers every morning. Feel obliged to be a bit more thorough than usual, in case they think I don't wash enough. The water's so *cold*, despite the fact that the taps are labelled 'C' and 'H'. Gerald says that 'C' stands for 'Cold', and 'H' stands for 'Horribly Cold'.

Thursday May 29th

What a night! Felt as if Giant Haystacks and Big Daddy were shaking our tent in shifts all night. About 2.00 a.m. I said to Anne, 'One of us ought to get out and check the guys and pegs, you know.'

Anne said, 'I agree absolutely. One of us quite definitely should. Yes, one of us should certainly get out and do that.'

Rather obvious snore from Gerald's compartment at this point.

Got up eventually and crawled into the darkness to face Giant Haystacks and Big Daddy. Everything secure. Anne and Gerald fast asleep when I got back. Had two nightmares when I finally got to sleep. In the first, I died and went to heaven, and found it was just like 'Let God Spring into Royal Acts of Harvest Growth'. Woke terrified.

In the second, I died and went to hell, and it was just like 'Let God Spring into Royal Acts of Harvest Growth'. Woke up sweating, and got up early to start collecting stuff for the launderette.

Talked to lots of nice people this morning from lots of different denominations. Had a really great chat in the cafe. Had to stop, unfortunately, or we'd have been late for the seminar on unity.

Friday May 30th

Everything dry this morning! Rather missed the usual launderette trip. Nearly went anyway …

Asked Anne this afternoon if she'd enjoyed it all.

She said, 'Oh, yes. Despite everything, it's good to be among all these people who are doing their best to do what God tells them. We're a funny old crowd though, aren't we?'

'Yes,' I thought, 'we certainly are that.'

Silently asked God to show me what really mattered in this strange world of tents and caravans, and Big-tops blowing down, and Celebrations and Christians and cold water and foul weather. As I opened my eyes, a figure passed our tent on the road. It carried a huge wooden mallet. The walk was a plodding, weary one. The young man was dishevelled and grimy. He'd probably been up for the last twenty-four hours at least, working all night in the wind and the rain to save some of the marquee tents. There was the faintest of nightlights still shining in his eyes as he walked. Somehow knew the weather would never quite put that light out.

'There you are,' God seemed to say, 'That's what it's all about.'

It was a steward.

Saturday May 31st

Camp communion today. As we sat waiting for the bread and wine to come round, couldn't help looking at Leonard and Richard and Gerald and Anne and Edwin and the others, and wondering why God's brought us all together. I'm glad he did, though. Felt quite a lump in my throat as I saw old Thynn screwing his eyes tight shut as he took the cup in his hands, and sipped his problem and its solution.

Talking of Leonard – that reminds me. Straight after this I'm going to grab him and make him tell me why he's been borrowing our blinking cat. …

*A major new novel by the best-selling author
of the Sacred Diary Series*

**Available
Now**

Ghosts

The Story of a Reunion

Adrian Plass

The strangest things happen when
friends are reunited after twenty years
apart. When together last, the friends
were members of the same youth
group and – on the whole – had life
to look forward to. Now middle-
aged, some are still optimistic but oth-
ers are worn-out and weary. One has lost his faith, and
another is struggling to reconcile the promises of his Christian
beliefs with the recent death of his wife.

When reunited for a weekend away, the friends find themselves in Headly Manor, reputed to be one of the most haunted
houses in England. What does it mean to stay in a haunted
house? Strangely warm beds on cold days, objects unaccountably
moving from room to room, and little girls in old-fashioned
clothes seen walking across the lawn? Or something more sub-
tle, but potentially much more frightening?

This engaging story blends Adrian Plass's rich style of humour
with his knack for addressing the deep issues we all face, such as
faith, grief, love, fear – and most crippling of all afflictions, the
fear of fear.

Hardcover: 0-551-03109-3

Pick up a copy today at your favorite bookstore!

ZONDERVAN™

GRAND RAPIDS, MICHIGAN 49530 USA

WWW.ZONDERVAN.COM

We want to hear from you. Please send your comments about this book to us in care of the address below. Thank you.

GRAND RAPIDS, MICHIGAN 49530 USA

WWW.ZONDERVAN.COM